On the Record

LUCIEN
BOUCHARD
On the Record

Translated by Dominique Clift

Stoddart

Published in 1994 by
Stoddart Publishing Co. Limited
34 Lesmill Road
Toronto, Canada
M3B 2T6
(416)445-3333

Original French edition published under the title
À visage découvert
by Les Éditions du Boréal in 1992

Published under arrangement with Les Éditions du Boréal

Canadian Cataloguing in Publication Data

Bouchard, Lucien, 1938–
On the record

Translation of: À visage découvert.
ISBN 0-7737-2801-5

1. Bouchard, Lucien, 1938–   .   2. Politicians —
Canada — Biography.   3. Diplomats — Canada —
Biography.   I. Title.

FC631.B68A313 1994   971.064′7′092   C94-930608-8
F1034.3.B68A313 1994

Typesetting: Tony Gordon Ltd.

Printed and bound in Canada

*Stoddart Publishing gratefully acknowledges the support of the Canada
Council, Ontario Ministry of Culture, Tourism, and Recreation,
Ontario Arts Council, and Ontario Publishing Centre in the
development of writing and publishing in Canada.*

To my father and my mother,
artisans of the past

To the future of my sons,
Alexandre and Simon

To Audrey, my wife, who is
the heart of this continuity

Contents

Preface to the English Edition

I began writing this book on July 1, 1991, the day after the founding of the Bloc Québécois. I thought I should answer questions people were asking about the consistency of my political career: How had I arrived at this juncture? What was the link between the admirer of the Liberal Jean Lesage, the disciple of René Lévesque, and the minister who resigned from the Mulroney government?

My purpose was not so much to convince as to describe the route I had taken. Retracing my steps as objectively as I could, I realized nothing is unique. Many people of my generation have had the same experience. In this sense, my return to the past may contribute to a better understanding of the way Québec society moves.

Since the book first appeared in French, in June 1992, two events have confirmed my political diagnosis: the failure of the Charlottetown referendum and the election of fifty-four members of the Bloc Québécois to the House of Commons. Regarding the latter, reality far outstripped my expectations. The sovereigntists of the Bloc Québécois now form the official Opposition.

The publication of an English translation is timely. More than ever, Québec's political behaviour is likely to baffle English Canada. How can one understand why, after massively supporting the

Conservatives in 1984 and 1988, Québécois decided they should be represented in the holy of holies of federal institutions by such a large number of sovereigntists? How is it that after worshipping Pierre Trudeau and saying no, in 1980, to Lévesque's sovereignty association, Québécois apparently stand ready to elect another Parti Québécois government?

To a very great extent, we Québécois are responsible for the fact that English Canada has misjudged our political reality. Even during the most intensive years of sovereigntist mobilization, we persisted in sending only federalist representatives to Ottawa. The delay in providing an alternative has created a persistent confusion about which we cannot justifiably complain.

This is what the last federal election changed. Jean Chrétien cannot claim, as Trudeau did, to represent Québec. Facing Chrétien's nineteen federalist Liberal MPs now are fifty-four members of the Bloc Québécois who will speak up for the sovereigntist reality of Québec, formerly hidden from view at the federal level. For the first time, the rationale behind sovereigntist objectives will come straight from the mouths of sovereigntists in Ottawa.

Before negotiations get under way, the elected members of the Bloc Québécois want to speak to English Canada. They want to say that Québécois sentiment of constituting a nation and the desire to give it shape in a sovereign state are not directed against anyone; that their goals issue directly from their wish to wield their own decision-making levers and shape their own social, economic, and cultural development; that, consequently, Québécois sovereigntists do not want to destroy a country but to build another one, fashioned on their aspirations and specifically dedicated to their progress.

Sovereigntists believe this new country springs from necessity. Even Québec federalists are seriously wondering about their support for a system that is inefficient and beyond reform. Those who, since Lesage, have sustained their federalist faith with the hope of constitutional change are now being asked to resign themselves to the status quo they have always rejected.

For Québécois, the most decisive thing to come out of the dual failure of Meech and Charlottetown has been this: English-speaking

Canadians, out of respect for their own national identity, out of loyalty to their vision of Canada, have refused to make any concessions to Québec. Validated in this manner, the refusal is indisputably legitimate. At the same time, this legitimacy matches and justifies the one that Québec sovereigntists espouse.

We are now in the realm of political facts, beyond acrimony and accusations of malevolence. Henceforth, it will be through logic that one becomes sovereigntist in Québec. Similarly, it is through logic that English Canada will have to come to terms with that fact. The two premises of the syllogism have been set: (1) Québécois, federalists as well as sovereigntists, want to develop as a distinct nation; and (2) Canada is viscerally incapable of integrating this demand into its federal system. Therefore . . .

We now must come to a conclusion. It is up to us Québécois to do so. Too often have we turned back, looking for other routes and coming up against a wall. I believe that what I say about my political course in the pages that follow is representative of the situation. We no longer can allow ourselves to vacillate from referendum to referendum, from one ultimate constitutional attempt to the next, from one federal-provincial conference to another. Charlottetown has done away with all ambiguity. A long journey has taught us that Québec has nothing to ask from anyone, that we must not lose ourselves in Byzantine negotiations condemned to sterility. The only thing these pathetic efforts have achieved is to convey the idea that we are politically irresolute.

Within two years, a referendum on sovereignty will ask Québécois to cut the Gordian knot. This will also be the moment of truth for English Canada. In the event of a sovereigntist victory, it will become impossible to find refuge in the status quo and the inertia of the political majority. Our mutual interests will require us, Canadians and Québécois, to define in a responsible way, from the point of view of our respective sovereignty, the relationship that geography, economics, and history are asking us to preserve.

LUCIEN BOUCHARD
January 1994

Prologue

May 22, 1990: The door slammed shut behind me. Night had fallen. I got into the car, and as we drove through the iron gates, I caught sight of *Globe and Mail* journalist Graham Fraser standing watch. But talking to the press was out of the question. I pretended not to see him. For the time being, all I had to say was in my letter of resignation from the Progressive Conservative party, which I had just read to the prime minister. I asked the driver to take me to my parliamentary office. Afterwards, I would get some sleep.

I had a lot on my mind.

I was well aware of the enormous personal repercussions of what was happening. The door of 24 Sussex wasn't the only one slamming shut. I had erased a whole part of my life, broken with countless friends, and irrevocably alienated circles of people who I knew would never forgive me. I did not fully realize then how my action would lead to the birth of the Bloc Québécois, which was destined to play a major role in Parliament following the 1993 federal election. But I could easily imagine people's reactions — unspoken or declared — ranging from surprise to sorrow, from bitterness to meanness.

I asked myself a lot of questions.

Was I right in believing that my father would have agreed with me? What would the outcome be, not only for me but for this whole psychodrama in which my own departure played but an insignificant part? But first, how had it all happened?

There comes a time of reckoning, a day when you must find the answers to all the questions. Yet, it would be futile to look only within oneself: we don't live in isolation. To find the answers, I must go back to the past, back to the characters and events that have marched through almost fifty years of my life. . . .

1

The Family on the Décharge Concession Road

My father and mother valued education above all else. As far back as I can remember, I can hear my parents expounding the merits of education. Where did this obsession come from? Likely it was the result of the brevity of their own studies. True, my mother had finished tenth grade. But my father never went beyond the four years at the concession school, which simply had nothing more to teach. Such was the baggage with which my father began adult life.

More than sixty years later, I saw him sit down at the kitchen table one summer evening to write to Roch, the first of my brothers to study in France. He was having trouble coping with Roch's prolonged absence. He sat there, pen in hand, concentrating. Suddenly, with tears in his eyes, he crumpled the sheet of paper he had been toiling over for almost half an hour and threw it away. An outburst triggered by the humiliating reminder of his own inability to write and the impossibility of communicating with the son who had left to follow his own dreams.

He loved his children more than anything, and he never seemed to tire of having them close by. During summer vacations and school holidays, he often piled us into the cab of his delivery truck. We would travel up and down the streets of Jonquière, Kénogami, Arvida, and sometimes even Chicoutimi, stopping here and there to unload lumber, nails, bags of cement, doors, and windows.

He used to laugh, put an end to our quarrels, talk about everything: other people, his father and mother, our uncles and aunts, trucks, the merits of Ford and International. He never could decide which was the better truck, switching allegiance from one to the other to the end of his life. Evenings, for a treat, he'd take us along on his rounds of the sawmills rimming the lakes around Jonquière. He'd load his truck with scrap timber, shavings, and sawdust, which he sold to clients in town.

I can't think of Lake Kénogami or Lake Long without seeing my father loading his truck with shovelfuls of shavings and heavy sawdust for hours on end. Of all the sensory impressions that form my memory of my father, it is impossible to forget the vision of this man who, as night fell after a full day's work, stood panting from exhaustion, harassed by mosquitoes and black flies. Yet nothing affected the good humour he showed on the way back. I can still hear him steering his truck in the night around the bumps and potholes in the bush roads, singing Tino Rossi's great hit, "As long as there are stars on the arch of heaven . . ." He sang the same song with mother accompanying him on the piano on Sundays and holy days.

After church on Sunday, four or five of us were always climbing on his back and knees, begging him to "tell us about life." He invariably complied, launching into a monologue that started with the words, "In life, my children . . ." and ended with deeply felt warnings and exhortations about happiness, work, and honesty. Of course, the lion's share was reserved for Education, which he praised as the means to personal development and progress in life. We were a good audience and lapped up every word. So good that these weekly sermons soon instilled us with solid convictions, almost all revolving around the need to study and to avoid "acting simple."

The ban on acting simple figured prominently in the family code, which stigmatized foolishness, sentimentality, vulgarity, and affectation. The expression is still very much alive in the Saguenay–Lac-Saint-Jean area, and is most likely of peasant origin. My grandfather, the farmer, always said anyone speaking or acting foolishly was "as simple as my cows." There couldn't be a harsher condemnation. My grandfather thought cows were the stupidest animals, as opposed to his horses, whose intelligence he praised endlessly.

My father had the same predilection for horses. As a young man, he spent many winters as a teamster in logging camps on the Lièvre River. And it was Chevreux, his favourite horse, who drew the sled that took him to Jonquière in 1940, sixty kilometres east of Lac-Saint-Jean on the south shore of the Saguenay River. Once settled there, the two of them started making home deliveries. Thus Chevreux became his first delivery "truck." Later, he would treat his motorized vehicles with the same diligent care he showed his horses — the horses to prevent illness, the trucks to avoid repairs.

For a long time, I shared this concern. My father had shown us how even a minor mishap with the Ford or the International could cost the equivalent of a week's salary, or even one or two months' wages. Work for my father meant drudgery from dawn to midnight every day except Sunday. The concept of holidays was unknown to him. Nobody ever saw him take any time off. Our worst fear was that something would happen to the differential, a spherical casing in the middle of the rear axle holding the transmission gears. Next to the motor, the differential was the most expensive part to replace. We always watched the heavy metal ball with mixed fear and reverence. It was particularly vulnerable when the truck traversed bumpy terrain. Yet it seemed as if our father went out of his way to travel with a full load on impossible roads.

In a way, our father never left the old family homestead. And neither did the rest of us. After we moved to Jonquière, we went back all the time, rarely skipping a Sunday visit. In the summer, I often went for long stays, as did my brothers later. It is not surprising then that the cult of family and all its myths so nurtured our imagination.

I use the term *family* in its broadest sense. Grandfathers, grand-mothers, uncles, aunts, and cousins were but the first circle. Great-uncles, great-aunts, and second cousins were also a part of our everyday life. I am always surprised to meet people who are unable to name relatives beyond their immediate families.

Even when we were very young, we had a near scientific knowledge of our genealogy. I always knew that my paternal great-great-grand-father was called Omer, that he lived in La Malbaie, that his son Sixte, my great-grandfather, had settled in Saint-Jérôme-de-Métabetchouan. I also knew that my grandfather Joseph had left the place, with my father, Philippe, still in diapers, to clear some farmland at Saint-Coeur-de-Marie, north and east of Lac-Saint-Jean. My maternal great-great-grandfather, François Simard, was a coastal boat captain at Petite-Rivière-Saint-François, and my great-grandfather Thomas and my grandfather Xavier left Charlevoix for Saint-Coeur-de-Marie. Every spring, Xavier went to Petite-Rivière for maple sugar, syrup, and taffy. In the fall, he brought back apples, plums, and eels.

On my father's side, Great-grandfather Sixte was the leading character in the family mythology. He was a prosperous farmer, a much-appreciated raconteur at family gatherings, and a stern patriarch with an inquisitive mind. In the 1920s, he set out to visit "the Europes," as people used to say. He had a profound influence on his next of kin and left behind not only his family name but his strange first name. The only other Sixte I know of was a pope whose name I read in the prayer book at church on Sundays.

Given the large number of Bouchards in the Lac-Saint-Jean area, and the even larger number of Tremblays, there has to be some way of telling them apart. Accordingly, we belong to the Bouchard-Sixte branch of the family. Nobody gets confused and nobody forgets it. I realized this during my first election campaign, the 1988 by-election in Lac-Saint-Jean. I had a serious problem: people in my riding were calling me an outsider. My executive assistant, Luc Lavoie, settled the issue decisively. He organized a photo opportunity with the prime minister at my grandfather's farm at Saint-Coeur-de-Marie. Everybody found out that I really had been born there and that I was indeed the grandson of Sixte's son Joseph, known for keeping his word, which was "as straight as the King's sword." Some time later, the mayor of Saint-Jérôme-de-Métabetchouan showed me a photograph in the town's hall of honour. There was Sixte, proudly posing as one of the former mayors of the municipality.

I never knew him, of course. All I remember is a tall man with white hair and grey eyes whom I met at Great-uncle Henri's place, on the Poste road in Saint-Jérôme. He was ninety-two and I was four or five.

No cult is complete without a shrine. Ours was the house on the Décharge concession road in Saint-Coeur-de-Marie. It was a large white building with green trim, surrounded by a wide veranda where generations of children raced endlessly, breathlessly round and round. The roof, bristling with gables, rose above a balcony at the front, leading to the room my parents occupied before they left for Jonquière.

The house was built in 1921, with lumber from my grandfather's land, by one of my father's brothers, Adélard, a nineteen-year-old carpenter's apprentice. This uncle left immediately after finishing the job to work on the construction of hydroelectric dams at Isle-Maligne and Shipshaw, and then the construction of the Manoir at Pointe-au-Pic. Later, he started a small carpentry shop in Jonquière. This modest establishment, known as Potvin & Bouchard, now managed by my cousins, became the largest distributor of construction materials in the area.

Today, I can well imagine that the land and the farmhouse were quite prosaic to my grandfather and all the others who wore themselves out clearing the bush and eking out a meagre living from the farm. However, for me, every trip to Saint-Coeur-de-Marie was a pilgrimage to a wonderland of mysteries just waiting to be discovered.

First of all, there was the land itself, about a thousand acres of it, a vast spread of fields and forest, broken by outcrops and gullies. We used to go picking strawberries, raspberries, blueberries, and wild cherries. Later in the year, we gathered hazelnuts. In winter, we cut down Christmas trees.

The farmland extended right to the Grande Décharge, the larger branch of the Saguenay River flowing from Lac-Saint-Jean. Another side bordered on the road between Alma and Dolbeau. It is exactly one mile from the house to the road. When my grandfather settled there in 1905, there was only forest and a makeshift home, where the family lived for eighteen years. My grandfather often told us about the challenge he had set himself, to cut down all the trees, over the width of two lots, so that one day he would have a clear view of the cars travelling up and down the road.

All this passed through my mind on a sunny morning in June 1988 as I looked back at the pack of journalists trailing behind the prime minister and me. We were making our "impromptu" visit to the farm. I was watching the traffic, barely visible, moving at the end of the immense field. Gazing over this remote bit of countryside, I tried once more to imagine how many swings of the axe, how many uprooted stumps, how many overturned stones it had taken. I remembered my father's reply when I asked him why he left the farm: "It was autumn. It was cold and rainy. I was in a swamp, pulling on a stump that wouldn't budge. We were all sinking in the mud. I stopped to catch my breath and began to think it over. Then I decided to quit."

While the contingent of cameramen, reporters, flacks, Mounties, and political aides jostled behind us, I tried to appear casual as I chatted with my famous companion. Then, with some uneasiness, I watched the prime minister heading for the cow shed. To avoid the usual comic mishaps, we had to zigzag our way along the path. At that moment, I heard a reporter asking my cousin André if I had ever visited the farm before. I realized that to these obligatory witnesses it was just an ordinary farm with its cow dung and mosquitoes. The only thing setting it apart that day were the two politicians using it for election purposes.

I wondered what my grandfather would think of it all. I doubt he would have liked the circus. Proud and independent as he was, he would not have been very enthusiastic about the prime minister visiting under these conditions. I was afraid that we were desecrating the land my grandfather saw as holy.

Nor am I sure how he would have reacted to the old homestead's transformation. No more horses, no more pigs. The bull, the sheep, the hens, and the turkeys had all vanished. As for the cows, milking was now computer-controlled, which, according to my cousin, did not make them any smarter.

The large house had also changed. The wide circular gallery had disappeared and new rooms had been installed on the second floor. Yet it still exerted the same fascination over me as it had in my childhood, evoking thousands of images, sounds, smells, and sensations.

Nothing was as exciting, back in my childhood, as sneaking into the large room on the second floor with the spinning wheel and the carded wool ready for spinning beneath the strings of onions hanging from the ceiling. There, in a cupboard set against the far wall, my grandmother kept her books.

She had received a good education from the nuns. On top of bearing and raising twelve children, she kept house and milked the cows every morning. She also read voraciously and wrote poetry, some of which has been piously preserved. Her books — there were at least a hundred of them — were the household's greatest treasure. They were huge tomes, many of them gilt-edged, with hard covers and bright colours, mostly red and blue. She had novels like *Le Juif errant, Une de perdue, deux de retrouvées,* and *David Copperfield.* There was also an illustrated biography of Napoleon, who, my father said, was master of the world for twenty-four hours. It seemed a very short reign to me.

My grandmother had been a beautiful brunette who never dropped her stern air. My father never talked about her without expressing pity for her and the harsh life she had led. Unable to fulfil her dream of becoming a nun (unlike one of her sisters, who helped found the order of the Antoniennes de Marie), she had gone to New England to work in a factory before returning to marry my grandfather.

She loved music. My aunts sang and played the piano. In fact, the whole family sang with varying degrees of talent. Whenever there was a *veillée,* an evening gathering of the clan, everyone knew what the person rising to perform would sing. One shone in "Les Blés d'or," another in "Douce France." I was known for my interpretation of "Mon beau sapin," while my brother Roch was regularly asked to sing "Pigalle."

Uncle Roméo, six feet five inches with a pinched moustache, was a champion brawler and Beau Brummell, and was famous for his imitations of Maurice Chevalier. My grandmother, who thought he was very funny, had a soft spot for him. She let him sing songs that would never be heard in church, such as "Elle avait une jambe de bois" (She had a pegleg). It was quite a spectacle, I must say, to see this big strapping man stiffen one leg and make the rounds of all the alarmed and delighted ladies while he performed this risqué song.

My father surpassed everybody with his great voice and large repertoire. When he came to the piano for my mother's advice on what to sing, we children thought we had the most incredible parents. Countless times, after having heard us sing, my mother would sigh and say, "How sad that none of you ever took after your father!"

Some, like Uncle Adélard, recited. One of his hits was "Paméla," the story of a trembling lover who dictates an absurdly passionate letter to his girlfriend.

The whole family loved and respected beautiful language; they would have had nothing but contempt for *joual,* an urban Québec dialect. They had a sense for the exact word and a good turn of phrase. My father never stopped correcting us at the dinner table and never hesitated to reprimand us for poor diction. I remember how my grandmother used to make me read her books out loud to check my progress at school.

Great-uncle Henri also did not rely entirely on the school system. Self-taught and a reader and admirer of Henri Bourassa, he applied himself equally to farming and carpentry. He had a habit of asking my brothers, my sister, and me all sorts of questions in front of our parents to test our knowledge. We dreaded his visits. One day on his return from an overseas trip he took advantage of an imposing Areopagus of uncles, aunts, and friends to quiz us about the dimensions of the doors of St. Peter's Basilica in Rome and of the Church of the Holy Sepulchre in Jerusalem. As usual, the cat got our tongues. The result was a litany of exact measurements, in inches and feet. "I measured these doors myself with my own carpenter's ruler when I was in Rome and Palestine," he told us. And then he added disdainfully as he turned to my parents, who were not terribly proud of their offspring at that moment: "I just wonder what they learn in school."

Uncle Henri's choice of questions reveal that in our family religion was never very far removed from education. Those who were destined for religious orders were sent to school. My father's five sisters entered a convent and stayed there. Their brother François is a Redemptorist priest. Two of my mother's brothers, my uncles Alfred and Armand, are parish priests. My father and my mother had countless cousins who were priests or nuns.

My grandfather especially was very religious. Grace before every meal and evening prayers were the rule. I can still hear, when I remember my summer holidays, my grandfather's voice launching into "Hail Mary, full of grace . . ." as he knelt in the dining room, forearms resting on the back of a chair. The whole family would reply, "Holy Mary, Mother of God . . ." And finally, as darkness descended on the large room, he would appeal for mercy in case death should take one of us in our sleep. My grandmother tended a flower garden in the front yard beneath a cross erected by Great-grandfather Sixte.

However, all these devotions never extinguished our taste for festivities, witticisms, and lively conversation.

Even though they were far from wealthy, these members of my family always had something to give to their fellow men. In the house on the Décharge concession road, there was a room, which we called "the beggars' room," that was occupied at one time or another by the destitute people who used to roam the countryside in those days.

In truth, the events of everyday life were bound up with religious practice. Even death itself unfolded in a way that joined the sacred and the profane.

My grandmother's passing was no exception. All the members of the family had been informed of the imminence of her death. My father left immediately for Saint-Coeur-de-Marie. He took me along, no doubt because I was the oldest and I was my grandparents' godson.

It was winter and I was fourteen. Of course, taking my grandmother to a hospital was out of the question. She would die where she had lived. They had placed her on a sofa next to the piano in the large living room, whose double arched doors were now open. She was half-conscious and near death. One of her daughters, a nun, and one of her sons, a priest, were taking turns reciting the rosary and the prayers for the dying. My grandmother was a long time dying, visibly tormented with pain. It was the first time I had seen someone die, and I wondered what evil she had done to deserve so much suffering.

The house was full of people, now talking softly, now responding to the prayers. Late in the day, Uncle Roméo, bigger than ever, just in from Passes-Dangereuses, came bursting into the room. His mother did not recognize him. He collapsed in a corner, sobbing like a child.

I can still see my grandfather kneeling at the foot of the sofa, his head resting on his hands. When his companion of more than fifty years drew her last breath, his shoulders shook with silent sobs.

He never recovered and neither did the rest of the family. Uncle Adélard and my grandfather died within four years. Then the others started falling like flies: Uncle Roméo, Uncle Rivard, and my father. Uncle Eugène, who undertook the modernization of the farm, held on until 1987.

Naturally, I often went back to the big house. But I knew it had lost its soul. Things would never be the same for the family. As for me, even though I was not yet an adult, I had the feeling my childhood was over.

2

Jonquière:
Classical Studies

This feeling was confirmed by the end of the following June, 1951. Summer holidays had just begun, and because I had been playing with some friends, I was late for supper. Fearing a reprimand, I ran home. The whole family was already at the table. My father got up, looking very upset. But to my great surprise, he put his hand on my shoulder and congratulated me. He asked me to read a letter he had just opened. It said: "Your son Lucien has been accepted as a student at the nonresidential college for classical studies, Externat Saint-Michel." The whole family had been anxiously awaiting the news since I had taken the entrance exams a few months earlier.

In those days, classical studies was the only road to higher education and a profession. Few people today remember the prestige accorded students of the classics. Everyone admired them for tackling the arcane disciplines of Latin, Greek, literature, apologetics, physics, chemistry, and philosophy. I remember the welcoming speeches at the beginning of the academic year saluting us as the "the élite of tomorrow" and congratulating us for keeping company with Aristotle, Titius Livius, and Corneille. The homily was embroidered with quotations from Sertillanges describing the challenge of intellectual work.

These words inflated the pride of unschooled boys who lacked particularly elegant backgrounds. In the more clear-sighted, such lofty expectations inspired feelings of apprehension.

But there was no denying the special prestige classics students enjoyed. After all, they were the future priests, or failing that, future doctors, notaries, and engineers. Or, at worst, lawyers, which was better than nothing.

Since most parents in Jonquière and Kénogami could not afford to send their children to the Séminaire de Chicoutimi, Externat Saint-Michel was the only entry into the rarefied world of classical education. The population of the two towns being mostly working class, there was a great crush to get in. Elementary schools registered their best seventh-graders for the entry exams, which covered French and general knowledge, plus IQ and aptitude tests.

Obviously, the system was terribly exclusive. Of the two hundred candidates, only thirty or forty of us were selected to discover the rudiments of Latin that fall.

For girls, the only option was the Collège du Bon Pasteur in Chicoutimi. But there, no truck driver's family could breach the money barrier, which is why our only sister — and so many other talented girls — gave up any idea of classical studies and university.

Today we easily criticize the public high schools and CÉGEPs created in the wake of the Parent Commission in the 1960s. But at least the system gives everyone an equal chance, which does not mean that we cannot improve it or thet we should overlook its shortcomings.

One thing is certain: without the Externat Saint-Michel and Collège de Jonquière, which replaced it, none of my brothers could have completed the schooling that eventually led to their doctorates in France, any more than I could have gone on to university.

These nonresidential schools seemed to have sprung from some sort of compromise. The three in our region covered only the first four years of the classical curriculum. Each year bore a name that still sounds strange after all these years: *éléments latins, syntaxe, méthode,* and *versification.* The four-year cycle ended with a fearsome examination called *Immatriculation,* administered and corrected by Laval

University's faculty of arts. Successful students boarded for the next four years in a "real" classical college, like the Séminaire de Chicoutimi. These years had equally evocative names: *belles-lettres, rhétorique, philosophie I,* and *philosophie II.*

The three *externats* in the Saguenay–Lac-Saint-Jean area seemed to be loosely attached to the Séminaire de Chicoutimi, which vouched for their academic performance to Laval University. In fact, religious orders ran all three: the Frères du Sacré-Coeur in Jonquière, the Frères de l'Instruction chrétienne in Arvida, and the Marists in Alma. The most famous Marist was Jean-Paul Desbiens, who wrote under the name of Frère Untel. He was directly descended — through his mother, a Bouchard — from Great-great-grandfather Omer, father of Sixte.

When will Québec society ever settle its account with the teaching brothers? I use the expression literally, in the sense of paying one's debts. But before we can pay our debts, we have to acknowledge them. We are being incomprehensibly stubborn in not doing so. Yet thousands of teaching brothers gave their best to the critical field of education, especially among the underprivileged. They did so humbly and, I would say, obscurely, seeking neither prestige nor power.

I always wondered why they did not receive the same respect as the nuns. Nuns are held in very high esteem, although they make the same vows and are on the same footing canonically. Perhaps it's because teaching brothers were considered inferior to secular and regular priests. Since women, on the other hand, were not admitted to the priesthood and could not be anything else but nuns, they were not subjected to hierarchical comparisons. It could not be said of nuns, as I have heard it said of brothers, that they were "failed priests."

I was an altar boy for a few years at Saint-Dominique Church in Jonquière. Some weeks, I served mass at six in the morning. As I passed by the Académie Saint-Michel at 5:45 a.m., I always saw a brother flooding the students' skating rink.

The brothers showed undeniable devotion. They organized hockey leagues, basketball tournaments, and track meets. They rehearsed plays and ran debating societies. But I think their greatest contribution was in setting up small libraries for each class. I made the rounds, devouring the books in one after the other. It is impossible to imagine today what pleasure it was for boys between ten and twelve who had never had books of their own to discover hundreds of new titles. I roared through a collection called *Signe de piste,* the adventures of Captain John's Biggles and Worrals, the works of Jules Verne, Carl May, and later Dickens, Balzac, and Victor Hugo. Some days, reading from four in the afternoon until late in the night, I managed to devour two books. I had loved reading since the age of five, when my parents made me read the illustrated weekly supplement of *L'Action catholique,* a paper they subscribed to.

However, school took precedence, and it was easy — until I landed in eighth grade and started Latin.

The superiors of the Order of the Brothers of the Sacred Heart must have sent their best teachers to the Externat Saint-Michel. The brothers had everything to prove by this incursion into a realm traditionally reserved for the clergy. The repercussions fell on us, since our teachers' success could only be measured by ours.

I must say their teaching skills lacked a certain sophistication. They never believed in magic formulas or easy solutions; they had an ironclad conviction that nothing came without effort. Everything was centred around work, intellectual stimulation, and emulation. They encouraged everyone to surpass his fellow students and urged the whole class to outdo the venerable Séminaire de Chicoutimi. Ours was a Spartan regimen of parsing, compulsory readings, compositions, and examinations. Everything was in keeping with the institution's Latin motto, which offered little comfort: *Illumino consumendo,* meaning "I shine consuming myself." The Séminaire's motto did not demand as much of our rivals: *Spes messis in semine,* "The crop's hope lies in the seed."

Every month, the students' grades were published in the *Ordo.* There was triumph for some, torture for others, but the gradings mercilessly crushed the aspirations and pretensions of the majority. Of course, parents were routinely informed. A prelate from the Séminaire was invited (unless he invited himself) to render judgement: "This one, first; this other, last." For, once inside the sanctum, we were not free from the rigours of élitism. In fact, it was even worse.

There was only one law, the survival of the best. A harsh law, we would all agree. For some, it is barely more acceptable than the closely related law of the survival of the fittest. Does surpassing oneself necessarily mean the subordination of others?

During the 1970s, that thought kept coming back to me as modern educators wanted to do away with examinations and promote self-expression and development. Whether the idea sprang from good intentions or laxity does not change reality: employers still hire the graduates with the best grades, university faculties apply the same criteria for admission quotas, and bursaries go to the best students. In life, as my father would say, it's the same thing: How can you prevent hardworking people and nations from pushing ahead of the others?

But let's get back to the story of the brothers and their school. Inspired by their students' academic success, they thought they could do more. They wanted to add the last four years of the classical course to the curriculum of Externat Saint-Michel. However, the ecclesiastical authorities flatly refused.

So all of us in the fourth year of the course faced the same problem our predecessors had: finding another institution to graduate from. At the last minute, the Oblate fathers, responding to an appeal from a group of parents, decided to found the Collège de Jonquière. The three *externats* closed their doors, and most of their students enrolled in the new college when it opened in 1955. At first it offered only the first five years of the classical course, but the other three were added as the students advanced. In 1959, we were the first graduates of the new college.

It is impossible to write about my education without talking about my alma mater. As we grew into manhood, this new school was growing into a college. We were well aware that we played a leading role in this dual development.

But in the beginning, there were only the Oblates. Having decided to establish themselves in the Jonquière area, the order took great care in choosing its pioneers. They were well-advised in their appointments. Pierre-Paul Asselin, the first superior, proved a true founder. Originally from Saint-Ambroise in the Lac-Saint-Jean area, he had spent his career until then preaching and teaching, mainly in community organizations. Before coming to Jonquière, he was chaplain of the Jeunesses ouvrières catholiques, the Young Catholic Workers Organization. Gérard Arguin, a passionate young philosopher with a keen interest in literature and a born educator, made an ideal dean of studies. And there was Émile Normand, professor emeritus and a knowledgeable educator, whose outward sternness could not hide his great love for his students. The fourth man on the team was Father Bilodeau. He played many roles: accountant, administrator, architect, and contractor. Between two daily masses and two readings of his breviary, he managed the operations and the almost spontaneous growth of the young institution with military precision.

Educators without match, the Oblates were also innovators. The campus, today one of the most handsome in Québec, mushroomed. The fathers received unconditional support from local people, led by the curate of Saint-Dominique's parish, Monsignor Luc Morin. Without him, the Oblates could never have overcome the misgivings of the bishop of Chicoutimi, who favoured the diocesan Séminaire.

It was impossible to extinguish the old rivalry between the Externat Saint-Michel and the Séminaire, which was fuelled by the competition between Jonquière and Chicoutimi. Especially since the Oblates wanted to give their teaching a social dimension, which could only set their own college apart from the traditional seminaries. The working-class population served by the college lent itself to this approach. The Oblates considered community development just as important as the students' individual development. Father Asselin's welcoming speeches focused more on our social responsibilities than on the privileges issuing from our future professional status. Taking advantage of the relative freedom allowed by Laval University's faculty of arts, the Oblates insisted on teaching courses in trade unionism, economics, and science. In a way, the college was a CÉGEP before they even existed.

Later, I realized the Oblates had set their priorities straight. They were uncompromising regarding discipline in work and academic performance. They overwhelmed us with homework, essays, and examinations. After the brothers of the Sacred Heart, I felt right at home. On the other hand, the Oblates showed unusual flexibility in freedom of thought and speech. We could discuss anything with them, including religion, without being branded iconoclasts. They also showed indulgence for the usual pranks: you couldn't make the honour roll by smoking in the washrooms but neither did they expel you for it, as they did in other well-kept institutions. Bringing beer to the house of retreat certainly got you two very bad moments, one at school and one at home. But the crime, worthy of infamy elsewhere, did not automatically lead to capital punishment.

The fathers were not afraid to slacken the reins when we showed initiative. They communicated a taste for innovation, free from the traditions that freeze action and smother creativity.

We created the traditions. The college was a vast building site. Outside, construction crews excavated, put up walls, and continuously worked on extensions. Inside, we worked feverishly, organized study groups, movements, and associations. With a classmate, I launched the school paper, whose name, *Le Cran* (boldness), said it all. Yves Villeneuve — later a brilliant engineer and executive at Alcan — and I wrote articles challenging the good fathers' tolerance to new heights. Without flinching, they even accepted my brother Claude's column, which never hesitated to mock their failings and mannerisms. Once, they shot across his bow an invitation to show more restraint. Carried away by his caustic wit, my brother had launched a personal attack on the bishop of Chicoutimi. A few years later, I noticed that the priests at Laval University were much more trigger-happy when it came to censorship.

From Ottawa, whose university they founded, the Oblates brought us a fascination with sports. They initiated us into basketball, gymnastics, football (my brother Roch found fame as a quarterback on the college team), and in track and field. And we excelled at hockey. My three brothers and I were all members of the college team. We won the finals against the best team of the "ordinary" schools of Jonquière, in spite of the insults hurled by their fans, who called us "college fairies." It was only after I left — possibly because of it — that the college team, now with only three Bouchards playing, defeated the champions, the Séminaire de Chicoutimi.

The Oblates themselves refused to get involved in local rivalries.

They had a larger vision than we did. Their most significant contribution was to open up an area that geography had condemned to isolation. The Kingdom of the Saguenay, as some people affectionately called it, is confined to a valley fifty kilometres wide, hemmed in by the Laurentians. To the east, the only outlet is the Saguenay fjord joining the St. Lawrence River at Tadoussac. To the west, it opens on the vastness of Lake Mistassini. The first passable road to Quebec City was not built until 1951.

Open to settlement for only 150 years, the area's population consisted of the overflow from Charlevoix. People migrated north, only to find even harsher land. But where else could they go, these gangs of woodcutters and logdrivers? The time had not yet come for the excess of sons and daughters of large families to move south to Quebec City and Montreal to launch artistic careers or grasp the levers of finance and economic power. (At least they occupied and developed Quebec's own territory instead of going into exile in the United States, as a million of our children have had to do.)

We often talk about the pride of Saguenay–Lac-Saint-Jean. I am aware these days that references to Québec pride are suspect to some, generally the same people who make faces whenever they hear a phrase like "the regions of Québec," immediately thinking of creeping regionalism. The truth of the matter is that regions do exist and they have never stopped feeding metropolitan Montreal.

The word *pride* does not frighten me if it corresponds to reality. We must distinguish between feeling pride and snapping our suspenders. I am proud of Hydro-Québec, but not of its environmental foul-ups. I admired the serenity of the crowds who paraded on Sherbrooke Street in 1990 and 1991. But I didn't care for the giants riding on floats in the Saint-Jean-Baptiste parade, who looked too much like fantasies born of an inferiority complex I thought we had left behind a long time ago.

Pride in Lac-Saint-Jean and the Saguenay is legitimate. People are proud to have survived on their own. They enjoy recalling the names of their fellow citizens who have become successful at home or elsewhere, in business, sports, and the arts. They have a traditional distrust of government, which, except for the Union Nationale, admittedly ignored them. Politicians remembered them only to bestow on *les Anglais* some timber limits, permits to flood farmlands, or hydroelectric rights on their rivers. And people in our families still remember how some of our grandfathers or great-uncles, during the Great Depression, refused to be on the dole or returned their old-age security cheques.

How can we avoid the hazards of withdrawing into our shell? The feeling that success has a high price, that it is always threatened by unemployment and the exodus of young people, helps us resist the temptations of complacency and village triumphalism.

Family sagas all tell of our forefathers' hardships: shacks for living quarters, food shortages, and workdays that lasted from dawn to dusk. With the return of summer, my father walked barefoot to the local school. In winter, in the first family home, he had to break the ice in the water bucket in his room to wash in the morning.

Above all, our people have always been aware of their isolation and its cost. Although from the beginning they had been selling their wood to the United States and England, and later their paper and aluminum all over the globe, as late as the 1950s they had little contact with the outside. For a long time, relations with the outside world and the management of industries were the privileges of an English-speaking élite. The woodcutters and the aluminum workers did not deal with international clients. At least, not in their own language.

Several attempts to break the pulpwood monopoly of Price Brothers failed resoundingly. The picturesque ghost town of Val-Jalbert and the monumental ruins of the old pulpmill in Chicoutimi are the only relics of our fathers' valiant attempts to endow the area with its own forestry industry.

Curiously enough, there was no acrimony towards English-speaking managers, no doubt because the Québec temperament is not a vindictive one. However, collective memory has certainly not forgotten anything. Otherwise, what is the explanation for the speed and consistency with which the region has responded to the appeal of sovereignty?

It was into this tightly knit community that the Oblates landed. Television had just arrived, but there was little contact with the world outside. I myself didn't look very cosmopolitan, having only been once or twice to Quebec City and never to Montreal. Understandably, my encounter with the humanities and the Oblates was a breath of fresh air.

I have never accepted the way the Parent Report, or its implementation, turned its back on the humanities, shortsighted vision bordering on irresponsibility. For most cultures in the West, the humanities lead us back to the sources of our civilization, surely the only way of nourishing and keeping our values alive. I understand and believe in the necessity of reforming outdated institutions, but I can't understand our eagerness to tear up our roots. Was there no way to weed the garden without uprooting the lettuce and radishes? Some pedantic fools in the Ministry of Education went so far as to eliminate history as a compulsory subject in secondary schools and, recently, in CÉGEPs. Bureaucratic constraints forced them to, they will tell you. Bureaucrats themselves, they are merely referring to their own turpitude. In any case, no pedagogical theory, no matter how hazy, can justify their actions. The net result of their irresponsible action will be to cut our children off from the foundations of Western thought — not to mention the others — as well as from the wellspring of their Québécois identity. Treacherous is the bliss of those who know not who they are or where they come from.

We must expand our intellectual frontiers as well as our economic ones.

As for me, at the age of fifteen, my horizons were so narrow and my motivation so undeveloped that I could only benefit from an intense intimacy with the Ancients. I cherished Greek and Latin and the access they provided to the treasures of antiquity. I would have been ready to pay for the privilege of translating Latin texts. My teacher, Father Reneault Poliquin (the brother of well-known Radio-Canada commentator Jean-Marc Poliquin), enrolled me in provincial competitions because I enjoyed them. Struck down by a heart attack during his best years, virtually between lectures, this eminent Latinist had won our esteem with his knowledge and his passionate efforts to get us to love the language of Cicero.

Father Arguin's French-literature courses were often inspired and always exhaustive. As the curriculum required, we spent a great deal of time in the company of seventeenth-century authors. Though these writers made the beauty of the language much more accessible to me, my youth and inexperience prevented me from sympathizing as much as I should have with the torments of Andromaque. Despite my father's lessons on life, I could not grasp as well as Father Arguin Rodrigue's motives for striking down his fiancée's father with his sword. Despite our knowing looks, what did we at fifteen or sixteen know of how love, ambition, honour, greed, and glory can ravage the human heart?

But right from the start I was a ready audience for Molière — who is less pretentious and closer to the people — especially after the priests took us to Québec City to see *Le Bourgeois gentilhomme* during the North American tour of the Comédie Française. With Louis Seignier in the role of Monsieur Jourdain, the play introduced me to the magic of theatre.

Our history lessons made little impression. It seems to me we dwelt too much on New France and raced through the nineteenth and twentieth centuries. It was as if we had ceased to exist after the Conquest. Will we never come to terms with this defeat on the Plains of Abraham?

Our science teacher, a Frenchman from Algeria, was a layman, and his influence went beyond the confines of his course. Maurice Scory surely inspired the scientific careers of many of my schoolmates. Taking a free hand with manuals, he went beyond formulas, which he made us find ourselves. He wanted us to enter into the spirit of scientific inquiry. The precision and elegance of his demonstrations demystified mathematics and opened wide the doors of physics and chemistry. We often gathered around him after his classes to discuss a range of topics. He had travelled widely, fought in the Second World War, and lived a full life. I remember one physics class that dealt almost exclusively with General de Gaulle's return to office. I have no idea what brought Mr. Scory to Jonquière, but it was a stroke of luck for us.

The teaching of philosophy was a scandal. The curriculum required our teachers to use a three-tome manual written in kitchen

Latin by a professor at the Séminaire de Québec, Abbé Henri Grenier. Apart from its failure to render justice to St. Thomas Aquinas, whose philosophical works sounded as if they had been condensed by *Reader's Digest,* this unintelligible scribbler and the way it was used amounted to a betrayal of philosophy.

Our Oblate teachers had studied in the faculty of philosophy at the University of Ottawa, one of the best in Canada, while at Laval the faculty was just a den of *intégristes,* people who believed in maintaining religion's hold on civil society. Doubtless unimpressed by Abbé Grenier, our teachers had us buy new books, all published in France. From the first moment, these books opened our eyes to the beauty of the queen of sciences. We plunged in, reading about and discussing Being, Free Will, and any idea that flashed through our minds. Alas, our eagerness was cooled somewhat by the results of the first examinations imposed on us by Abbé Grenier's successors. Most of us failed miserably, while others just passed by the skin of their teeth.

Only one student came out of it with honour: I think he even scored 20 out of 20. His older brother at the Séminaire de Chicoutimi had warned him about the Oblates' approach, which was based too closely on the Socratic method. And he had given him a tip: just learn Abbé Grenier's pointless commentary by heart and then spit it out word for word.

After recovering from the shock, teachers and students alike began to drone out Abbé Grenier's simpleminded and definitive answers, like schoolboys reciting the catechism. We answered questions like "What is socialism?" or "Why must we reject it?" Such gibberish as *Socialismus rejiciendus est* or *Minor patet ex dictis* resurfaces from time to time — hiccups of memory.

As for their own responsibilities, the Oblates took every opportunity to expand our minds. They invited tenor Raoul Jobin, who, despite being at the end of his career, gave a superb recital. Missionaries passing through told us about Africa, Japan, South America, or the Canadian North. Explorers, filmmakers, writers, and businesspeople described their work. Cardinal Léger visited us just after his appointment to the high rank of Prince of the Church. He had the language and the bearing for it. I have no trouble remembering him: the fathers had me compose the students' address and read it to this august personage.

For other reasons and on a less elevated plane, I have a vivid recollection of a ballet recital the fathers decided to hold one day. A dancer, a young woman from a touring company performing in the area, executed some steps from *Swan Lake*. She was a graceful, raving beauty and built like a goddess. Her triumph owed as much to lust as to aesthetics. The Oblates concluded that our initiation into ballet should go no further. From then on, basketball was the only activity allowed in the great school hall.

The fathers handled partisan politics with even more caution than they did ballet. I don't remember ever hearing a politician at the college. Although the fathers had great respect for the public good, their consideration apparently did not extend to politicians and electoral activities. They preferred talking about the common good and the role of every individual in promoting it. They approached politics from the angle of the Church's social doctrine and of the duties assigned to every Christian. However, they were not ready to join the political struggle waged by Dominican priest Georges-Henri Lévesque, another son of Lac-Saint-Jean, who fought Duplessis and who founded the faculty of social sciences at Laval University. To Father Asselin, for example, working for the public good was primarily a moral obligation, which might or might not lead to public service. Then again, it seemed that commitment to the public good assumed greater value when it was turned towards public service. It is no surprise, therefore, to see so many graduates of the college working as civil servants in Québec City and elsewhere.

The fathers never denounced the Union Nationale régime. While this was the result of their sense of obligation to be reserved with civil authorities, there was probably also an element of prudence. They had dipped into their own coffers to build the college, but they also needed government grants. In any case, they showed no inclination towards nationalism and scrupulously kept their distance from it.

This noncommittal attitude hardly contributed to our politicization. As for me, particularly towards the end of my studies, I was more preoccupied with my own future and torn by the decisions I had to make about where my life should go.

For a while I believed I was destined for the priesthood. During the summers preceding my entrance into philosophy class, I got a job in the bush after applying, in my best English, to Price Brothers. The last summer, though living in camp with forty other men, I buried myself in Bernanos and thought very seriously about the priesthood. Others had guessed as much from how seriously I took my studies, my taste for austerity, as well as the relative distance I kept from girls, which was more the result of shyness than design. One day, in the presence of my parents, Monsignor Morin placed his red biretta on my head and said, "Lucien will be our cardinal." My mother didn't ask as much and would have been happy with an ordinary priest — as long as he did not "act simple."

When I eventually dropped the whole idea, I had hardly any time to make new plans. We were only a few weeks from graduation. At the ceremony, we were to pin on colour-coded ribbons denoting our chosen profession: white for the priesthood, red for medicine, and so on. At the last minute, I managed to register at Laval University in medicine, science, arts, and social sciences. After discovering I could get a BA after one year in social sciences, I decided to spend my first year in that faculty to give me time to think about my future.

That is how, in the fall of 1959, I left for Québec City.

3

Québec City:
Years of Ferment

I was leaving behind both my family and the region that had been my home. It was a shock arriving in Québec City, where I knew only the zoo and the Capitole Theatre. Suddenly, I had to contend with a large city and a university.

The city was the easier to deal with. In my endless walks, I discovered the autumnal beauty of the Plains of Abraham and the lively bustle of rue Saint-Jean with its taverns, cabarets, and shops. I loafed for hours in the Place d'Youville, which had not yet been disfigured by the horrible pink cube that was to replace the Hôtel Montcalm. This harsh architectural judgement is probably due to my regret over the disappearance of the hotel itself, which, although not particularly elegant, was the only place a penniless and starving student could enjoy a sirloin *beurre noisette,* everything included, for $1.65. With those prices, it wasn't surprising that the hotel had to close its doors.

I frequently passed the front doors of the Château Frontenac and the Clarendon Hotel. I was both intrigued and intimidated by their doormen, who were costumed and brocaded like imperial marshals.

The Château Frontenac's surroundings immediately became my favourite area. They still are. Few panoramas are comparable. From the heights of the Citadel, I could see the Québec bridge,

Saint-Romuald, Lévis, the tip of Ile d'Orléans, and the Beaupré coast as far as Mont Sainte-Anne. Level with the Château, I could see the old post office, one of the city's most beautiful buildings. Little did I suspect that one day I would be working there as minister of the environment, in the very office Louis Saint-Laurent used when he was prime minister of Canada.

The boardwalk of the Château Frontenac was Quebec's Champs Élysées. People from all over, from Yves Montand to Mathée Altéry, strolled there. Every student knew that the city's most beautiful girls would walk there in the evenings, that they could do so without losing social status. Dressed in their Sunday best even on weekdays, they were said to be unassailable fortresses. They had a reputation for refusing to leave the city, even after marriage, making a lie out of the proverb "Who takes a husband takes a country."

The terrace was also the scene of less mundane activities. I often went there to study on beautiful spring days, sitting near the railing and occasionally glancing at the ships below. Yvon Marcoux (who became president of the General Financing Corporation and later went to Provigo) and I later engaged in peripatetic school exercises there, rehearsing questions and answers on civil law and procedure in preparation for bar examinations as we walked.

I was not the only one starting a new life. There were many of us from outlying areas. The only university northeast of Montreal, Laval drew students from most regions of Québec. In every faculty, each class was a mixture of people from Beauce, Gaspé, Trois-Rivières, and elsewhere. The *bleuets* (blueberries, as natives of Lac-Saint-Jean are called) were out in strength; far from home, their rivalries faded and their natural solidarity came to the fore.

Old college friendships survived. Two classmates from Jonquière and I rented rooms from Madame Saint-Pierre, who, since the death of her husband, lived with her elderly father in a large apartment on rue Claire-Fontaine. I was there four years, leaving only when the building and the rest of the block were torn down to make way for the Grand Théâtre. The beautiful elm tree that kept the sun from my window still stands there, rather lonely at the edge of the parking lot.

Bernard Angers and André Tremblay were marvellous companions during these years, and Madame Saint-Pierre treated us like sons. In no time, we revived the studious atmosphere of our alma mater. After evenings of hard work, we indulged in interminable discussions about the fate of the world. Both of my friends went on to lead successful professional lives. André became a professor at the University of Montreal and Premier Bourassa's constitutional law adviser. Bernard earned a master's degree at the London School of Economics and began a career in Québec's public service, where he eventually rose to the position of deputy minister of revenue.

My early days in social sciences were not so successful. I was disoriented right from the start. First of all, the school's layout did not correspond with the grandiose idea I had of the university. Academically speaking, the faculty was a poor relation. It occupied two rundown houses on narrow rue de l'Université, across from the Séminaire de Québec. These impressions may sound superficial, but they affected me, particularly in light of the medical faculty's sumptuous building on the new Sainte-Foy campus. I felt I had lost status in relation to my former classmates who, like me, had worn the red ribbon of medicine but, unlike me, had not had a change of heart.

I was also disappointed in the first semester's program. I had the unpleasant feeling I was starting my classical studies all over again. Social philosophy seemed so close to the lectures on Saint Thomas Aquinas in Jonquière that I felt Abbé Grenier's ghost was hounding me. We were also subjected to a repeat of our lectures on the social doctrine of the Church. Mathematics advanced hardly further than Maurice Scory's lessons. Political economy was barely a sketchy introduction; I learned more from reading Samuelson's text. Our initiation into sociology bored me to tears. I remember it as an endless series of definitions to learn by heart. The professor, probably distressed at being unable to impart all his knowledge, ended his lecture one day by saying, "This then, pathetically telescoped, is what I had to say on this topic."

I also wondered how the program could ever help me earn a living.

Matters improved in the second semester. Professor Marc-Aurèle Thibault, an unpretentious and very competent man, opened my eyes to the views and complexity of microeconomics. The faculty scheduled two courses by sociologist Guy Rocher. They dazzled me. I followed his lectures with unwavering attention and got a glimpse of what sociology is really all about. Too bad the faculty had not scheduled Professor Rocher during the first semester. While his presence might not have changed the history of sociology, it might have changed mine.

For it was too late. I had missed my appointment with the social sciences. Later, I discovered it wasn't until the second year that one came to the heart of the matter. The first year was simply an overview allowing students to choose between sociology, economics, industrial relations, and political science. But I missed, by one year, my appointment with the authentic social sciences that effectively transformed Québec society.

The fault was all mine. I let timidity get the better of me instead of speaking up to my teachers about my concerns. I never dared to approach them. I just studied as best I could and handed in my assignments.

There was another motive, one that did not surface at the time. From the recommended readings and courses emerged a picture of Québec that left me totally confused, so different was it from the naïve and sentimental one I had formed within the family nest and the sanctuary of college. Father Lévesque's faculty did not make it its business to mask the truth about Québec. On the contrary, statistical, economic, and sociological analysis stripped away the layers of ignorance deposited by generations of complacency and the propaganda of the Union Nationale. The faculty's vision of the Duplessis régime was not as bucolic as that of my father and grandfather, who faithfully perpetuated a long line of *bleus,* as Conservatives are called in family discussions in Québec. The advent of electricity and farm loans to rural Québec, considered giant steps forward, scarcely deserved the name of progress in the eyes of urban intellectuals. What we heard about Duplessis and his associates in our lectures and hallway discussions did not compare these heroes of rural politics favourably to Plutarch's illustrious models. Nor did the merciless description of Québec society have anything to do with the delights of Arcadia, with which we were familiar from our Latin homework. For example, I never found in Marc-Adélard Tremblay's seminar on the working conditions of lumberjacks the epic image I had of my father's sojourn in winter lumber camps.

Without my realizing it, these disorienting perceptions probably contributed to my decision to leave the program.

On the other hand I observed that my roommate, André Tremblay, found the study of law gratifying and absorbing. I seemed to be more interested in his studies than my own, captivated by the rigour and intelligence this ancient discipline placed at the service of justice. I often daydreamed of judicial eloquence. Overstimulated by the arduous decoding of their speeches against Philip of Macedonia and Catiline, my imagination was haunted by Demosthenes and Cicero. A preposterous idea occurred to me: neither of them had ever thought to end a plea with "This then, your Lordship, pathetically condensed, is my argument."

So it was that during my first semester, I decided to give up social sciences and start law the next year. This decision did not stop me from working hard right to the end. I even received an award for excellence. Learning of my decision, Professor Thibault urged me to continue my studies the following year in the department of economics. But the dice had been rolled. I had found my calling and was determined to become a lawyer. However, the year had not been a waste of time. Besides expanding my mind, I had discovered history. My year in Québec City started with the death of Premier Duplessis and ended with a visit by General de Gaulle. One year was not too long to move from one to the other.

When Duplessis died, I was part of the crowd gathered across the square from the Basilica of Québec on the mound with the statue of Cardinal Taschereau, watching the arrival of the funeral procession. I had the sense that I was seeing not so much the death of a public figure as the end of an era. I saw all the dignitaries and officials of the "province" (which is how people used to refer to Québec), with their black hats and grey gloves, emerge from the limousines and follow the casket into the church. People around me were naming the eminent figures they recognized among the procession.

I thought of my grandfather, who in 1956 had risen from his deathbed to vote one last time for Duplessis. I also thought of my father, who said the premier had drafted all the laws of the province with his own hand. "Even the most insignificant laws?" I asked him one day. "All laws are important," he answered.

The crowd waited for the end of the service to see the procession come out. Many had bared their heads. All were silent.

The logic of chance is sometimes curious. It was fit and proper, after the departure of a provincialist eager to keep his little nation isolated from the world, that there should come a giant of the twentieth century, a man determined to restore the province's status of a great nation.

I had already read much about General de Gaulle. I had also devoured *Les Mémoires de guerre* and *Le Fil de l'épée*, a short book on the exercise of power he wrote in 1932. To me, he, along with Churchill and a few others, was the embodiment of history. I was not going to let this opportunity pass. Knowing he was bound for City Hall, I took up a position on a street he would be taking. Several rows of onlookers had already gathered here and there along the way, like human hedgerows. As the general came closer, I could hardly see him through the crowd in front of me. He seemed to be shaking hands right and left with people lined up along the route. I pushed them aside and rushed right to the edge of the street. However, I failed to see the steel wire strung high along the route. Momentum carried me forward. The wire struck me in the face, digging like a bit into my mouth. Needless to say, I was in great pain. At that very moment, the general saw me, and whether he took pity on me or just appreciated my enthusiasm, he held out his hand. I grasped it eagerly. I couldn't help noting how fine and smooth it was. They say the general's entourage thought his welcome had been rather cold in Québec. They certainly can't blame it on me.

After these events, I spent the summer at home with my parents, preparing for law school.

* * *

Jean Lesage and his Quiet Revolutionaries came to power in June 1960. In September I reported to Laval. The law faculty, located in a solid stone building at the foot of the Côte Sainte-Famille, between the Séminaire and the ramparts next to Bassin Louise, still had a façade of immutability. The spacious and functional premises were not luxurious. Their virtuous austerity conveyed with a certain haughtiness the impression that this venerable institution had an authenticity that did not require the architectural ostentation of celebrity and civic pride.

An exclusive preserve of Québec's *haute bourgeoisie,* the faculty was the keystone of a sociopolitical system that had endured for generations. Ecclesiastics and magistrates were equally represented among men of the gown, and were often recruited from the same families. To wear the gown, you had to attend the faculty of law and become a lawyer. From law to politics and politics to government were just a few quick steps, particularly if you had the talent to go along with the family name. The next step was an appointment to the bench. Somewhere along the road, an academic chair might become available. As late as the 1960s, almost all law professors were drawn from private practice and from the ranks of judges and former cabinet ministers. Their availability governed the course timetable: lectures were from eight to ten in the morning and from four to six in the afternoon; this enabled lawyers and judges to go about their professional business according to the hours of the courthouse, which were from ten to four.

Families such as the Choquettes, Galipeaults, Dorions, and Lesages had many sons in the magistracy, both behind and before the bench (judges and prosecutors), who made frequent incursions into politics and academia.

Consider the Taschereau family. Two members, Henri-Elzéar and Robert, were justices of the Supreme Court of Canada; Henri-Thomas was chief justice of the Québec Court of Appeal; a fourth, Louis-Alexandre, was premier of Québec. When I entered the faculty, Jacques, another family member, a future president of the Chamber of Notaries and a man of great reputation, was teaching there.

Roland Fradette, with whom I would soon be practising law in Chicoutimi, used to relate how in 1924, on arriving from his father's farm in Saint-Nazaire in Lac-Saint-Jean to enrol in the faculty, he was asked by one of his professors, "Is the law really for you? Why don't you leave it to our children?"

In other words, the faculty of law was the antithesis of the social sciences faculty. So, I was not feeling very confident when I took my seat in my first class.

I knew none of my classmates. My deskmate, more affable and outgoing than I was, introduced himself: Michel Cogger. He was from Québec City, spoke both French and English, and had just graduated from arts. All this I discovered within the first few minutes of class.

My talkative deskmate also told me that the lanky blond fellow sitting not too far from us was the grandson of Arthur Meighen, a former prime minister of Canada; that another student, Peter Kilburn, was the son of the president of Greenshield's, a large brokerage firm; that another's father was the son of Senator Léopold Langlois. Among this profusion of sons of lawyers, judges, doctors, and engineers, there was the great-nephew of Louis-Alexandre Taschereau and the son of the mayor of Québec City. As my new friend did not know everyone, he eventually came to a stop. We were also somewhat distracted by the professor, who persisted in his lecture. However, one thing struck me above all else: the large contingent of anglophones, mainly from Montreal. I soon learned that this had never happened before in the faculty.

It was 1960 and Québec was waking up. Obviously, the newcomers were eager to understand contemporary events and to integrate into the new society that was about to emerge. Another anglophone group appeared the following year, and the one after that, with the arrival of Conrad Black, George McLaren, and others.

We had enormous sympathy for them and welcomed them with open arms. Our relations went beyond the usual group dynamics. Never did we refer to one another as anglophones or francophones. It was always simply the class, within which we formed friendships according to personal affinities, regardless of language and wealth.

Of course, not everyone in that class of eighty had blue blood in their veins. Many, like me, were of humble origin ("modest but proud," we hastened to add), either from working-class families, such as Jean Thibeault (later secretary general of the Confederation of National Trade Unions), or from rural families, such as Yvon Marcoux. I was surprised to find similar distinctions among my English-speaking classmates. Through circumstances, until then I had only met anglophones who were wealthy and in positions of authority. I assumed that all the students from Westmount and elsewhere came from well-to-do families. I later discovered this was not the case for one student, a fellow from Baie-Comeau.

I did not link up immediately with Brian Mulroney. My first contacts were with Michel Cogger, Paul-Arthur Gendreau, Pierre De Bané, Peter Kilburn, and Michael Meighen.

Although we were very different from each other, Paul-Arthur Gendreau and I got along well. We were generally on the same wavelength. I am not referring to politics, which has nothing to do with friendship and sometimes ruins it. Paul came from Rimouski, where his father practised law before his appointment to the Superior Court. He lived in Québec City with his two sisters, who were also at the university. I was often with all three, which allowed me to rediscover the pleasures of family life.

In Pierre De Bané I found a generous heart and a deep sense of friendship. His background was European, and he did everything with passion. I admired Peter Kilburn's intellect. I approved of the idealist in him, but dreaded the rigorous moralist. He had just returned from a year in India, and he shared his experience with us.

Michael Meighen, the epitome of that untranslatable expression *golden boy,* had everything. Name, fortune, bearing, intelligence, and success with women. We often said he would become prime minister of Canada and would be in office longer than his grandfather. He and Kilburn spoke impeccable and even refined French, apparently acquired in Europe. Mike, as we called him, invited me to his parents' home in Westmount. He also got to know my family. His father, an eminent Montreal-establishment lawyer, had preceded him at Laval's faculty of law. He had been a classmate of Mr. Fradette, whose son Paul was in our class. What chance meetings life arranges for us!

Within a few months I had greatly enlarged my circle of acquaintances: Yvon Marcoux, a man with clear ideas and a head for law, whose heart was in the right place; Raynold Langlois, whose combativeness and fearsome arguments turned him into an outstanding lawyer; Bernard Roy, a model of honesty and generosity; Peter White, a man with a discerning mind and an enterprising temperament, a probing observer of Québec society; Bruno Bernard, the youngest in the class, who was warm and resourceful; René Croft, a Séminaire de Chicoutimi graduate, with good judgement, disarming amiability, who was a notary and a son of a notary.

I could go on about most of the others. Without a doubt, the group was restless, brilliant, and ambitious.

I will not readily forget our participation in the 1964 Winter Carnival. We were in fourth year; during half of the year we received practical instruction and the other half was spent articling in a law office. I had the luck to be accepted as a clerk in the prestigious law firm of Létourneau, Stein. At the instigation of Eugène-Marie Lapointe, who was a lieutenant in the Canadian Armed Forces, we decided to celebrate Carnival with a commando raid on the most popular local radio station. The objective of the operation, under Eugène-Marie's command, was to seize the station *manu militari* and broadcast our revolutionary message. The impetuous Lieutenant Lapointe put into it all the joyous ardour associated with the spirit of Saguenay–Lac-Saint-Jean, and the mission was conceived, planned, and executed instantly. The lieutenant, at the head of his shock detachment, burst into the studio and grabbed the microphone. He harangued the people, making liberal use of the energetic and pictur-esque vocabulary of his military training. Many people in Québec City thought our prank had gone too far and some were scandalized.

I was terrified myself. The lieutenant had requisitioned Létourneau, Stein's switchboard for the campaign's communications centre. A clerk, an accomplice, let us in. I might have feared for my career, or at least my reputation, had my superiors not been very understanding about how we had used their offices. They were even more magnanimous with Bruno Bernard, one of the authors of the coup; he is now a partner.

In spite of everything I owed my classmates and despite my pleasure in being with them, I was never able to overcome a certain tension. The competition among us was fierce: to attain the best grades, the widest influence, the most credibility, the most enduring popularity, the most important jobs, and, supreme ambition, the most brilliant career.

The leading factor behind this competitive spirit was the diversity of the group, which represented a cross section of Québec society with all its regional, rural, urban, social, and linguistic elements. This diversity stimulated dialogue and the exchange of ideas. Another factor was the coming together of two educational systems, anglophone and francophone. I may be excused for thinking — I am not so sure — that our contingent's classical training must have had something to do with the competitiveness, too. We were the last to graduate before educational reform. And let's not forget that the collective turmoil of the 1960s was also a powerful catalyst. It revolutionized Québec. It transformed us just as it overwhelmed the old faculty of law.

Naturally, politics also allowed our competitive spirit to run free. In fact, it soon became clear that many of us were destined for such a life.

No graduate of the class of '64 was surprised to learn that Michael Meighen, André Ouellet, Pierre De Bané, and Clément Richard were taking the plunge. Like many others whose entry into politics seemed perfectly understandable, they had shown considerable interest in public affairs. No one was really surprised by the subsequent activities of Peter White, Michel Cogger, and Jean Bazin in the Conservative party. Bernard Roy's case, however, was different. He came on the scene much later, apparently because of his personal ties with Brian Mulroney. These ties were close, and very old, going back to our first year in law.

It took me some time to establish a strong relationship with my classmate from Baie-Comeau. At first, I kept my distance, concentrating on my studies and perhaps even taking refuge in them. But this Irishman could not be ignored for long.

Now that he has written his name in the annals of history, it is difficult to be realistic and objective about him, particularly as the annals are still being written, and not only by historians. The only solution is to return to the vision I had of him in that particular period.

His most striking quality was his charm. There was no hesitation in his outgoing manner; his natural ways and lack of pretension put everyone at ease. His sense of repartee and his disarming smile won him enduring popularity among a growing number of classmates. Those with more insight saw a trace of vulnerability that made him even more appealing. In his first contacts, he never imposed his views or showed off. On the contrary, everyone had the impression that he was happy to have others teach him something. One thing he needed to learn was French; most of the other anglophones in the class had a better command than he did. He set about learning it with such eagerness and application that he made rapid progress. He was never offended when people corrected him and was always searching for new words and expressions, which he would try out at the first opportunity.

As you got to know him better, his ambition became more apparent, as well as his determination to follow the path of politics. His drive, by no means an isolated phenomenon in our class, shocked no one. His ambition had a romantic aura: he saw the world as something to conquer rather than to change, as a place where cruelty spared a few individuals who happened to be more resourceful or fortunate than others. If one can't change the world, one can try symbolically to compensate for the misfortunes of a whole nation, in his case, Ireland.

Brian Mulroney is Irish to the bone. I am thinking not only of his charm, his sentimentality, and his passionate tenacity. In spite of his good humour, occasionally broken by impatient explosions, he knows injustice exists — and that for a very long time it struck his own people very harshly. I always thought that deep down he felt the same way as a French-speaking Québécois would if he lost his language and his country. Deprived of primordial loyalties, he stood alone to realize his dreams and aspirations. For such a person, apart from faith in oneself, the most vital and precious things are family and friends who have inherited the obligations and the privileges of the clan.

This is why Mulroney's secret wound is probably the sorrow he feels that his father, whose memory still haunts him, did not live to see him fulfil his great ambition of becoming prime minister of Canada. It is also why he never spoke with greater emotion than when he implored English Canada, in 1984 and 1988, to right the injustice done to Québec by the constitutional rebuff of 1981–82.

Everyone in the faculty realized the extent of the influence Mulroney had already acquired in political circles when he persuaded Prime Minister John Diefenbaker to make an official visit to the faculty just before his 1962 defeat. No one doubted that the dreams of this well-connected and sociable classmate would be realized through politics.

But it was not until the fourth year that I truly perceived the full magnitude and intensity of his dreams. Circumstances, not very favourable until then, now brought us together. We came to know each other well, talking and walking in the old town, he improving his French while I obstinately refused to speak English because I was paralysed with shame because of my ignorance.

I can still see him in the park next to the law school, poring over a bronze plaque, reading with proper oratorical intonations the words of Georges-Étienne Cartier: "In a country such as ours, all rights must be safeguarded, all convictions must be respected." I later discovered in Donald Creighton's book on the life of Sir John A. Macdonald that the episcopal building, the site of the Québec Conference and the signing of the confederal pact of 1864, had stood on this very spot.

I also remember a pleasant trip with Mulroney to Montreal, in my Volkswagen, to visit Peter White.

We were not in the same social group and even belonged to different camps. Some of his friends worked to defeat me when I ran as faculty representative to AGEL, the students' association of Laval University. Another time, there was a conflict, even an altercation, over a matter submitted for arbitration by the student council.

It was a time when public opinion classified people as being on the left or on the right. Not that we were torn by ideological confrontations or transcendental quarrels. It was a simple question of sensitivity and attitude. I supported Henri Brun and Jules Brière, our seniors by one year, who were campaigning for educational reform in the faculty. They wanted to replace private practitioners with career professors. They also wanted to do away with exegetical learning (article-by-article study of the civil code, with no overview) in favour of a Cartesian approach based on theory and fundamental principles of law. Apparently, that made leftists of us.

There were also occasional hostilities arising from my articles in *Le Carabin,* in 1961–62. *Le Carabin* was the official student newspaper at Laval. My experience with *Le Cran* had given me a taste for journalism. The summer before my year in social sciences, I had the good fortune to be hired by *La Presse.* Under editor Jean-Louis Gagnon, the paper was expanding outside Montreal and opening new bureaus across the province, one of them in Jonquière.

Since they paid me by the inch, I filled column after column with news stories, reports, interviews, anything the desk in Montreal would accept. My haunts were municipal council and school board meetings, and baseball games in Jonquière, Kénogami, and Arvida. During lulls, I told the story of the great Saguenay fire of 1870, the epic flood of Saint-Cyriac, and the life of Sir William Price. I also wrote an architectural series on modern churches in the area, and special reports on the pulp and paper industry. The Jonquière telex clattered ceaselessly. Stimulated by the mode of remuneration, I larded my stories with historical references, social commentary, and local colour. Some of them were so long that the desk in Montreal had to choose between the wastepaper basket and serial publication. But during the summer doldrums, the paper used them most of the time, adding immensely to my gratification when I tallied the copy I had delivered during the week. I was now measuring in feet. Never in my whole life had I earned so much money. My superiors, impressed with my productivity, hired me again the next summer, putting an end to my career as a lumberjack. I owe *La Presse* for teaching me that, in the processing of forest products, it is more profitable and less tiring to scribble on paper than to fell trees in the suffocating heat, harassed by mosquitoes.

As soon as I arrived in Québec City, I offered my services to *Le Carabin,* in which all extravagant minds and would-be writers liked to see their bylines. But getting in was not easy. The editors looked down with scorn at any scribbler fresh from the country.

It took me two years to get established at *Le Carabin*. True, there were a few mishaps. The first year, I barely had time to submit two brief articles before the whole staff resigned in solidarity with one of its members. University authorities had castigated Rémi Savard, a sociology student, for an article entitled "Collusion in Power." To someone who had tasted the liberalism of the Oblates, the text was not particularly offensive. However, attacks on the clergy's complacency during the Duplessis régime offended academic authorities who were still very close to the Archbishop's Palace and the Séminaire de Québec. Almost as soon as I arrived, I had to join the protest and sheathe my pen.

Back at Laval for my first year of law, I knocked on the door of *Le Carabin* again. But I was jinxed. The sword of censorship soon struck another contributor, this time for publishing an article deemed indecent. It was an erotic poem praising the charms of Dora — the poet's girlfriend, no doubt. The author, a medical student by the name of André Blanchet, went into exile at the University of Montreal. The message was clear: if we lacked the virtue to repress our amorous outpourings, we should at least refrain from setting them down in *Le Carabin.* I do not quite remember what happened after that, but again I had to bide my time.

The next year, my second one in law, the timing was right. The student council decided that Denis de Belleval and I should take over *Le Carabin,* as publisher and editor, respectively. I did not know Denis very well. He was in political science. However, I have never ceased to rejoice in the fact that our paths crossed. Our collaboration led to a friendship that owes everything to goodwill and nothing to interest, one sustained by vigilant and unrelenting frankness.

His energy and intellectual abilities played a leading role in the success of "our" paper, *Le Carabin* of 1961–62. It won the Bracken Trophy for the best editorial page of all student newspapers in Canada. It also won the *Le Droit* prize for the best French-language student newspaper.

We had brought together a remarkable team, which included

some of our classmates: Peter Kilburn, Pierre De Bané, and Georges Dubé. The paper ran columns, reports, and studies on the arts, student affairs, literature, love, economics, and social issues. We encouraged controversial writing, as long as it stayed within the bounds of propriety. Satire appealed to some writers. However, our favourite topics were education and politics, always from the angle of questioning society's values. Our tone was one of protest rather than of militancy. In fact, we disliked militancy for its unyielding, and often ambitious attitude. The political clubs tied to the Liberal, Conservative, and Union Nationale parties were our favourite whipping boys. We ridiculed organizations with names like Young Liberals or Young Conservatives. We enjoyed referring to them as "Young Seniors."

We were living in the midst of the Quiet Revolution. Its leading personalities were often seen in the old city and around Parliament Hill. René Lévesque often went to a restaurant called the Aquarium on rue Sainte-Anne. Cabinet ministers Eric Kierans and Paul Gérin-Lajoie didn't mind stopping on the street to answer our questions. I remember meeting Daniel Johnson Senior on the Grande-Allée one evening. Seeing our small group, he stopped to chat. He told us a political anecdote that had us in stitches and made us forget for a moment that we didn't like the Union Nationale.

We were part of the scene. *Le Carabin,* and our group discussions around a huge round table in the great hall of the law school, echoed the debates of the legislative assembly and the controversies of the day.

Educational reform was a hot topic. The law faculty greeted with consternation a bill granting public service employees the right to strike. It was enthusiastically applauded in social sciences. Those in favour argued that union leaders, as responsible citizens, would never exercise their right in hospitals. Those who were opposed predicted that we would indeed soon experience interruptions in health care. The "national question" was already on the agenda. A group of us went down to the railway station to welcome Marcel Chaput, who had been invited to speak in Québec City. Within the class, there were stormy debates on Québec's constitutional demands and the viability of the federal system. Brian Mulroney, Michael Meighen, and Peter White organized a symposium on the theme "Canada: Failure or Success." Many political celebrities participated: André Laurendeau, Jean Lesage, Davie Fulton, and René Lévesque.

As for me, I was not yet committed to independence, though I was an ardent nationalist. In my articles, I did not go as far as Denis de Belleval, who openly advocated independence. I was counting on current reforms, particularly in education, to change the face of society. Many had similar expectations. It was reasonable to believe that a democratic educational system would end Québec's shameful waste of talent and intelligence.

I thought with indignant sadness rather than hurt pride of my father, my mother, my ancestors, and all the others who had never been allowed to shine. Gray's verses, memorized when I was fifteen, came to my mind:

Full many a Gem of purest Ray serene,
The dark unfathom'd Caves of Ocean bear:
Full many a Flower born to blush unseen,
And wastes its Sweetness on the desert Air.

I thought the courage and perseverance of our own people, enhanced by the full development of their intellectual capabilities, would lead them irresistibly, whether under federalism or not, to fulfil their destiny as a nation.

Québec was moving, and in the right direction.

The government created a ministry of education and appointed the Parent Commission to map out the reforms that eventually bore its name. The government also set up the General Financing Corporation, started work on hydroelectric dam Manic 5, and was on the point of nationalizing electricity and making Hydro-Québec the largest public corporation in Canada. Already it was considering setting up a financial institution to manage public pension funds. During this heady period, when everything seemed to be speeding up, it was never far from dream to reality. In 1964, Jean Lesage signed an agreement with Lester Pearson that led to the Caisse de dépôt.

There were new social programs, particularly in the area of health care. The foundations of a modern public administration emerged with the creation of the Treasury Board, a nonpartisan public service, and the beginnings of a salary policy. Nowadays we tend to forget how critical these steps were. Two examples demonstrate this.

The possibility of hospitalization was a universal concern, since hospital bills were beyond the means of the ordinary worker. After the illness of one of its members, it was not unusual for a whole family to go into debt for years or to have their salaries garnisheed or furniture and homes seized for nonpayment of medical bills. From the doctor to the lawyer.

Roch Bolduc, at the time a young civil servant and recent graduate of the University of Chicago, says that, starting in 1953, he saw Premier Duplessis himself revising civil service salary lists. "So and so, this much more. This one, nothing," and so on. The list went back to the appropriate department, with the initials "M.L.D." (Maurice Le Noblet Duplessis) beside each name. In other words, we had an embryonic state that was completely provincial and amateurish. There was even a time when the premier of Québec considered himself inferior to a federal cabinet minister.

Well, Québec was momentarily living in a state of grace; the best minds were answering the call. Arthur Tremblay, Roch Bolduc, Louis-Philippe Pigeon, Yves Pratte, Michel Bélanger, and Claude Morin were already at work. Guy Rocher had joined the Parent Commission. Jean Marchand, whom many of us saw as our next leader, was head of the progressive Confederation of National Trade Unions, which was waging the good fight on many fronts and identified itself with the future of Québec. Jacques Parizeau, Yves Martin, and many others trained in the greatest universities of the world would soon be joining them.

When Québec awakens and thrives, it does not withdraw into its shell. It opens up to the world.

The artisans of the Quiet Revolution, most of them disciples of Father Lévesque, believed that it was up to us alone to manage our development within the federal framework. They practised affirmative action before its time. They believed that an educated community, master of its own economy and supported by the resources of a modern state, could push its way through all constitutional barriers. They postulated that their Canadian partner would have the political maturity and openness of mind to accept this evolution. In any event, natural forces would eventually bring English Canada to accept the structural changes giving rise to a modern society that was economically strong and politically self-determined.

I thought so, too, more or less. In other words, many people, as the future would show, had illusions about the attitudes of English Canada as well as about the virtues of the Quiet Revolution. They underestimated the debilitating effect of federal constraints.

We said these things over and over as we wrote our articles and laid out the paper with the whole team every Monday evening in the Pollack building. Our articles were handed to others whose merciless editing might have owed something to the savage treatment previously given their own work. Regularly putting one's thoughts and attitudes on paper is a tough discipline. Once a week that year, we experienced the intimate correspondence between thought that feeds writing and writing that ordains thought.

Censorship was now more discreet. We were summoned two or three times by professors angry about some article, but we had no real problems. I had already taken the lead by denouncing the inclusion of several books on the Church's Index of prohibited books. University authorities, no doubt having learned from their past mistakes, were showing more flexibility. They had organized a joint management committee to which I was appointed. But we did not manage a thing. As students we were no match for university representatives who, like André Bisson, easily manipulated us.

The Monday-evening sessions were exhilarating. Denis de Belleval and I had the power of life and death over articles submitted, which gave us an exaggerated sense of our own importance. We would not have been prouder putting to bed the editorial pages of the *New York Times*. Two days later we would be checking proofs at a printing shop in Lévis. This was a real printer, like in the old days, one who worked with lead, hands stained with ink.

It happens that some images stand out from a long list of routine activities. One is of a trip Denis and I made to Lévis one afternoon in April. The ferry was cutting through the ice, while the stone façades of the old city receded into the distance, warmed by the young sun. It was springtime in Quebec City.

After *Le Carabin,* I was involved with Laval's *Cahiers de droit,* of which I became chief editor. I regularly published legal commentary and studies, which brought me into close contact with several professors, among them Marie-Louis Beaulieu, Louis Marceau, and André Desgagnés. The reformists who were campaigning against the law faculty were not complaining about the quality of their professors but about their teaching methods and a system that deprived them of support. After-class discussions or explanations were not possible when professors had to rush off to court to plead an important case.

On the whole, however, our professors were distinguished jurists: Louis-Philippe Pigeon, constitutional law; Yves Pratte, commercial law; Robert Cliche, practical instruction on formal legal interrogation and pleading; André Patry, international law; Jean-Charles Bonenfant, Roman law; Julien Chouinard, corporate law; and Antoine Rivard, appeals procedure. Three of them were later to sit as judges on the Supreme Court of Canada.

I was closely acquainted with Professors Beaulieu, Marceau, Desgagnés, and Patry. Marie-Louis Beaulieu was an old-fashioned gentleman, always available and had a politeness that left us with the impression that we were his equals. He had given up the practice of law to teach. A brilliant intellectual worker, he liked to write and loved his students, who often took advantage of his easygoing ways. Without any sense of false modesty, he would quote legal decisions that had gone against him. He was an expert in land claims and knew all there was to know about fence disputes in Beauce.

Professors Louis Marceau and André Desgagnés, the only career professors we had, were the rising stars of the faculty. They had earned doctorates in Paris and had introduced a new form of teaching founded on legal principles rather than on the memorization of legal codes. They put a great deal of fervour into their work, particularly Marceau, a specialist in civil responsibility. One of his lectures, given with unusual passion, we called "The Tragedy of the Mandate."

Desgagnés was versed in public law and taught administrative law. This otherwise warm and civil man was ferocious when he graded examination papers, cutting a wide swath of victims.

The new faculty was built around these two young professors, as career academics trained in France, England, and the United States gradually replaced the old faculty.

André Patry stood out in this circle of jurists. Originally from social sciences, he taught international law, but his culture and erudition went beyond the strict limits of his lectures. Patry discussed diplomacy, NATO, geopolitics, and France's André Malraux, my idol of the moment. I went without many a sirloin steak to acquire the Pléiade edition of his complete works. Patry had actually met Malraux, and had even been invited to his home. I had never come close to anyone who had read and travelled so much.

He used to invite Denis de Belleval and me to sample, with more appetite than refinement, the exotic cuisine of the Nanking restaurant, which later burned down, and that of Kerhulu's, a magnificent establishment that was demolished to make way for progress. Patry, with staggering erudition, dissected international politics, conversed about Italy, painting, and water-level agreements on the Great Lakes. But his main purpose was to raise our expectations.

He did not hide his disapproval when I told him I would be returning home to practise law. Most of my friends had opted for Montreal and Québec City. But I had taken several summer workshops in the offices of Fradette, Bergeron, and Cain in Chicoutimi. I had enjoyed them and had developed a good relationship with the partners. Though five years in Québec City had expanded my horizons, my ties with my family and my home region were as strong as ever. I was also very serious about a young woman from Alma.

My parents travelled to Québec City for my graduation, during which I received my law degree and a few awards, including one from the Québec Bar Association. My father, already suffering from the illness that would eventually kill him, demonstrated his approval by taking my mother and me for a hamburger-steak dinner at the Laurentian restaurant in Place d'Youville.

Before leaving the city, I had the opportunity to make my first political speech, during a demonstration in front of the legislature where the 1964 federal-provincial conference was convening. While the first ministers were meeting inside, several hundred students, from every university in Québec, had gathered outside to shout slogans and brandish placards.

It was agreed that I would speak for the students from Laval. When my turn came, I climbed onto the base of the statue of the Indian standing in front of the main doors of the legislature. I tried my best to persuade my audience to support Jean Lesage in his demands to the federal government and English Canada. (The Caisse de dépôt was one issue under discussion, and Québec won.)

For the first time, I experienced the unique sensation that comes from communicating with a crowd, which responded to my questions with shouts and noisy approval. Obviously, everyone liked my performance.

Everyone, that is, but Pierre Marois, who was representing students from the University of Montreal and succeeded me on the base of the statue. I was distressed to hear him say he deplored my shortsighted speech, in which I had been content to call for solidarity with Premier Lesage. Marois said the real struggle was for social justice and improvements in the conditions of the underprivileged. I admired Marois and was mortified by the cold water thrown on my burgeoning eloquence. I even pushed aside a furtive regret for not having taken law at the University of Montreal.

However, I would not be going to the big city for a while. Soon I was loading up my Volkswagen and heading in the opposite direction, towards Chicoutimi.

4

A Lawyer
in the Making

The professional reason for my return home bears a name: Roland Fradette, a man totally unknown outside Saguenay–Lac-Saint-Jean and the dwindling circle of judges and lawyers who had seen him at work.

Of course, this is not surprising since there is nothing about the practice of a profession like law that appeals to the media. Such factors as the privileged nature of the client–lawyer relationship and a professional association that has the status of a private club keep a wall between the public and the lawyers. The greatest lawyers, largely known to the public when alive, are totally forgotten once dead. Eloquent words fly away and the most skilful pleas do not survive beyond the final judgement closing the case. And the profession wants it this way. Only recently has it lifted its ban on personal advertising. The better the lawyer, the less he needed it.

A lawyer like Fradette was doubly condemned to anonymity, for he exercised his profession in a region considered remote by those who never go there. Yet he was one of the finest courtroom lawyers of his generation. He brought much to bear on his legal arguments: a full command of the language, an impressive knowledge of the law, his culture, and his lively mind.

Seldom have I heard anyone speak French so well. We all know the lessons in humility orators can derive from reading transcripts of their improvised speeches. Who has not looked in vain in such a jumble for the object or point of a muddled sentence? Who has not cursed the pet words, the repetitions, the barbarisms that find their way into a discourse? In Fradette's case, although he had a very large vocabulary, his sentences were always clear and grammatically flawless. His elocution was without equal: he was charming when he needed to please and unfailingly rigorous when he needed to convince.

Fradette always said that cases were usually won or lost during examination. He had a gift for cutting through the defences of the most recalcitrant witness. He played all registers: bonhomie, indignation, fierceness, and seduction. His favourite prey were the expert witnesses who earned high fees for defending the viewpoint of the cheque-signer. He engaged in contests in which he took great pleasure in finding them at fault on some technical angle or in making them contradict testimony given in another case.

Fradette always knew exactly when to end his interrogation. Lawyers too eager to press an advantage often fall into the trap of asking one question too many, the one that allows the witness to recover and provide an answer fatal to the case.

Though Fradette professed the deepest respect for justice and all who render it, he was also unsparing of judges. Judges respected and feared him. They knew that it was his principle never to accept a judgement that he thought was wrong, which explains why he so often appeared in appeal courts in Québec City, Montreal, and Ottawa. Robert Cliche and others confirm that, during the 1950s, professors at the law faculty often urged their students to sit in on the Court of Appeal when one of Fradette's cases was on the roster. Endowed with an exceptional memory, he read a huge number of legal reports and retained their substance.

Fradette was nondescript, except that his face and eyes exuded intelligence. He was fearsome at chess, unbeatable at bridge. Like Saint-Simon with the French nobility, he could describe the family trees of his acquaintances and unearth the most remote alliances. "So and so? But you are related to the seventh degree." And he could prove it with a long chain of marriages and births.

To his associates and articling students, one of his most precious gifts was his ability to teach. He loved to share his knowledge and train young people. He let nothing pass. Screening our legal opinions and our research reports, he laid bare their logical structure and corrected their language. He resented tediousness in speech and in writing. Nothing annoyed him so much as a statement that started with the tail and ended with the head.

He had learned about life the hard way. Originally a lumberjack, he had to go back to work on the family farm after wounding his leg. The parish priest, noting his lively mind, taught him the rudiments of Latin and Greek and paid for his studies at the Séminaire de Chicoutimi. Fradette finished the course in six years. At Laval, he stood first in his class and articled with the father of Louis-Philippe Pigeon, another government legal adviser. Returning to Chicoutimi to practise law, he literally starved during the Great Depression. A voracious reader, he was particularly knowledgeable about seventeenth-century French literature and French political history. He spoke of Georges Clémenceau, Aristide Brillant, Jean Jaurès, Raymond Poincaré as if they had been personal acquaintances, and he could recite excerpts from their speeches in the National Assembly. He knew by heart long passages of the pleas delivered during the Dreyfus Affair and the trial of Marshal Pétain. He was something of a freethinker. Though he occasionally read Voltaire during Sunday mass, he was on good terms with ecclesiastical authorities.

Fradette had little respect for politicians, except for Wilfrid Laurier, Henri Bourassa, and Armand Lavergne, whose speeches he liked to quote. Whatever respect he might have had for politics he lost along with his deposit in the 1935 general election. He was an unfortunate Liberal candidate; his opponent hired bullies to pull down his placards and disrupt his meetings. After that, he stayed away from politics. It probably cost him the bench, for he never became a judge. He did not need the salary, having accrued wealth through professional success. Being too proud to solicit a nomination, having no contacts in political circles, and living in an isolated region, he was deprived of the opportunity to give his full measure and ensure that his name would live on, if only because of the decisions he might have rendered.

In the privacy of his home, Fradette was even more engaging. His conversation was an intellectual feast. He grasped things quickly and was quick on the rebound. His natural, authentically French playfulness sparkled in this remote part of the country.

Though he spoke endlessly of France — of its literature and its great figures — he had never been overseas. He only travelled once, when he went to New York with his wife to see Édith Piaf perform. Later, a widower and retired, he lived with his dreams, which he never mentioned but which likely remained unfulfilled. Education, talent, and professional success were not enough for regional people of that period.

Need I say I loved and admired the man?

I joined his firm in July 1964. I already knew Pierre Bergeron, his trusted nephew, who was himself an excellent lawyer and is now a Superior Court judge. Bergeron became friend and ally after the marriage of his youngest sister, Lise, to my youngest brother, Gérard. The other partner was Michael Cain, an Irishman with the bearing of a gentleman. He was perfectly bilingual, a talented lawyer who was so attached to his profession that he returned to it after a brief stint on the Superior Court.

According to tradition in Fradette's firm, a lawyer worthy of the name was first and foremost a courtroom lawyer. So often I heard him say, "A lawyer may belong to a firm with a hundred partners, but he must stand alone before the court and show the fire in his belly and his head." Fradette ran rings around unwary colleagues arriving unprepared from Montreal or Québec City with expectations of fun and games. Another aspect of the lawyer's solitude is that he can only rely on himself. "You have to be cook, ship's mate, and captain," he told me repeatedly.

Fradette had little respect for lawyers who never stepped into a courtroom. He thought they were not true lawyers, period. So I was sent to court to plead cases. It wasn't long before I realized the truth of the adage, *"Nascuntur poetae, fiunt oratores"* (Poets are born, orators are made). Neither Maurice Garçon's book on judicial eloquence nor Cicero's treatise on eloquence could make an instant orator of me in the courtroom. My knees shook under my gown the first time I had appeared in moot court with a motion for a medical examination, a simple formality, as lawyers know.

Not all judges have infinite patience with young lawyers, particularly those eager to impress them with their erudition. Pleading my first real case, I was devastated by a remark one of them made. After examining the witnesses, I rose to make my plea, which I thought would make me immortal. The judge cut me short, saying, "You, young man, remain seated. You have a good case, don't spoil it."

A courtroom teaches you modesty, and I must say I took a lot of lessons in it. You get the feeling everyone else is an opponent: the other lawyer, paid by his client to point out your mistakes and ignorance; the other party's witnesses, who think you are the devil in person, which is exactly what you are trying to be; the judge, who rejects your frivolous objections and your leading questions, and reproaches you for failing to understand the rules of evidence; and your own client, if you happen to lose his case. Accordingly, I always dissuaded members of my family eager to see me at work.

I spent the first four or five years in court, pleading as many as four cases a day, most of them damage suits related to automobile accidents. This was before Lise Payette introduced no-fault insurance, effectively killing the goose that was laying golden eggs for the legal profession. Not only were damage suits lucrative, but they allowed young lawyers to expand their courtroom experience, their interrogation skills, and their knowledge of witness psychology.

* * *

I feel honoured to have had such excellent teachers. For important cases, they often took me along so I could see them in action. I learned the rudiments of a profession that I still think is one of the most satisfying. Even as an ambassador, cabinet minister, and member of Parliament, I often wrote "lawyer" as my profession when I filled out airline landing cards or signed hotel registers; that's how much I missed the profession I had practised too freely and joyously for twenty-one years.

In 1966, I was married for the first time.

These were studious years. I was unknown, particularly in Chicoutimi, where I had never resided or studied. I did not go out much and spent most of my spare time reading. Having read all of Chateaubriand's books, I embarked on Michelet, and then plunged into the complete works of Saint-Simon and Proust. I devoured every word from the first page to the last. I have read *À la recherche du temps perdu* twice, along with commentaries and biographies, one being the unequalled work of George Painter, and another the remarkable book of Ghislain de Diesbach. I read Gibbon's monumental *The Decline and Fall of the Roman Empire* as well as a number of biographies of eminent personalities from France, Britain, and the United States. I had been reading in English for a long time, ever since I was fifteen, when a cousin of my father's, Roland Eleffson, who worked at Alcan, started sending me old issues of *Time* magazine. Eventually, I subscribed to it for several years and read it regularly with the help of Webster's dictionary.

While I lived in Chicoutimi, I read everything I could get my hands on. I read in the evening, late at night, in buses, planes, and hotels. Books were always an important part of my life. They communicate, at the desired time and rhythm, the thinking and creativity of the greatest minds of all time. Reading is something no one can take away from me.

Gradually, I started handling more important cases. I became familiar with the laws of real estate, school and hospital administration, bankruptcy, communications, labour, and injunctions. I sensed, rightly or wrongly, more consideration from judges. Perhaps they appreciated the work behind the presentation of my cases. One of them once even asked me to handle a civil case in which he was personally involved.

Then, in 1968–70, I was presented with a couple of exciting new opportunities.

My partner, Pierre Bergeron, moved to Montreal for a year in his role as hospital negotiator. He transferred three of his hottest cases to me. The first one concerned the ministry of social affairs' purchase of Chicoutimi Hospital, which was owned by the Chanoinesses hospitalières. The second was the transfer of the Séminaire de

Chicoutimi, now a CÉGEP, to the ministry of education. The third was the rental of the orphanage of les Petites Franciscaines de Marie by the Université du Québec for its Chicoutimi campus. I was representing vendors and had to deal with all three cases at the same time.

I had already conducted labour negotiations for private-sector employers, but I had never handled such an important and complex case. And certainly not three at once. The corporate owners were very old religious communities and had to take into account a great many internal imperatives. Discussions were prolonged and arduous, particularly in the case of the CÉGEP and the seminary, and enlivened by political interference.

It was the first time I was called on to deal with civil servants. They wanted to pay the lowest possible price. After a long series of ups and downs, for which I had to travel across Parc des Laurentides to Québec City more than a hundred times, the three transactions were equitably concluded. The proceeds from the sale of the seminary made it possible to continue operating the private college, which is still called the Séminaire de Chicoutimi.

However, the decisive breakthrough gave me responsibilities throughout the whole of Québec. A fairly long chain of events had set my career on a new path. The first links were based on one of the requirements of the Quiet Revolution — equitable public services across the province.

This objective required uniform working conditions in health care and education. In the early 1960s, local bargaining along with the setting of salaries and work standards by arbitration, had introduced wide disparities into the system. There now existed a mosaic of arrangements. To end the resulting inequities and inconsistencies, the government resolved to integrate all existing collective agreements within two broad provincial ones, for health care and education. The 1966 negotiations gave rise to innumerable conflicts as authorities enforced the new arrangements. To break the deadlock in health care, the government appointed Yves Pratte ad hoc administrator of all institutions authorized to determine working conditions.

In education, a more elaborate mechanism was put into place.

Bill 22 created an administrative tribunal presided over by Judge Jean-Charles Simard of Chicoutimi. The tribunal would determine how to integrate each case into the provincial framework. The operation led to the negotiation of a province-wide agreement on uniform working conditions for teachers. The two parties signed the agreement in November 1969, but could not agree on an arbitration system for grievances. It was a serious problem because as yet no sector had centralized grievance arbitration. Since both parties in education were eager to centralize arbitration jurisprudence and reduce costs, they agreed to a single tribunal with jurisdiction over all of Québec.

According to the system they had in mind, both parties were expected to draw up a roster of judges from the Superior Court and the provincial court. One of the judges would serve as first president. Each judge, known as a president, had to preside over specific arbitration tribunals, along with one union and one management adviser. The idea was to promote a spirit of collegiality among judges through the first president, who would assign grievances. The first president would also preside over arbitration sessions where he believed new jurisprudence would arise.

The project ran into an unforeseen obstacle. The National Assembly, in the process of amending the law on judicial tribunals, ordered judges not to stop their current assignments in common law to engage in arbitration. Discussions stalled when the government, the unions, and the Federation of School Boards and CÉGEPs had to resort to using lawyers and could not agree on the choice of a first president. The problem with well-known lawyers in Montreal and Québec City was precisely that they were too well known. Former cases, either on behalf of employers or unions, made them suspect in the eyes of other parties. At the time, nothing was more Manichaean than the world of labour relations.

Finally, Judge Jean-Charles Simard, before whom I had appeared on several occasions to plead either civil cases or labour grievances, proposed my name. The parties, none of whom knew me except perhaps by word of mouth, agreed. I therefore became, in April 1970, the first president of the arbitration tribunals for the education sector.

The appointment was an interesting one for a thirty-one-year-old lawyer who, in addition to keeping his private practice and his home base in Chicoutimi, now had the opportunity to travel all over Québec, acquiring experience and meeting a wide network of people in a key social sector. At the same time I would enter circles new to me.

We were starting from scratch: establishing the clerk's office, setting up a filing system for hundreds of thousands of cases, organizing the individual tribunals, preparing the rosters, beginning the hearings, distributing cases among the various presidents on the list, determining the principles of jurisprudence, publishing the decisions. Chance led me to an extraordinarily able and devoted civil servant, Lionel Labbé, who became court clerk.

My first task was to take over most of the initial cases in order to set norms of jurisprudence. Everyone was eager to avoid conflicting interpretations, so that there would not be conflicting decisions in cases heard by one president versus another. Though the first president's office was in Québec City, I saw to it that hearings were conducted as much as possible in the plaintiff's town. I visited most regions of Québec, from the Magdalen Islands to Abitibi, hearing grievances and meeting the leading players in the worlds of education and labour relations: administrators, union leaders and staff, negotiators and lawyers.

The cases I heard allowed me, albeit indirectly and through the distorting prism of conflict, to take the pulse of the schools and probe the motivation of teachers, who were under severe stress as a result of the bureaucratic proliferation already gripping the educational system. Curiously enough, the better schools were those where administrators and teachers had agreed to work outside the excessive minutiae of the collective agreement. In fact, my task was to decipher what Lise Bissonnette called that "book of spells." I despaired of ever being able to understand such esoteric problems as the "half year of schooling."

Where do we get this mania for forcing the finest aspects of teaching into a straitjacket? Measuring minutes, dividing tasks into countless components, using Byzantine regulations to distribute teaching assignments, and hundreds of other constraints, often inapplicable even by their originators, have desiccated the lively and creative act of teaching.

Our decisions often had serious financial repercussions, particularly one that I rendered on the meaning of a retroactivity clause. At stake was about thirty million dollars.

An interesting aspect of my job was overseeing my colleagues, the fifty tribunal presidents. This is when I saw Robert Cliche again and got to know him better. He had been one of our teachers in law school. I also worked with Roger Chouinard, Marc Brière, both now judges, and Stanley Hartt, whom I was to meet again as Mulroney's chief of staff.

My friendships with Cliche and Jean-Roch Boivin, later Premier Levesque's chief of staff, and Guy Chevrette, a union assessor and currently House leader in Québec's National Assembly, date from this period. There is something instructive about the world of labour relations. People speak directly, without worrying about sensitivities. I had a few jolts myself. One day, Viateur Dupont of the CEQ, the teachers' union, said in the middle of the hearings, "If you weren't so stiff and starchy, you would understand us better."

* * *

Discussions became increasingly spontaneous with these people who were active in politics and social reform. My contacts with them and my new experience intensified the doubts I already had about my political beliefs.

For several years I had been a Liberal-party supporter. In 1967, André Ouellet, then Guy Favreau's political assistant, asked me to join Paul Hellyer's staff at the Department of Transport. I declined. But this did not prevent me from being an early supporter of Pierre Trudeau when he sought the leadership of the federal Liberal party. I was happy about his going into politics. But the person I thought was truly a breath of fresh air was Jean Marchand. His integrity, intelligence, and passionate loyalty to his people had at first led me to believe that he might stay in Québec and succeed Jean Lesage. I accepted his move into federal politics, thinking that for once, English Canada would see in Ottawa something other than the usual mediocre and serviceable French Canadian intellectuals who were ready to trade whatever personal assets they had — or didn't have — for pensions and plum appointments. I thought Marchand and Trudeau (I did not know Gérard Pelletier very well) would show the whole country what brilliant Québécois, with independent minds eager for change, could achieve. When Marchand's star began to fade as Trudeau's was rising, I was seduced, as everyone else was, by the latter's command of two languages and keen intellect.

The upshot was that, in 1968, I participated in the federal election campaign, supporting the Liberal candidate in Chicoutimi. Besides joining the organization, I made a speaking tour of the riding with the candidate. I sang the praises of Trudeau in Chicoutimi, Saint-Fulgence, Sainte-Rose-du-Nord, Anse-Saint-Jean (a town proud of its covered bridge, which appears on thousand-dollar bills), Petit-Saguenay, and Rivière-Éternité. Those who stayed right to the end of my speeches were invited to salute the arrival in Ottawa of a new generation of Québécois able to impose our views and promote our interests. The tune is well known, particularly to contemporary ears.

My partner François Lamarre campaigned with me. After the Liberal victory, we received several proxies from Ottawa to represent various government departments in the area. We returned them all with a rather arrogant letter indicating that we had not campaigned for personal gain and did not lack for work.

Our attitude apparently shocked no one in the Liberal party, for some time later, I was appointed vice-president of the political committee of the party's Québec wing. The president was Jean Gérin, a relative of Paul Gérin-Lajoie. When the leadership of the provincial party opened up, I was invited to attend a meeting at the home of Gérin-Lajoie. He was toying with the idea of running and wanted to gauge his chances of success. I remember seeing Guy Rocher there. I don't think that Gérin-Lajoie found the meeting very encouraging.

After Robert Bourassa's accession to the leadership of the Liberal Party of Québec, political organizers in Chicoutimi set out to find a candidate for the 1970 elections. No Liberal had been elected there since 1931, and party members felt it was time to change things. Several party brokers approached me, saying they would support me if I ran. I refused because nothing in the world could persuade me to give up law.

The Liberals finally convinced Adrien Plourde to accept. Well known in the area, he was a forceful public speaker and president of the powerful aluminum workers' union. He seemed unbeatable — on paper. But the merchants on rue Racine, Chicoutimi's main street, had long memories: they had seen their revenues decimated by a four-month strike that Plourde and his union had set in motion in 1957.

I campaigned for the Liberals, who gave me responsibility for communications in all the area ridings. Two or three weeks before the polls, we were leading everywhere but in Chicoutimi. The central organization sent some help in the person of Jeanne Sauvé, who knew Adrien Plourde, perhaps through Jean Marchand. It was not a bad idea. Her charm, her blue eyes, her class, and her distinguished manner of speaking would please Chicoutimi's bourgeoisie. But she didn't stand a chance because the incumbent, Jean-Noël Tremblay, a cabinet minister and Union Nationale candidate, was also a brilliant speaker. His speeches were jewels of perfection. He was reelected. I had no idea that he would later be writing speeches for the Governor General of Canada and that that person would be Jeanne Sauvé. Or that, one evening, all three of us would meet again, in formal attire, at a gala dinner in honour of the Governor General at the Paris apartment of writer Maurice Druon, perpetual secretary of the Académie Française.

The night of the election, I invited several big Liberal organizers to my home to celebrate the favourable results we anticipated for the whole of Québec. Roger Chouinard, a lawyer friend and now justice of the Court of Appeal, was there, as was Gaston Ouellet, a close friend since our days in *La Presse*'s newsroom.

As expected, the Liberal candidate in Chicoutimi lost. Otherwise, these dyed-in-the-wool Liberals had much to celebrate: We had elected seventy-eight candidates out of 108. It was party time. But the festivities were suddenly interrupted by the sobs of my first wife and the wife of a friend as the announcement came that René Lévesque and Jacques Parizeau had gone down to defeat. I saw the Liberals exchanging questioning looks. Another defeated candidate was the Parti Québécois standard bearer in Chicoutimi. He was a lawyer, a few years older than I. Marc-André Bédard had waged a good campaign and he spoke more movingly than Adrien Plourde. I won't mention Jean-Noël Tremblay, whom everyone liked to hear but never remembered anything he said.

Marc-André Bédard was already practising law by the time I arrived in Chicoutimi in 1964. Almost all the lawyers in town had their offices at 100, rue Racine. Bédard and I were among them. We all met in a neighbouring restaurant where political discussions were usually the main dish on the menu.

Lawyers are interested in politics. They follow it closely and like to comment on it. However, contrary to popular belief, they do not generally have a high opinion of those among them who enter politics. The thought was always just under the surface that if these colleagues had been successful in their chosen profession they would not have embarked on such a sticky venture. Who would give up a lucrative profession, built over years of effort, only to be torn to shreds by political commentators, stalked by journalists, and loathed by the public? And lawyers do not always welcome as prodigal sons those who have lost their cabinet posts and want to return to the fold. Examples abound of ex-politicians who have had to knock on many doors before finding something worthwhile.

Most of my new colleagues were either Liberal or Union Nationale. You could count on the fingers of one hand those who were for independence. For a long time, and certainly until 1976, the brotherhood of lawyers thought poorly of those who had joined the Parti Québécois. Bédard, who had been a member of the old RIN (Rassemblement pour l'indépendance nationale) was perceived as a marginal figure because of his sovereigntist commitment.

Nevertheless, everyone liked him. He took part in all our discussions. He had a special way of listening to others, of never upsetting anyone, of discreetly pushing forward his arguments. His selflessness and his love for Québec were indisputable, as were his patience and instinctive understanding of human reactions. I found it hard to fight him in 1970. But he did not hold it against me, and our relations remained intact.

Then came the October Crisis with its kidnappings, murder, and War Measures Act. My compromise with federalism, already fragile and tenuous, was shaken. I was horrified to discover how easy it was for a small group to push a government into repression and a whole society into psychosis. Travelling on business, I saw the army in Montreal. I witnessed the imprisonment, without charges being laid, of innocent people. I was overwhelmed that Saturday night when they discovered Pierre Laporte's body in the trunk of a car in Saint-Hubert.

I did not recognize my country nor its idea of justice. Moreover, I was deeply disillusioned by the people I had helped, albeit modestly, get elected to Ottawa and Québec City. Today, I understand less than ever how the democratic reflexes of Trudeau, Marchand, and Pelletier could have collapsed so completely. Speaking of collapse, Robert Bourassa did not seem any more honourable, since it was then that he contracted the habit of calling the federal army into Québec.

I had to concede that René Lévesque was the only one to stand up and embody the democratic values of Québec.

Then Trudeau revealed once and for all, with a persistence that bordered on provocation, his determination to keep Québec a province, a simple module, like the other nine, in a system controlled from the centre. The Quiet Revolution was over. It could not go any further, obstructed by the rigid structures condemned to immutability by English Canada's intransigence. I recognized the validity of Lévesque's arguments about the necessity for Québécois to assume their own fate as a nation and to take control of their own affairs. I thought the slow unfolding of our community could only lead to its having full political powers and responsibility.

An unconscious process of maturation led me to the idea of independence. I can't remember the day or the week, because there was no critical turning point. I did not call a press conference to spread the good news or lead an assault on federalism. It was a private matter.

Some time after I chose sovereignty, Parizeau showed up in Chicoutimi. I signed my Parti Québécois card in front of him. It was in 1971 or 1972. I told my friends and relatives about it and broke with the Liberals.

Bourassa called for elections in October 1973. I accepted the task of campaigning for Marc-André Bédard and gave up my annual three-week vacation. I wrote speeches, organized communications, and addressed political rallies. Towards the end of the campaign, I even spoke on television. In short, I gave everything to the campaign, at the end of which Bédard was elected. I was happy for him, but disappointed by the Parti Québécois's defeat across Québec.

Another disappointment was waiting for me, this time in my law office. I was coolly received by some of my partners, who were possibly shocked or offended by my visibility and passion during the campaign.

Fradette was no longer there. However, he had impressed strong family tradition on the firm. Since we formed a family, the actions of one would necessarily reflect on the others and might even compromise them. Several partners were federalists and had reacted negatively to my political commitment, which they feared would rub off on them after my public participation in the campaign. They wanted to insert a clause in the partnership agreement putting limits on political activism. I refused. Though I still kept my esteem for my ex-partners, I left the firm where I had been happy for almost ten years.

So it was that in December 1973, I found myself an unemployed Péquiste. I turned down overtures from Montreal and decided to start my own law firm — a rather extravagant word for the small office I fixed up the next month, alone with my first wife, who for a few months was receptionist, bookkeeper, and secretary.

Clients eventually did show up, a few at first, but later in sufficient numbers to allow me to take on a partner, then another one, and so on.

One of my first clients was Hôtel-Dieu, a hospital in Alma on whose behalf I pleaded a grievance in 1974. In the midst of the court hearings, I was informed by a messenger that there was an urgent phone call for me. With the court's permission, I ran to take it.

5

The Cliche Commission: Knights and Knaves

G uy Chevrette was on the line. "Lucien," he said, "I'm with Judge Cliche and Brian Mulroney. We have a proposal for you." After chatting briefly, he passed the phone first to Mulroney, then to Cliche.

You didn't need to be a mind reader to figure out what they were doing together. It was only a few weeks after the riots on the James Bay project. Hydro-Québec and its subsidiary, the SEBJ (Société d'énergie de la Baie James), suspended all work on the construction of the dam and improvised an airlift to evacuate the construction site.

Rioting, violence, arson in the bunkhouses, wrecked equipment — a leader of the construction unit of the Québec Federation of Labour had driven a D-9 Caterpillar into the giant generators — had caused heavy damage, and the consequences were enormous. The episode had exploded like a bomb in Québec, leaving people dazed and perplexed.

Premier Bourassa's government appointed a commission of inquiry to determine the cause of the disaster and to identify the guilty parties. But this was 1974, when the labour movement enjoyed great moral authority in Québec. Mindful not to incur accusations that it was mounting a repressive operation against the unions, the government took great care in choosing the members of the commission.

The chairman was Robert Cliche, chief justice of the provincial court of Québec. Still wearing the halo of prestige as former head of the NDP in Québec, he had just inaugurated the small claims court and put it through its paces. It proved to be a great success with the public. Well connected among intellectual and progressive circles, Cliche was on familiar terms with most union leaders. He had enjoyed a successful career as a litigation lawyer and was versed in all aspects of judicial examination. In a word, Cliche was a dream chairman.

For balance, there had to be one member each from business and labour.

In the first case, the government's choice fell on Mulroney, who specialized in labour law and negotiations. He had represented various employers, including the Port of Montreal, mining companies, and the daily newspaper *La Presse*. His appointment to the Cliche Commission was his first important one related to the public sector. It put him in the public limelight. He had impeccable credentials. Moreover, he was from the prestigious Montreal law firm Ogilvie, Renault. His excellent relations with the English-language community completed the picture.

The appointment of a union representative posed several problems. The announcement came after the other two. Both the Québec Federation of Labour and the Confederation of National Trade Unions had members on the LG-2 construction site when the rampage broke out in April 1974. I suppose neither felt too keen about investigating their own unions. Finally, Guy Chevrette, a vice-president of the Québec teachers' union (CEQ) accepted the appointment. He was a teacher, a union adviser, and a union president in the Joliette area. He had covered a lot of ground before becoming vice-president of the CEQ. Of the three commissioners, he had the most to lose. Obviously this was not the labour movement's finest hour. Chevrette's responsibility for meting out justice would not make him a hero in union circles.

When they called me in May, the commissioners were about to make one of their first decisions: the choice of legal counsel. They thought of Arthur Gendreau and me, whom they all knew. Mulroney had been in our class at Laval, Cliche had taught us law, and Chevrette had worked with us on the arbitration tribunals for education.

The government knew about my Parti Québécois leanings and opposed my appointment. But the commissioners held fast, threatening to resign if they had to. After all was said and done, the roster consisted of Crown prosecutor Jean Dutil, Nicol Henry from Québec City, Paul-Arthur Gendreau from Rimouski, and me. Jean Dutil became chief counsel.

My work with the commission proved of great human and professional interest. First and foremost, I discovered the extent to which institutions, such as labour unions, businesses, and governments, were vulnerable to violence and blackmail.

Until then, my knowledge of such matters had been theoretical. I had read about the union corruption uncovered by the McLennan Commission, in which John and Robert Kennedy had participated, and about the scandals in the Union Nationale. But these were from another place and age.

I was in for a shock. For a year, I felt I was taking part in a scene out of cinéma vérité, pushing characters on stage, where their confessions drew a nightmarish picture of union, government, and business circles.

The first part of the inquiry dealt summarily with union officials, mainly those of Québec Federation of Labour (QFL)-Construction. Television cameras were freely admitted to the hearings at crucial moments, so all Québec witnessed the parade before the commission, a menagerie no novelist could have invented.

We saw a pimp with a diamond-studded tooth that glittered under the television lights; union loan sharks who, after lending their members money at rates of 256%, battered delinquent borrowers and then cashed in their Workers' Compensation cheques; recycled wrestlers and boxers on union staff; habitual criminals and other shady characters going about union business with baseball bats, .25, .38, and .45 revolvers, and M-1 submachine guns; well-dressed businessmen and union officials accepting cash bribes, with a special affinity for thousand-dollar bills. We learned about people drawing up hit lists and others putting out contracts on rival union leaders; and union heads rewarding subordinates for criminal acts with $6,000 cheques. These are just random examples. Most of the 355 pages of the commission's report reads like a catalogue of horrors.

However, the commission also unearthed corruption in business and government.

At that point I was head counsel, replacing Jean Dutil after his appointment to Québec's provincial court.

We heard ample evidence showing employers had joined the bribery ring, distributing envelopes to union blackmailers who ran protection rackets on construction sites. When the commission started looking into the government's own involvement, its disclosures were no less edifying.

A member of the Minimum Wage Commission secured his appointment with a $2,000 payment as part of a scheme involving the chairman of a Crown corporation and a minister's chief of staff. A deputy minister ordered his ministry to pay out $45,000 following union threats to slow down the construction of a large government office complex in Québec City. A Ministry of Education employee extorted $2,500 from the director of a professional training school in search of a permit. The chairman of the Public Service Commission admitted getting his position after helping a protégé of the régime obtain a strategic post supervising personnel at James Bay. A gang of thugs successfully put an end to parliamentary committee hearings, right in the parliament building itself, without ever being brought to justice.

The rest is in the same vein. Names, dates, and amounts appear in the report. With supporting evidence, the report shows the QFL-Construction was rotten to the core, that a large number of business people had come to terms with it, even contributing to the system, while people in high places in government held their noses and plugged their ears.

Obviously, the lawyers had their work cut out for them. For the commission, while it sponsored research and studies on theoretical questions, was in every way a commission of inquiry.

In conjunction with the Sûreté du Québec (provincial police) and the Montreal police force, we were instructed to investigate the largest construction sites in Québec, from James Bay to Mount Wright, from Mirabel to Ultramar's refinery in Saint-Romuald. We held hearings, behind closed doors and in public.

After the first series of hearings took place in Québec City in September 1974, primarily for the hearing of briefs, the commission moved to Montreal. For almost five months, it sat in the same room in the Parthenais Building. Its lawyers interrogated witness after witness. Often, they brought their own lawyers, which led to many confrontations on legal points, the soundness of a motion, and even the right of a witness to remain silent. Day after day, I faced a good number of Montreal's masters of the court.

It was a hard struggle, and not everyone was pleased with our efforts. André Desjardins, known as the Construction King, had charmed many with his force of character, intelligence, and steadfast-ness on behalf of the labour movement.

The inquiry's lawyers, with the support of the commissioners, conducted forceful interrogations and showed the sort of enthusiasm that many of our colleagues preferred to call aggressiveness. Many did not hesitate to say that my energetic examination of government officials stemmed from my péquiste leanings. I summoned witnesses and flooded banks, companies, and other institutions with *subpoena duces tecum* to get my hands on cheques and other documents. We also issued many search warrants.

A good number of these hauls yielded cheques paid to the Liberal party's election funds, which I produced before the commission. I summoned Paul Desrochers, the *éminence grise*, who came to blink before the TV cameras and undergo prolonged questioning. The commissioners also authorized me to summon two cabinet ministers, Jérôme Choquette and Jean Cournoyer. Next on my list was Robert Bourassa. However, the commissioners felt differently about that, and the premier did not have to testify.

Everyone showed considerable determination. Our indignation mounted as the inquiry progressed. Judge Cliche was not above the occasional outburst. To a union lawyer asking for the postponement of a witness, the judge shouted out in front of everyone that granting the motion was out of the question because he did not want his witnesses ending up in Montreal's Back River. One day as I questioned the chairman of the SEBJ, I was interrupted by Michel Chartrand, a well-known union activist, from his seat in the audience. He started hurling abuse and accusing me of being soft on management and hard on the unions. There was a great hullabaloo. Judge Cliche, putting aside his judicial reserve, was unable to resist a cockfight. He suspended the hearing, which did not prevent him, crimson-faced with anger, from "seeing" Chartrand to the elevator. I also remember a noisy argument between Mulroney and Michel Bourdon, who accused the former of being pro-management. As we say, everyone was uptight.

When the Ministry of Labour delayed the commission's first budget appropriations, we all chipped in personally — commissioners and lawyers — and advanced the funds to begin our work.

The atmosphere was full of nervous tension, partly due to the inquiry's revelations of violence. Our chauffeurs were armed, and after receiving threats, the commissioners were placed under police protection. The inside of my next-door neighbour's home in Chicoutimi was completely destroyed by vandals. The police were never able to prove anything against anyone. All I know is the poor man, a quiet computer programmer, had no insurance, and that from then on he wouldn't look at me.

One of our research assistants always carried a revolver, which instilled more fear in us than the hypothetical danger he sought protection from.

One night, a Sûreté du Québec corporal woke me at two in the morning to tell me they had found a man's body in the trunk of a car parked in a shopping centre near Montreal. The man's lips had been sewn shut with steel wire and a construction union badge was pinned to his jacket. Early next morning, Guy Chevrette viewed the body at the Parthenais morgue. He had to skip breakfast and, for the rest of the day, looked as if he wore a papier-mâché mask. A check showed that the victim's name was not on our list of witnesses. The crime remains unsolved to this day.

Never before had I worked in the kind of tension brought about by the combination of threats and violence. For most of us, there were two other elements of surprise: cooperating with the police and the constant presence of the media. Our first contacts with the Sûreté du Québec were polite but cold. This was not their first commissioned inquiry. They did not exactly know who we were and they probably wondered about our purpose. Would this turn out to be just a sham inquiry, destined only to placate public opinion until it blew over and the files could be quietly put away? Would the inquiry dare go after the sacred cows and follow the trail to union power and the government itself?

I later realized the police had stood by in waiting mode while they figured out our intentions. They diligently met all our requests but went no further. The police, by definition, are suspicious. They know they are unloved by a society wanting security and protection from them. Hard experience has taught them they are first to be blamed and last to be praised. Since this was an inquiry into union criminality and its ramifications on business and government, one can understand how the Sûreté needed to know which way the wind was blowing.

The turning point was René Mantha's return from Zaire in October 1974. The Sûreté let us in on the secrets of the gods and gave us the means to lay bare the truth. Mantha was the business agent of Local 791 (heavy machinery operators) during the LG-2 riot. A few weeks later, he was hired in Zaire under a contract with the Canadian International Development Agency. Incriminated as a result of testimony given to the commission, he came home immediately. On his arrival at Dorval, he said he was coming to defend his honour before the commission. He was invited to do so the very next day.

That evening, after preparing for my examination of the witness and checking our files, I realized the evidence against Mantha was rather thin, except for allegations by other witnesses. I went back to my hotel (the Queen Elizabeth, where we all stayed). I had just fallen asleep when a member of the intelligence squad of the Sûreté called, asking me to come to his office. When I arrived, he informed me the police had launched a wiretapping operation, code-named Vegas 2, and that Mantha was one of its targets. He played a recording of

Mantha's telephone conversations, proving without a shadow of a doubt Mantha's part in organizing an assault on a person in Hull.

The next day, balky and indignant, Mantha denied participating in roughing up a rival union leader's young son. But he looked crestfallen when I played recordings of a voice he recognized as his own. He heard himself giving instructions on the very operation he had denied, after swearing on the head of his mother.

It was just the beginning. The ice was broken with the Sûreté. Until then, progress was tough. We had to pit one witness against another and work on uncooperative witnesses. Things improved bit by bit after the Sûreté's intelligence section started passing us information they had gathered by electronic eavesdropping. Many witnesses, counting on the nonexistence of incriminating evidence, came to the witness stand with a self-confidence that soon crumbled under the weight of the evidence from their own telephone conversations. The tactic proved even more effective with later witnesses, who, instead of risking public embarrassment, took the initiative by confessing the truth.

The wiretapping operation preceded changes to the Criminal Code in July 1974. Parliament banned all wiretapping not specifically authorized by a judge according to prescribed conditions. It had not been like that before. Indications are that authorities had taken advantage of the law to engage in widespread eavesdropping, particularly after the October Crisis in 1970.

Admittedly, without evidence gathered this way, the Cliche Commission could never have proved half the facts it disclosed. Public interest in the hearings had its effect. The press thrived on the drama and on the inquiry's unexpected twists. The media, who overwhelmed the building, soon grew to understand just how rich the whole issue was. I just hope they were paid by the inch, because for several months the commission made daily headlines.

The commissioners themselves quickly grasped that the press played a leading role in kindling public awareness. Part of their mandate was to institute true democracy in the unions and to purge the labour movement of undesirable elements. The commissioners' personalities aided the task at hand. All three were effective with the media. On top of getting across well, they also understood better than anyone else how the media operated, their limitations, the reasons behind their interest or indifference. Furthermore, the commissioners' humour, enthusiasm, and sincerity impressed the most blasé journalists.

Cliche loved the journalists. Seduced by their irreverent spirit and spontaneous conversations, he acted in a way that would facilitate their work. Lawyers had instructions to take deadlines into account when questioning witnesses. If a question was expected to get a headline-making response, we were requested to ask it before the TV reporters left to prepare their reports. Sometimes, wrapped up in my questioning and delayed by the resistance of a particular witness, I forgot the time and the desired sequence of questions. The commissioners soon called me to order, pointing imperious fingers at their watches.

I am not sure such a relationship with the press would be possible today without being deemed incestuous. Cliche realized this before his death. With a straight face, he told Mulroney and me a fictitious anecdote: "Listen guys, I just had a call from Premier Bourassa. He wants me to chair another commission." We asked him what his reply was. "Well, Mister Premier, I accept on condition that I can choose my topic, my commissioners, my lawyers, and my journalists."

It wasn't only the media who loved this warmhearted man. We all adored him. He inspired us, communicated his enthusiasm to us, made us laugh at our own failings and vanities, all the time mocking his own. It was impossible to be bored in his company. He was not a man of fixed ideas, nor of a single state of mind or purpose. A day with him meant going through several different moods.

This man from Beauce had kept his habit of getting up at the crack of dawn. Every morning we met in his suite, reading the papers, commenting on them, going over the previous day's events, and putting the last touches on the day's strategy. Mulroney, who lived in Montreal and so did not stay at the hotel, never missed these early-morning meetings. Cliche gave us advice, encouraged us, reassured us occasionally, but refused to get complacent. Those who had not done very well in the proceedings of the day before had to be prepared for criticism: "Listen, kid, you didn't do very well yesterday.

You were lucky to be in Montreal, because in Beauce they would have pelted you with tomatoes." Then, turning to another lawyer, who thought this was funny, he said sternly, "And you, instead of laughing at others, would be better off preparing yourself for today's work."

Though he could never resist a well-timed quip, he presided over the hearings with dignity. He had a natural exuberance, but always kept it in check as he carried out his duties, subordinating it to his exalted idea of justice, the courts, and their decorum. His respect for judicial institutions had its roots in family tradition. His father, brother, and uncle were magistrates either in the Superior Court or provincial court.

He revered his father. He spoke of him as a living person whose expectations he must meet. Austere and respectful of the established order, Cliche Senior was probably instrumental in his son's high regard for the state and its institutions, for Cliche Junior spoke of the state only in serious, even solemn tones. The state was his secular church.

Another institution he thought needed protection was the labour movement. I am not sure this one would have been endorsed by the father, who lived in a time when the rural middle classes did not see the organization of workers into unions as a priority. The value Robert Cliche attached to the labour movement came from his own social conscience.

It took courage and clearheadedness to lead an inquiry that would tell the public how corruption undermined certain unions and government agencies. He often expressed his fear of destabilizing the Québec state, which he felt had not yet sufficiently recovered from the trauma of the October Crisis. At the same time, he was most sensitive to criticism from certain left-wing elements who might accuse him of playing into the hands of the right by discrediting the labour movement. For these reasons, he never accepted malevolent attacks on unions and the government. He saw himself as a surgeon cutting off the gangrene.

He was a complex individual, a little too conscious, perhaps, that all things are relative, who never resolved his ambivalent feelings. Even though he had long believed in federalism, I do not think he would have rejected Québec sovereignty. Like many of his generation, he probably wished for it but felt apprehensive about the break with Canada. Volunteering for service in the Royal Canadian Navy during the war, he served on board a corvette escorting convoys in the North Atlantic. He retained fond memories of the camaraderie among crew members. He liked to recall the night vigils he spent contemplating the stars while looking out for enemy submarines. In politics, he had always supported federalist parties. I can say no more, except that he was undergoing a conversion and was thinking of running for the Parti Québécois in the next elections in 1976.

That spring, René Lévesque made several bus trips from Montreal to Québec City, where he met with Cliche and Alfred Rouleau of the Mouvement Desjardins. He hoped to persuade them to join him. In the end, both declined. Cliche invoked reasons of health. Neither Lévesque nor the majority of his friends believed him. Who would have thought that this dynamo, this athlete who on weekends skied thirty miles cross-country on his farm in Saint-Zacharie during the busiest months on the commission, would collapse two years later. But Cliche knew his days were numbered. Several months earlier, he had made arrangements with a funeral director. His wife, Madeleine Ferron, must have known, too, because in referring to her husband's commitment to the Parti Québécois, she once told Lévesque: "The plane is waiting at the end of the runway; all the engines are running, but it can never take off."

Possibly, this was why Cliche urged us so insistently to enter politics. Twice, in 1965 and 1968, he suffered defeat as a New Democratic candidate. Knowing he would never play a return match, there was nothing left for him but to find his political heirs. He designated them from both sides of his ambivalence. He would tell us in his hotel room: "Listen, kids, it's your turn now. You, Brian, you're going to Ottawa and you'll be prime minister of Canada. You, Guy (Chevrette), you get elected in Québec. You two (he meant Gendreau and me), stop thinking only about making money and attend to your civic duties."

One wonders whether his fellow citizens did not do him a great service by refusing to elect him. He had so many romantic ideas about the state. Elected and brought to power, he would likely have lost his illusions. You can't charm bureaucracies, and petty politics have hamstrung more than one idealist.

Mulroney, whom Cliche influenced like a second father, also took his first steps into politics with a romantic and oversimplified vision of power. His theory went something like this: "We are going to be tolerant and generous; the people will love us, even the press. We will do great things, and I will go down in history." He would later discover there is nothing poetic about fighting the hydra of deficits, and nothing generous about cutting unemployment benefits. The time of romanticism is past in Ottawa. No future prime minister will ever experience the exhiliration of setting up Via Rail, creating Radio-Canada, and founding Petro-Canada. Prime ministers are now subject to orders from accountants in the Ministry of Finance who instruct them to chop the first, slash the budget of the second, and eliminate the third. For a generation of leaders overtaken by mutations affecting the whole world, the exercise of power won't amount to anything greater than handling scissors and organizing fire sales. Cabinet meetings in Ottawa will be increasingly concerned with answering the question, Who will we hurt today — seniors, the underprivileged, or women?

Cliche was not born for the politics of budget-cutting. He belonged to the race of nation builders. I cannot go further without losing myself in conjecture. He left before it was time to make the ultimate decisions about the future of Québec. In Québec we can no longer count the number of people whose lives have ended without realizing their ideals — certainly this is true of the contemporaries who inspired me. Perhaps this is normal, and will continue, as long as Québec does not achieve its goal. That Cliche, who had so much to contribute, will not see that day is a great pity.

Those privileged to know him remember him as a man who looked everywhere for poetry and tenderness. Not finding them too often, he would laugh to hide the sadness he felt. I have never met anyone so curious about people, so skilful in spotting their faults, and so sensitive to their lack of delicacy. Yet he was eager to forgive them because he only wanted to see the best in his fellow man. The public identifies his name only with his commission, which died once it was out of the news like a flame deprived of oxygen. Only God knows whether he had more in him that a simple inquiry commission.

In any event, the commission was a success. On May 2, 1975, less than a year after its creation, the commission tabled its report. The recommendations led to at least four laws redefining the qualifications required of professional contractors, creating the Office de la construction, imposing trusteeship on three unions, and reforming the system of labour relations in the whole industry.

Many people were found guilty or pleaded guilty to criminal acts. Unions, employer organizations, and ministries involved went ahead with the necessary purges. Violence and corruption have now practically disappeared from construction sites. And the people of Québec have perhaps also learned something about the fragility of democracy and the need for unwavering vigilance. It would be easy enough for the whole problem to start up again, in Québec or elsewhere, if people were simply to lower their guard.

Even though the inquiry and the hearings were over, the last few weeks of the commission were not entirely restful for Gendreau and me. Not satisfied with the drafts submitted for the final report, the commissioners asked us to lend a hand. We locked ourselves in offices at Place Ville-Marie, and the two of us wrote almost two-thirds of the report.

After that I returned to Chicoutimi to pick up the threads of my law practice.

6

The Negotiation Game

During the Cliche Commission, I had returned to Chicoutimi on weekends to look after urgent matters and discuss pending files with my associates. But on returning for good in June 1975, I plunged back into private practice and became more deeply involved with the Saguenay Bar Association, of which I was president. As such I was a member of the Québec Bar's General Council, which in turn appointed me to its Administrative Council. The president was Guy Pepin. From both a professional and human standpoint, I found the internal activities of the bar most stimulating.

Law is the only profession whose members are systematically pitted against one another. The proceedings of the bar, however, provide opportunities for working together on training future colleagues, on new legislation, and on the profession's ethical standards. In an atmosphere free from the confrontations arising from defending clients' interests, lawyers can enjoy the sociability of their professional association and discover new sources of self-motivation. For the time I held office, I participated as much as possible in the bar's workshops, committees, and conventions.

One of the advantages of a general practice lies in working on several fronts at once, broadening the scope of topics and fields of professional interest. It is the lot of courtroom lawyers to move from bank loans to airplane crashes, from corporate litigation to inheritance cases. Circumstances also led me into a relatively new field at the time, negotiations and labour law. At one point, I was simultaneously first president of the arbitration tribunals for education, negotiator for employers in the private sector, and attorney for some twenty hospitals, community centres, and residences. I alternated between the public and private sectors, and between education and health care.

I often pleaded cases in the latter. It was not rare for a single hospital to accumulate a hundred grievances. Teams representing employers and unions would agree to meet on the premises, resolve most grievances amicably, and refer the rest for arbitration before a tribunal presided over by a lawyer-arbitrator flanked by union and employer advisers. Hearings lasted a week or two at the hospital and were public, so that there were always large groups of employees and managers in attendance. I met many people active in health care. It may seem paradoxical, but in spite of the acrimony of the discussions and conflicting viewpoints, I wove strong ties of comradeship with my adversaries. The rules of the game are unwritten and simple: respect for one another's word and no backstabbing.

Travelling and group meetings often led to extraordinary encounters, such as the one with a Breton priest who ended his career as a chaplain of the Hâvre-Saint-Pierre hospital, where he had symbolically run aground. I spent four or five evenings with him in the top-floor apartment the nuns had provided for him. In fine weather he said he could see as far as Anticosti Island.

Father Le Lannic had devoted a large part of his life to the Inuit of the Far North. This mystic loved, with equal passion, his compatriots Chateaubriand and Renan. He spoke of one with pride and the other with sadness, as of a beloved brother gone astray. Many years later, Father Léger Comeau, a champion of the Acadian cause who happened to be passing through Paris, helped me locate Father Le Lannic. He was still alive, and we resumed our correspondence. However, he was unable to finish his last letter, dying a short while after starting it. His roommate forwarded the letter as he found it.

This cultured man, exiled to our most barren and hostile lands, did not belong to our century. He never spoke of money, cultivated his image, or stretched out under a sun lamp. He did not howl into high-decibel speakers strumming a power guitar. So we punished him, like all other heroes of everyday life, by letting him rot in obscurity. The proof he was out of sync is that he seemed happy anyway.

In the spring of 1976, I turned down a government offer to act as negotiator at the hospital workers' bargaining table. The Confederation of National Trade Unions (CNTU) represented the employees. However, I did accept ad hoc appointments, such as drawing up working conditions applicable to police officers and a review of the layoffs in health care during the 1976 negotiations.

The air was heavy with politics. By the end of 1975, the electoral agenda was almost ready. Reports of patronage and the Cliche Commission's revelations had shaken the government. Moreover, the outlook for negotiating with the Common Front of public-sector unions seemed rather stormy. It was becoming apparent that Robert Bourassa would again call on voters before the end of his mandate.

At that time, I had a meeting with Jacques Parizeau. It told me much about the vexations of political life. On a beautiful Sunday evening in the summer of 1976, I answered a phone call from Marc-André Bédard. He wanted me to join him at the Hôtel Champlain in downtown Chicoutimi. "Jacques Parizeau has just arrived from Montreal and will be going back tonight. Come, it's an important meeting," he said. There were ten of us militants in a poorly lit room, surrounding Parizeau, who was rumpled after six hours on a bus.

"I am here for *Le Jour*," he said. "Each day's run is a miracle, and our suppliers insist we pay them on delivery. We need $10,000 for tomorrow."

I now understood why there were ten of us. But I was thinking about the career the man might have had if only he had followed the beaten path of federalism: governor of the Bank of Canada, prime minister of Canada, everything was within the grasp of his talent, education, background, and perfect bilingualism. But there he was, pleading to prolong for two or three more days the agony of the Parti

Québécois's daily newspaper, which had been launched with minimal financial resources.

Bédard, in a tone of irresistible sadness, called around the table: "You're good for a thousand dollars, aren't you? And you? And you?" He came to a friend of ours, a doctor and ardent nationalist, whose words struck consternation: "Well, I'm not so sure. I must say, Mr. Parizeau, I didn't like your last article on the demands we doctors made in our negotiations with the government." And Parizeau, ill at ease and wiping his forehead, started to explain and argue his point. He went on for a good ten minutes, until our friend finally decided he would contribute his share.

As our visitor climbed aboard the bus to travel overnight back to Montreal, I reminded myself that anyone eager for the political pilgrim's mantle should think twice about it.

However, Bédard wanted me to run in Jonquière, where I had many friends and relatives. Chicoutimi was out since Bédard already represented the riding. One more time, against my inclination, I had to consider the possibility of going into politics. Pressure reached its high point when Lévesque asked Guy Chevrette and me to come to Montreal, to recruit us.

Corinne Côté, Bédard, and his wife, Nicole, attended the meeting at Sambô's Restaurant. I had never met Lévesque face-to-face. My admiration for him and his shyness as well as my own were the required ingredients for an embarrassing interview. Moreover, he was obviously ill at ease at having to plead with us. I had a passing thought that he might take my presence to mean I would not expose him to the disappointment of a refusal. Unless someone had already told him it was in the bag.

I had the impression that Chevrette, who was farther down the sovereignty road, would say yes.

The weirdest thing about the meeting was the surroundings. The meal took place in the midst of a fashion show. Models regularly came to parade around us, as if our table was one of the markers for the show. Each time one of these gorgeous girls stopped next to us to make a pirouette, our male eyes converged on them, bringing the conversation to a stop. These apparitions overwhelmed Lévesque's loquaciousness no less than our own. Each time, we tried as best we could to get back on track after the goddesses had turned their heels.

Once again, I measured the force of my attachment to the legal profession and my lack of interest in political life. Cliche's refusal to enter the fray reinforced my views. After refusing to run myself, I joined Bédard's campaign during October and November of 1976.

The party organization asked me to introduce him to religious communities. Many of them were clients: the Chanoinesses hospitalières, the Soeurs du Bon Conseil, the petites Franciscaines de Marie, the Soeurs du Saint-Sacrement, the Ursulines, not counting diocesan authorities and parish officials. I took Marc-André to several. But an overeager organizer added the Antoniennes de Marie to the list. I had no objections. Not only were they my clients, but I had an aunt as well as several other relatives and friends in the order.

They received Bédard with all due consideration. I introduced him to the nuns who had assembled in the great convent hall to listen to the candidate's message. To all appearances, the reception was polite and attentive. Obviously satisfied with his performance, Bédard invited questions from the audience. After a long moment of silence, I saw with a sense of foreboding my friend, the order's financial officer, rise and ask very softly: "Mr. Bédard, I have read your party's platform. I would like to know if I am wrong in believing that you intend to eliminate grants to private schools? You know, if it is true, we will have to close the Apostolic School."

Bédard turned ashen. His left leg started twitching, a sign of real agitation. A disaster! Everyone had forgotten about the Apostolic School, a jewel among the private schools in the area. It was an elementary school established fifty years earlier. Every middle-class boy in Chicoutimi had attended the school. Bédard's four sons were enrolled there. The devil only knows if the reverend sister got the drift of Bédard's reply. He spoke about the Parti Québécois, which was one thing, and about reality, which was another, without leaving out the Apostolic School, a magnificent institution, and so on. I don't know what the Liberal candidate, an alumnus of the school himself, told the nuns when he saw them the following week, but he must have had a very easy time of it.

Two impressions remain of Lévesque in Chicoutimi at the end of the campaign. After his speech, a small group of us accompanied him to a restaurant. Hearing one of us vituperating against Bourassa in very aggressive terms, he said curtly, "Careful you don't underestimate him. He is very intelligent." A few hours later, in the midst of a snowstorm, he arrived at Bagotville airport. Someone came up to him saying, "Mr. Lévesque, I am afraid the snowstorm will prevent the plane from taking off." Lévesque tensed, made a gesture of exasperation, ran to the chartered old DC-3, which took off in the blizzard. This impatient man must have known that for once he was flying to victory.

A few months later, as premier, he asked me to meet him in his Québec City office, where he offered me the post of deputy minister of labour. Once again, I found myself in the position of having to say no. He didn't seem to mind too much because in the spring of 1977, he asked me to join a commission, chaired by Yves Martin, for reforming negotiating procedures for public and parapublic sectors. I accepted and, with Michel Grant of the Québec Federation of Labour, became commissioner.

For more than ten years, negotiations in the public and parapublic sectors had led to unrest in Québec society. During those tense times, illegal strikes in hospitals and schools, and interruptions in government department operations were common occurrences. At one point, the Bourassa government had even jailed union leaders for refusing to obey a Superior Court injunction.

On the whole, the Parti Québécois, in 1972 and 1976, had supported the Common Front of public-sector unions. Its political base depended to a large extent on organized labour. Feeling it had a strong hand, the party expected that, once in power, it might succeed where previous governments had failed. It hoped to reform the bargaining system and shorten time spent negotiating. It was asking a lot to think that improving the quality of dialogue, based on the credibility of the Parti Québécois, could improve things.

First, we had to restore a more constructive climate, find some common ground, and bring the necessary changes to the bargaining process. This was the mandate given the commission to which I was appointed, later named the Martin-Bouchard Commission (Grant resigned before the report was drafted).

The commission held public hearings until the end of December 1977. It heard several dozen briefs. After eight weeks of uninterrupted work on the report, Martin and I sent the report to the premier in the middle of February 1978.

We were aware that many people in government were expecting radical proposals. They were counting on some ingenious means to "depoliticize" the bargaining process and bring discipline to the use of union power. Some said openly they hoped we would recommend abolition of the right to strike in the public service.

After six months of consultations, study, and reflection, Martin and I came to a different conclusion. It seemed to us the dynamics of the situation were political in nature. Changing the mechanics of the bargaining process would not achieve very much. In fact, the problems we wanted to correct did not spring from a bad choice as such. The government never really had much of a choice, anyway. The conduct of negotiations was dictated by inescapable political imperatives.

Even though it was called "quiet," the revolution of the 1960s was the direct cause of the upheavals and the crises that have attended each round of negotiations with the Common Front. The initial choice made by the government carried the germ of centralization and politicization of the bargaining process.

The winds of social justice were blowing across Québec. Stifled until then by a mentality that feared the future and by a political order hostile to collective action and responsibility, Québec's social conscience was coiled like a spring. Suddenly released in 1960, it set off an irresistible wave of reforms, all aligned on equal access to education and to health care. The rest would flow from the implacable logic of necessity. The democratization of education and the universality of health care required the equalization of resources and services.

From then on, all the government needed were proper fiscal and administrative structures. The task of defining the normative and financial conditions for different categories of personnel had a primary role in the system's financial equilibrium and smooth operation. For equal services, there had to be equal work and, obviously, equal wages, too. Whence the centralization of the process determining working conditions, the only way to ensure parity.

Only one problem remained: Would the State determine working conditions by itself, resort to arbitration, or negotiate directly? It rejected arbitration. This was necessary since only the state itself can make decisions committing half its financial resources. It is unthinkable to have an arbitrator, a nonelected person coming under pressure from both sides, ruling indirectly on budget allocations for economic development and social programs.

However, from the moment that public-sector unionism first emerged, with its primary justification being the struggle against favouritism and arbitrary decisions, a negotiated settlement was inevitable. Premier Jean Lesage, on Louis-Philippe Pigeon's advice, believed he could hide behind an old adage from the golden age of the British monarchy: "The Queen does not negotiate with her subjects." In reality, the premier was concerned about the right to strike, the moving force in the traditional bargaining process. In the end, the government pretended to believe Jean Marchand, then president of the Confederation of National Trade Unions, when he himself feigned to promise never to have a hospital strike. The law granting the right to strike was passed in 1965.

Consequently, the Martin-Bouchard report told the government that it could not modify the basis of the collective bargaining process without bringing into question the universality of health services and the democratization of education. On the other hand, the report proposed a more effective timetable. But we had few illusions, knowing full well that the unions rarely respected bargaining time limits framing the right to strike. As for that right, we suggested keeping it, but under stricter conditions.

Where the report was innovative was in the field of essential services. It recommended giving the unions a key role in defining them. However, the cabinet had the authority to prohibit a strike should the level of services prove inadequate.

When I explained the main thrust of the report to Lévesque, I had the impression he was disappointed. In fact, we were lobbing the ball back to where it should have been. The state is not an employer like any other: it is responsible to the community. It is the community that is committed every time the government negotiates with its employees. Lévesque certainly understood that no technical gimic could ever exempt the state from its responsibility. But did he anticipate then to what extreme his duties as premier would lead him one day, or at what political cost?

As for me, I thought my own responsibilities would end with the commission itself. However, a few months later, Jean-Roch Boivin called me to Québec City to ask me, on behalf of the premier, if I would be the chief government negotiator at the central bargaining table in the forthcoming negotiations. "You thought you could tell us what to do and now you'll be the first to know whether you were right," he told me. Subsequently, I met with Treasury Board secretary Jean-Claude Lebel, who would be coordinating government strategy within the public service. I was then summoned by Parizeau, the undisputed head of the whole operation.

He was in fact more than that. Never had so much power been concentrated in the hands of one minister. Besides holding the purse strings of finance, he was revenue minister, chairman of the Treasury Board and member of the Priorities Committee. He controlled every aspect of public finance. He was the tax collector. It was he who prepared the government's budget and controlled departmental allocations, borrowed money in the name of the government, and approved public expenditures.

As chairman of the Treasury Board, he held court every Tuesday morning. No minister could undertake the smallest expense, even for funds already figured into the budget, without justifying it to the board. Many left empty-handed. He surrounded himself with top graduates from Montreal's élite business school, the Hautes Études Commerciales. They liked to repeat: "The Treasury Board plays an essential role: it keeps its hands on the spending brakes."

True, other important ministers — Camille Laurin, Bernard Landry, Pierre Marois, Robert Burns — if placed at the head of key ministries, might have opposed his will. But they ran ministries of state without front-line responsibilities, confined to policy decisions in priority areas. They did have some initiative, as shown by Dr. Laurin's accomplishments in the realm of language. But on the whole, while they consulted, called meetings, deliberated, and drafted reports and white papers, Parizeau, who sat in Duplessis's former office, made fifty decisions a day, and did the governing.

Lévesque, who hated administrative routine and bureaucratic power, had in fact handed day-to-day government operations over to Parizeau. The government held no secrets for Parizeau, for the simple reason that he had designed most of the system himself. He played it for all it was worth, like Menuhin on a Stradivarius, even choosing the score.

Parizeau was aware that the first test would be the next round of negotiations with the Common Front. Again, he was superbly prepared. He had had a front seat during all the negotiations of the 1960s. Trusted adviser to at least three premiers, Parizeau had made the first calculations of the government's total wage bill, calibrated the initial wage scales, and established the parameters for the monetary clauses. He liked negotiations with their dramatic turns, opposing strategies, and surprise countermoves. For the first time, he would lead the entire operation.

For all these reasons, he wanted to choose his chief negotiator and spokesman personally, someone with a lot of experience. However, I had never participated in negotiations with the Common Front and had been appointed by the premier's office. Unaware of all the subtleties of the situation, I was surprised at his cool reception the first time I met him. Parizeau greeted me with tones of perfect civility, saying, "They tell me you are interested in negotiating with the Common Front."

* * *

At last, I reported for my post. But the first few weeks were difficult, civility not always sufficient to mask the finance minister's reticence. I discussed this with Jean-Roch Boivin, and asked him whether it might be useful to speak to the premier about it. What I got was a demonstration of the legendary frankness of this man from Saguenay. His little speech was replete with expletives that reminded me of my lumberjack days in Pikauba. "Do you think for a minute that if he had to choose between his minister of finance and a greenhorn like you, Mr. Lévesque would have one second's hesitation? Get down to the job and learn to work with Jacques Parizeau. It's part of your job to win his confidence."

Once I recovered from Boivin's tongue-lashing, I resolved to give it another try and put all my energy into the job at hand. I discovered there was only one way of pleasing Parizeau: delivering the goods. Gradually, my relationship with him improved.

The stakes were enormous: for the duration of the three-year contracts, the total wage bill was close to thirty billion dollars, nearly half the government's budget, shared among 300,000 employees, fifteen percent of the active labour force in Québec.

The operation launched that spring of 1979 was full of pitfalls. As our preparatory studies progressed, it became clearer and clearer that the dynamics of these negotiations would prove different from earlier ones. The 1966 and 1969 negotiations were catch-up operations. Public servants, teachers, and hospital employees were underpaid. Union strategy concentrated on redressing inequities and injustices. In 1969 teachers won a single scale of remuneration for men and women, with parity from one region to the other. In the area of social affairs, union members won the concept of posts and promotion by seniority; in 1969 they obtained job security with two years' seniority.

The years 1972 and 1976 were normative and monetary breakthroughs for the unions. The 1972 negotiations lightened teaching loads for elementary schoolteachers and introduced a formula protecting teachers from layoffs in times of surplus personnel. Starting the same year, all public and parapublic employees got their own pension plan. It was also in 1972 that the government was among the first employers to index income in the form of lump-sum payments. The government also accepted the compression of wage categories, to the benefit of wage-earners at the bottom of the scale, by means of larger increases in the base rate. Often, the unions receiving these gains forced the government to impose them by way of decrees.

The 1976 negotiations gave all salaried employees sizeable monetary and normative gains: four weeks' vacation after one year, job security for teachers, detailed job descriptions, teacher-student ratios specific to the different types of institutions. The package also allowed for generous compensation rates, including increases, structural adjustments, and incorporation of lump-sum income protection. As well, the year 1976 marked the first appearance of indexing clauses integrated into the wage scales themselves.

As negotiated gains outstripped private-sector wage levels, the unions discarded their initial idea of a catch-up operation. Public-sector bargaining was presented as an instrument of social advancement, something that would pave the way for later improvements in the private sector.

Similarly, the tone became more and more political. Politicization occasionally even brought about systematic attacks by the union on the party in power. Paradoxically, this was the case in 1976, when the unions actually made their greatest gains, increasing the gap between public and private sectors to sixteen percent. Wage increases averaged twelve percent, and went as high as twenty-four percent.

Obviously, things couldn't continue this way much longer. Without resorting to rollbacks, adjustments had to come, particularly in the round of 1982. Tax revenues were falling, while interest on the debt was rising.

The surge of wage concessions, amplified by inflationary trends, had eaten into the government's resources for meeting other responsibilities. Moreover, the problem of wage disparity with the private sector was attracting considerable attention.

It was about time that government and unions remembered that it was the taxpayers who actually paid public service salaries. No matter what union leaders might think, the question was: "Why should a private-sector employee pay, through his taxes, a public servant doing similar work a salary higher than his own?" Not to mention the job security, nonexistent in the private sector. Moreover, the carryover from one sector to another had never taken place. As the engine of social progress, public service unions had left the rest of the train far behind. Some advantages, such as lower workloads for teachers and the concept of posting, were hardly transferable to the private sector. Nor could private employers match the monetary gains of the public service.

These problems and the policies needed to resolve them brought little cheer to a government that had confessed "a favourable prejudice towards the workers." Everyone recalled the words "Hang in there, guys" that Lévesque had said a dozen years earlier, as minister of natural resources in the Lesage government, to striking employees of Hydro-Québec. It is harder to turn the screws on friends than on enemies — especially when the friends happen to be political allies.

It so happened that the Parti Québécois was pursuing unusually demanding political goals. The party was not only different from other parties simply because it managed the state from a more left-wing perspective, but it also promoted Québec independence and was committed to a referendum on sovereignty association. The whole referendum process needed the support if not the approval of the Common Front.

The government saw a preview of future events when it published its white paper on sovereignty association in 1979. Everybody saw unionized public servants on television throwing the document into the fire.

It was naïve to think union support of independence would moderate the unions' stand. Not even Lévesque and Parizeau believed that for long. However, unionized government employees identified their own interests with the cause of independence. As far as they were concerned, the government had not yet reached the limit of its ability to pay. As for the unions, they could hardly be expected to give up a mode of pressure that had proved so effective in the past. Strategists and bureaucrats in union organizations continued to believe in the virtues of confrontation.

After some initial bitterness at union intransigence, the government adopted the only solution possible — it decided to bargain forcefully and openly, counting on the realism and mature judgement of the workers and their leaders.

The government came straight out with its objectives: to bring public service wage increases in line with the cost of living, thereby reducing the wage gap between public and private sectors. In exchange, it made it known it was prepared to make certain concessions. But the choice of concessions was crucial: they had to meet basic union concerns and harmonize with government policy. The choice eventually narrowed down to improvement in working conditions for women, who represented two-thirds of the Common Front's membership. For the first time, we established a separate forum for women's issues, besides the central bargaining table, which negotiated wage levels and coordinated the sectorial bargaining tables. It was soon clear that improvements in maternity leave benefits would be the key to a settlement.

As expected, the bargaining was tough, exhausting, and punctuated with crises. The most significant crisis took the form of an illegal hospital strike, which collapsed after Lévesque appeared on television. Reviving the format of his old television program, *Point de mire,* he stood before a blackboard, chalk and pointer in hand, and spent half an hour demonstrating the seriousness of the government's offers and the illegitimate nature of the work stoppage. That very night, during an emergency meeting at the bargaining table, I could see from the union leaders' faces what effect Lévesque's words had had on their troops.

However, the incident did not free us from going through all the traditional bargaining motions.

Like a Greek tragedy, negotiations unfold in four acts. In the first, the characters come on stage and describe their grievances: this is the exposition. The second act presents the fundamental reasons behind the conflict and maps out a battleground: this is the crux. The third act concentrates on denunciations, threats, strikes, and the use of force: this is the action. The tragedy ends with the resolution, either with an agreement or with the intervention of the legislature as a *deus ex machina.*

Here, the comparison stops. Talks at the bargaining table are not at the same heights as the dialogues of Aeschylus. There is no unity of time, place, and action. The actors gesticulate on forty different stages at the same time, while the real action takes place behind the scenes. Cacophony replaces the music of the strophe. Journalists in jeans take the place of the chorus. Victims do not cry out in pain on stage but meet their fate in the silence of everyday life. They sit in the bleachers, deprived of public services and of any voice in the matter. Above all, there is no hero; only negotiators with deep shadows under their eyes speaking some jargon even more hermetic than ancient Greek, sleeping for only a few hours at a time and always by day, living at night like vampires in smoky hotel rooms littered with empty coffee cups and uneaten sandwiches.

It is in such rooms and conditions that the final texts are written. It will take years for hundreds of arbitrators to unravel their meaning. Such is the fruit that falls from such a tree. The unbelievable weight of the structures put in place for the negotiations leads to confusion and paralysis. They seem to be designed to hamper resolution. There are more than forty bargaining tables and hundreds of participants. The process is plagued by diverging interests, from one union to the next, none wanting to sign anything before their peacetime rivals for fear of being stuck with more serious problems than the others. At the centre stands the coordinating table vested with the responsibility of negotiating wages for 300,000 service employees. The people at this table have no real hold over sectorial blockages, except at the last moment. The end comes when the government, its defences breached, feels the anger of the taxpayers, the whiplash of the opposition, the vituperation of editorialists, and the harassment of its own caucus. Then it decides to dynamite the logjam with special laws and concessions.

Just before Christmas, the central bargaining table came to an agreement on wages. As expected, our proposal on maternity leaves (twenty-one weeks with pay after giving birth) carried the day. To resolve conflicts on normative clauses, we had to accept a fifty-kilometre travelling restriction for people on availability lists. On the other hand, we managed to align salary increases with consumer prices. The agreement reduced the wage gap between the public and the private sectors from sixteen percent to about eleven percent.

Right at the end of salary negotiations, the government agreed with the union's proposal to add six months to the normal duration of collective agreements. The agreements would now expire on December 31, 1982, instead of June 30. A salary increase, indexed to inflation, was scheduled for July 1, 1982. No one realized it at the time, but we had sown the seeds for the crisis of 1982 that terminated the nonaggression pact between the Parti Québécois and the labour movement.

During the first weeks of 1980, forty-three collective agreements were signed without the government having to threaten legislative action.

Now, the referendum debate on sovereignty association could begin in a climate of social peace.

7

Defeat on All Fronts

The outlook for the 1980s was auspicious: everyone was happy with the way negotiations had gone with the Common Front, and the yes campaign for Québec sovereignty was off to a good start.

Québec had made enormous progress since 1960. After setting up an educational system, social programs, a modern public service, a state organization with the proper tools for economic development, many thought it would make sense to raise anchor. It seemed logical for the revolution to find its quiet accomplishment in sovereignty. From June 22, 1960, to May 20, 1980, it had been a beautiful trip. An aura of inevitability gave it the elegance Einstein sought of a mathematical equation describing the perfection of the laws of nature. However, the contours of political reality are never that clear, and they seldom conform to functional aesthetics.

Unlike others who noticed the growth of the no side, I believed right to the end that the yes side would win. However, it's true that I tended to be optimistic because the majority in Saguenay–Lac-Saint-Jean favoured the yes.

I was stupefied by the results of the referendum. Several images survive: Pierre Trudeau, at the other side of the world, reacting yet again with strange detachment; Claude Ryan, with a grimace of bitter rejoicing; René Lévesque, pathetic and small against a giant backdrop, stunned with pain but trying nevertheless to convey hope for the nation he had been so proud of four years earlier.

For people of my generation, who had, throughout the 1960s, spoken and written solely in terms of hope and pride, it was the end of an era. I know that history never ends, that new hope can spring from the ashes, and that the fate of nations does not hang on states of mind. However, no one experiences each moment as a historian or a political scientist. In any case, for me May 20, 1980, marked a break with the past.

The next three years confirmed this conclusion in several ways. At the collective level, the break stemmed from the infamous unilateral repatriation of the Constitution in 1981–82 and the rupture between the Lévesque government and the labour movement. At the personal level, whatever modest professional part I had played came from both these social and constitutional setbacks, and from the discouragement that gripped me due to personal fallout from these events.

A few months after winning the referendum with a promise of radical reforms in the Constitution, Trudeau showed his true colours. In October 1980, he made public his unilateral repatriation proposal accompanied by a charter of rights that reduced the powers of Québec's National Assembly. Yet another lesson in *Realpolitik* for the people of Québec who had given him carte blanche, believing that the forthcoming constitutional changes would be beneficial to them.

Evidently, the federal government had decided to make the most of the advantages conferred by its referendum victory. The no vote placed the Lévesque government in a desperate situation. Lacking further political recourse, it had no option but to seek intervention through the courts. It set up a team of legal experts headed by former Supreme Court justice Yves Pratte to refer the legality of the unilateral repatriation to the Québec Court of Appeal. I was part of the team, along with Georges Emery, Colin Irving, and Paul-Arthur Gendreau, then assistant deputy minister of justice. I was the only Péquiste in the group, the government feeling that it might be best to keep a safe distance between judicial initiatives and politics. As for the federal government, it was represented by Michel Robert, Raynold Langlois (another classmate from Laval), and Gérald Beaudoin, a future Conservative senator. The case was heard in January 1981.

We were still waiting for the court's decision when, great misfortune, the Lévesque government was reelected on April 13. One wonders why the electorate returned it to power after having refused to support sovereignty association. Was it a consolation prize after the no vote of May 20, 1980? Was it the expression of confidence for a good government? Was it to punish Québec Liberals guilty by association for the anti-Québécois schemes of their referendum ally Trudeau? Or was it a repudiation of Ryan's leadership? Any hypothesis is valid. But one thing is certain: the reelection gave Lévesque his passport to hell.

It is easier today to see the Parti Québécois's vulnerability to the federal postreferendum offensive. Trudeau could easily attribute the least resistance to ill will. A party that had tried to "destroy" Canada and, worse, had been called to order by voters in Québec held little credibility in negotiating seriously or repelling the federal offensive. And if, in the end, Québec was isolated, Ottawa and its nine allies would be free to tear up the pact of 1867 and impose its will on the recalcitrant province.

At any rate, the Parti Québécois existed for the sake of Québec independence. It was not at ease in this new role that went against its very nature: negotiating the "renewal" of Canadian federalism. The Parti Québécois had to guard against two equally perilous hazards: success or failure. The first would turn the Parti Québécois into a resolutely federalist party. The second would imply it had negotiated in bad faith. Either way, because it was politically impotent, the Parti was exposing Québec to cruel setbacks.

Our worst fears were realized. In this misadventure we lost our right of veto (which everyone recognized) and a large part of our jurisdiction over language. It was as if Québec had sent its champion into battle with his hands tied behind his back.

Two days in power, and the disasters began to pile up. The Court of Appeal rendered a decision supporting Ottawa's case and confirming the legality of the repatriation proposal.

The next day, Québec signed a solidarity pact with seven other provinces. Then, putting its last hope in the Supreme Court, it instructed us, its lawyers, to appeal the damaging decision. We pleaded the case in Ottawa in June. On September 28, the Supreme Court rendered a decision that stood on the border between law and politics. It held that repatriation was legal but illegitimate because it lacked the consent of the majority of the provinces.

Federal authorities responded with lightning speed to recover from what was in reality a political setback. Within the hour, Chrétien rushed before the cameras and the microphones claiming victory and celebrating the court's decree that no "legal" obstacle stood in the way of repatriation. Of course, he was careful not to grant any importance to the political condemnation expressed in one of the court's conclusions. To the great distress of the group of lawyers representing Québec, the Lévesque government lost the information battle, underestimating the political card the court had put in its hand. It was already clear that the British Parliament would never consent to repatriation after the highest court in Canada had called it illegitimate.

From then on, events moved quickly. On October 2, the National Assembly adopted almost unanimously (111 to 9) a resolution condemning the federal project. However, the provinces' common front was already crumbling. It was naïve to think that seven English-speaking premiers would compromise themselves by staying on side with a separatist government and go to the extreme of confronting the national government. Our seven allies couldn't drop Québec fast enough after using it to bargain with Ottawa from a position of strength. They used Québec to obtain the concessions they wanted: an opting-out clause, suppression of the "national" referendum, and the right to withdraw without compensation.

To say the least, the outcome lacked class. The final deal was made in the middle of the night, behind the backs of the evil separatists lodging in a hotel on the other side of the Ottawa River. Not belonging to the gentlemen's club, Québec's representatives did not have the right to fair play. A few months later, the Supreme Court decided that what had not been legitimate when eight provinces opposed it, was legitimate against Québec alone. The Trudeau government was thus able to ignore the issue.

Would they have done this to Ontario, Alberta, or even Newfoundland? Probably not. But they didn't hesitate to do it to Québec.

I will never forget the epilogue, fixed visually once again in my memory: the spectacle of the Queen of England (she was also our Queen that day), Pierre Trudeau, Jean Chrétien, and André Ouellet, gathered on April 17, 1982, on the lawn of Parliament Hill to affix their signatures to the bottom of a constitution that had orphaned Québec.

This to me is the key event triggering all that happened and will happen, the breach through which Québécois democracy will escape from a régime that violated its moral commitments. By severing the bonds of trust, the partner himself liberates us. From now on, we can no longer exhort ourselves to respect the achievements of John A. Macdonald and George-Étienne Cartier. Cartier's name did not carry much weight during the night of the long knives. The English-speaking provinces preferred to substitute the signatures of Jean Chrétien and André Ouellet. They will have to live with that choice.

I ended my legal foray into the constitutional issue with a taste of ashes in my mouth.

But there was nothing euphoric about my other mandate in the fall of 1981, either. I had accepted for the second time an appointment as the government's chief negotiator with the Common Front.

It was in the cards that after their reelection, Lévesque and the Parti Québécois would have to drain the cup to its dregs. They were engaged in a standoff with 300,000 public service employees and their unions that had all the earmarks of civil strife.

Even before their election victory on April 13, 1981, the péquiste cabinet ministers knew that future public service negotiations could be disastrous. The recession, which was drying up tax revenues, was accompanied by a bout of inflation. Rates topped ten percent for the period between July 19, 1981, and June 30, 1982.

The Treasury Board rang the alarm bells early in 1982. Secretary Robert Tellier and I prepared a memorandum for chairman Yves Bérubé's signature that outlined the government's financial situation and the leeway it had in the forthcoming negotiations. The memorandum made it clear that the salary increases scheduled for July 1, 1982, would increase the government's deficit by $725 million. There were only two possible solutions: borrow that amount or don't pay the salary increases. Borrowing meant risking Québec's credit rating on Wall Street. Refusing to pay was easier said than done.

Robert Tessier and I attended the interministerial meeting where Bérubé introduced the document. The messenger and the message were badly received. In the midst of the constitutional fiasco, the Lévesque cabinet saw with trepidation the storm clouds gathering in another direction, the social climate.

The government had already decided to launch an initiative to make economic and social decision-makers better aware of the precarious state of public finances. It all came together at a summit meeting in April 1982. Numerous speeches and courteous discussions did not alter the intractable reality: the government did not have the money to pay what it had promised union members, and the unions were not going to budge. I was asked to make one last tour of union federations and social action groups. My mandate was to explain to them, with supporting figures, that the government was financially incapable of honouring the July 1 wage increase, which had swelled to unmanageable proportions after being indexed to the rate of inflation. With the help of a team from Finance and the Treasury Board, I drafted a scenario of catastrophic measures (we even said "apocalyptic") that the government might adopt if forced to pay the increase in its entirety. One measure, for example, would be to lay off 17,000 employees.

I was met with a categorical refusal. The unions absolutely refused to reopen the contract or to accept a $521-million cut in the wage increase scheduled for July 1. Consequently, the government returned to its basic function: decision-making.

Suddenly, time was running short. The finance minister was due to table a balanced budget before the end of May. Lévesque convened a meeting of all the ministers and deputy ministers concerned (Finance, Treasury Board, Education, Social Affairs, Public Service, and Justice). Louis Bernard, Jean-Roch Boivin, Robert Tessier, and I were also part of the group that met one evening in a private dining room at the Continental restaurant in Québec City.

There was only one item on the agenda: Was legislation necessary to cancel the July 1 wage increase? That was the Treasury Board's proposal. Opinions were divided. Jacques Parizeau did not accept that the Québec government would repudiate its signature. Others, like Bérubé, argued for the need to balance the budget without compromising Québec's credit rating. But Parizeau's arguments and influence had their effects on the premier: the raise in salaries would be made as promised.

Since the option to borrow was closed, there was only one expedient: pay the higher wages until December 31, 1982, then recover the money the very next day with drastic pay cuts. The strategy didn't fool anyone, least of all the union members. Without a doubt, they would sooner accept a law depriving them of a wage increase they had not yet seen than get a wage increase that would later be withdrawn. The latter alternative would give them the feeling they were victims of a hoax.

The government passed Bill 70, which stipulated that if there was no agreement with the unions within three months, the government would take, starting January 23, $521 million through massive pay cuts. By December 31, 1982, the wage gap between public and private sectors had jumped to fifteen percent. Bill 70 forced the gap down to six percent. Almost simultaneously, the National Assembly voted in another law imposing drastic cutbacks in pension benefits.

After that, nothing worked. Meetings of the central bargaining table turned sour and sometimes led to altercations. The days dragged by. Union representatives were not afraid to tell us right to our faces what they thought of us. They felt they had been betrayed, wrongly treated, and mugged by their friends.

All "negotiations" having failed, Lévesque brought down Bill 108 in December. It touched on every aspect of the collective agreements, normative as well as monetary. The government and its partners (schools and hospitals) took advantage of the situation. It unilaterally modified the normative clauses, particularly teachers' workloads. The best paid (generally members of the Québec's teachers' union) were hardest hit by the financial recovery operation. Salary cuts were as high as nineteen percent. In constant dollars, it took years for many people to climb back to their salary levels of December 1982. Moreover, they resented the disparaging remarks of some cabinet ministers about their average age (over forty) and their workloads compared with their colleagues in Ontario.

The union's reactions were as brutal as the government actions had been: illegal work stoppages, open rebellion against the law, personal attacks, and even violence against Minister Camille Laurin.

But it was Premier Lévesque who bore the brunt of union reaction. Paraphrasing the name given Klaus Barbie, head of the Gestapo in Lyon, union members referred to him as "the butcher of New Carlisle."

What was going through Lévesque's mind while he was under attack from all sides? After twenty years of political and social mobilization, Québec society, now stronger than ever, had arrived at the last roadblock. No one knew it better than Lévesque. But he also realized that, at the last moment, Québec had reared up and withheld the effort he demanded. In a way, Québec had said no to him. This no vote had left him to founder in disarray and with a vulnerability without precedent in the face of federal blows. Now, circumstances compelled Lévesque to use what little strength remained of the Québec state to fight the very people who had supported his vision of sovereignty. The ultimate reversal would have been to see the teachers' union declare void the law governing salaries because of the government's failure to have it translated into English!

Most of those who knew Lévesque agree that he did not readily confide in others. I can only confirm this observation. Indeed, I always had the impression that I learned more about him from his speeches than from his conversation. Inscrutable in private, in public he touched everybody's heart. It was as if he could only give of himself that which he shared with all Québécois. Perhaps this is why they recognized themselves in what he said. The rest, what was personal, he kept for himself, except, I imagine, when he was with intimate friends. But I was not one of them.

Nevertheless, I saw him fairly often during the confrontations with the Common Front. He tended to blame the union apparatus, instead of the membership, for the indifference that met his appeal for solidarity during the budget crisis. Lucid above all, loving people but without any illusions about human nature, he knew exactly what his firm stand would cost him. However, he had decided to wage a fierce war to preserve the health of public finances. If one element had to be saved for the future of Québec, it would be the foundations of a solvent state.

Exhausted by Trudeau, betrayed by his allies in the other provinces, abandoned (could he have believed it?) by Québec on May 20, 1980, Lévesque probably felt that, after all, he could not possibly lose every battle. Once the unions had refused to reopen the collective agreement, he settled into an unshakeable determination. The escalation of union pressures made him even more determined. From that time on, he became increasingly impatient with philosophical discussions about "task parameters," the "costs of the system," and "scale compressions." One day during a meeting, I saw a minister hand him a technical note on a problem under negotiation. He glanced at the first few lines and then furiously threw it to the floor. "Can anyone explain to me in French what this means?" he asked. Parizeau came to his colleague's rescue, improvising a brief explanation.

Lévesque admired his finance minister's brilliant talent. For his part, Parizeau worshipped the premier and his office. But their relationship was not warm. There was absolutely no camaraderie between them. Neither was given to pouring out his heart to others, and they both shunned the meaningless and interminable conversations that most politicians seem to enjoy. Between them they used the respectful pronoun *vous*. In serious moments, they exchanged letters, generally relayed by Jean-Roch Boivin, long their essential link.

The best political teams consist of opposites because truth can only emerge from the collision of the different realities that make it hard for everyone to work together. Lévesque achieved this miracle of equilibrium with Louis Bernard and Boivin.

The imperturbable Bernard drew every decision from a cascade of premises. He managed crises during office hours without allowing them to deviate his plans. Leaving a promising career, he came to the public service in search of a grand design. Somewhere, then, he had strong passions, but no one could have known it from his behaviour or conversation. He never lost the equanimity with which he accepted good news or bad, or ideas whatever their source. When he made up his mind, he seldom changed it, although he was a team player who could execute a decision that went contrary to his views.

He practised intellectual rigour and honesty as if they were religious vows, which made him a formidable opponent in any debate. "What is Bernard's position?" cabinet ministers and deputy ministers would ask when wondering what to do about a problem or project referred to the premier for decision. Everyone knew that Lévesque gave tremendous weight to the opinion of this totally disinterested adviser.

Bernard was made to measure for the job of executive council secretary, whose functions bridged the line between politics and public administration. The secretary must be a politician who inspires the confidence of public servants; he must also be a public servant who has the support of politicians. In him are brought together the interests of state and government. In a way, he is a man torn by having to decide ten times a day where loyalty to the party ends and service to the state begins. Louis Bernard, who believed in sovereignty with all his heart and soul, was devoted to Lévesque right to the end. But he never lost sight of the respect due to institutions and the moral conscience and elevation of mind they call for. That probably earned him the complaints I occasionally heard about lapses of political judgement.

If Bernard reflected the rational component of Lévesque, Boivin exhibited more his instinctive side. All comparisons are faulty and all images are oversimplifications. Even so, I would risk saying the one served the premier and the other served Lévesque, who happened to be premier.

Twenty-five years in Montreal as a student and lawyer had not smoothed the rough edges that must have lacerated in Québec City more than one civil servant, journalist and politician. Boivin was direct in his approach: he did the strong-arm jobs, he was blunt and crude, and he enjoyed good food and fat cigars. Lévesque more than anyone avoided unpleasant meetings. It was left to Boivin, then, to reprimand cabinet ministers, tell them to give up pet projects, impose on them a deputy minister they did not want, order them to cancel long-planned European tours, or inform them they would be dropped after the next cabinet shuffle. He was both slave driver and whipping boy of overpaid and ambitious ministerial assistants who, from one government to the next, act as if they are cabinet ministers.

There is no better way to become unpopular.

By nature and tradition, the job of the premier's chief of staff is a thankless one. He takes the blows others would not dare level at the premier. He is accused of giving the premier calamitous advice, of isolating him, and of protecting him from reality. Considered the guardian of the régime's most sordid secrets, the chief of staff is naturally suspected of harbouring the blackest designs and held responsible for all the government's failures. Like his predecessors, Boivin had to bear these affronts.

A thick skin is necessary equipment. This was especially true for Boivin, who carefully concealed under his the sensitivity of an artist and the discipline of a moralist. His bond with politics was Lévesque and his passion for Québec. Together they had walked out of a 1967 Liberal party convention and founded the Mouvement Souveraineté-Association, and had been together ever since. They got along famously and could understand each other without talking. There was a lot of respect and affection between them, but even more, they could criticize and be honest with each other.

The premier expected Boivin to confirm his intuitions. Boivin either liked or didn't like a speech, an idea, a strategy, or a situation. He would grasp issues right away without having to weigh, examine, and dissect them. I saw the premier during a working session turn towards his chief of staff, after a long and learned exposition by one of his ministers, and ask, "What do you think, Mr. Boivin?" I was not the only one to overhear the answer: "Mr. Premier, he's full of shit." After that the tedious discussions were cut short, much to Lévesque's satisfaction.

Bernard and Boivin should have gotten along like cats and dogs.

They had strong personalities and overlapping responsibilities, and both reported directly to the premier. Conflict is not rare on prime ministers' staffs. People are at each other's throats to have the boss's ear, to control access to his office either physically or by phone, and to monitor his correspondence. I saw this sort of thing in both Ottawa and Paris. All the biographies of American presidents point to the power struggles that took place around them in the White House. In general, peace comes only after the victory of one over the other.

However, nothing like that ever happened between the two close advisers of the premier. No one was ever able to say which had the greater influence. Neither sought to cut the other off. This was probably because they had no ambition or aimed no higher than what they were. Equally motivated by the cause of sovereignty, they combined their personal qualities and resources to provide the premier with an efficient and harmonious environment.

This attitude continued during this stormy period when the government, moving from crisis to crisis, was losing support.

Boivin sometimes came to see me in the middle of the night in the suite where we were having our palavers with union negotiators. We were desperately seeking some way out of the deadlock. When failure was inescapable, his nocturnal visits became more frequent, as if he wanted to comfort me. I would have liked to have had a freer hand so I could budge the unions and avert the looming disaster. But we were faced with reasons of state, which necessity had made more unyielding, and which Lévesque's bitter-end determination had made implacable.

In Québec City, dawn was still rosy-fingered, as it says in the *Iliad*, even from our lofty suite full of smoke and dirty plates, and even to antiheroes like us who sometimes had not left the hotel for a week and slept for three days. We waited for the dining room to open so we could gulp down our breakfast before resuming what we now called "the negotiations" only with derision. Meanwhile, in the attic of the Treasury Board, dozens of people were pushing paper by the ton. Keeping one another going night and day, they were drafting some fifty collective agreements that were to be imposed by decree.

A barrage of special legislation, recriminations, and political uproar ended the whole business. I was personally singled out for my expenses, although I had reduced by ten percent the hourly rate stipulated in the original contract. A taxi slip in my name for an official return trip to Montreal (a $200 expense for two civil servants and myself, much less than the cost of three plane tickets) started a public debate. An anonymous civil servant also leaked a twenty-dollar invoice I had submitted to the Ministry of Justice for a pair of formal pants that I had rented to conform to the dress code of Newfoundland's Court of Appeal. I was representing the Québec government in a case concerning Churchill Falls. We were contesting a bill before Newfoundland's legislature cancelling (unsuccessfully, as it turned out) a contract supplying electricity to Hydro-Québec, a multibillion-dollar trifle. I read sarcastic newspaper stories alluding to the Vautrin affair — Vautrin was a minister in Taschereau's government whom Duplessis had stigmatized for billing the province for a pair of pants.

In short, I was stung and humiliated as never before in my life. I resolved never again to accept a government appointment with an honorarium. There was little merit in it since I made more money from my private practice.

I did not feel very cocky on my return to Chicoutimi, before the Christmas holidays. I was licking my wounds when, the day after New Year's, the government let me know that union representatives were asking to meet with me. They wanted to negotiate the applications of the decrees just promulgated. I could not refuse, but I did insist on one condition: I would do it at my own cost and without remuneration. I did not want to see my name listed in the public accounts anymore.

Mustering my courage, I returned to Québec City. When I arrived, an incident arose that would otherwise have been unimportant, showing that in the search for guilty parties people in the government were also picking on me. I was with Jean-Marc Boily, assistant secretary of the Treasury Board and my companion in misfortune during these tribulations. As we entered a restaurant, a mandarin (they are not all in Ottawa) from the Executive Council said frostily before turning his back to me: "Thanks for the great social climate."

It took three months of "volunteer" work to draft what we coyly called "readjustment agreements." The union leaders wanted to soften certain changes the decrees had unilaterally brought to the normative clauses. We were hoping that these new agreements would confer an appearance of legitimacy to our strong-arm tactics. The government had not seen any union signatures for a long time and was happy about this last-minute substitute. In the end I earned a mocking compliment from the premier: "You are more persuasive when we do not pay you an honorarium."

After which, I left Québec City for Chicoutimi, where I hoped to stay for good.

8

A Calculated Risk

I had just turned forty-five. Professionally, I had been through a rough time, and a personal problem needed to be resolved. For some time, my wife and I had lived apart. Easter was approaching. I buried myself in the *Confessions* of St. Augustine and then in those of Jean-Jacques Rousseau. Just before Easter 1982, I took them with me to the Capuchin monastery at Lake Bouchette for a weeklong retreat. Back in Chicoutimi, I acknowledged my faults, returned to live with my wife, and resumed my law practice.

I imagine many people in Québec at that time felt they had been sent back to attend to their domestic and professional affairs. The political road, for supporters of sovereignty especially, seemed blocked, and for a long time to come. Triumphant federalists in Ottawa were biding their time before the next provincial elections freed the Péquistes from their Calvary. Political impotence gripped the government that had shown such creative enthusiasm during its first years in office.

Gone was the joyous fever that produced Bill 101, agricultural zoning, registered stock-saving plans, no-fault auto insurance, popular financing, and water purification. Time had cooled the satisfaction these able and cultured people had felt in fulfilling the dream that had brought them to politics. Members of the cabinet committee for the first Common Front negotiations used to insert Latin quotations in the discussions or show off their literary erudition. I once heard Jacques-Yvan Morin correct a colleague who was quoting Boileau:

> *What is well conceived is clearly expressed*
> *And the words to say it* come *readily.*

"No, not *come* but *arrive,*" Morin said. An argument ensued, ending with a wager, which was won by the minister of education — as well it should be.

These intellectual games were certainly over. Members of this cabinet, probably the most brilliant ever assembled, sank into moroseness. They shared the misery of some colleagues and lamented the departure of others. Fate spared them nothing, not even the tormented end of an admired leader. They continued to come up with perfectly valid projects, such as the building program, but fate was against them. The end of a régime always has something inexorable about it.

I observed everything from afar and by proxy, and felt comforted by my decision to stay in my tent. For this reason, I refused the offer to become deputy minister of justice when my friend Pierre-Marc Johnson became justice minister. Similarly, I gave Guy Chevrette a friendly "no" when he wanted me to chair a commission to revise social and health programs. I really believed my public career was finished even before it had really started.

I concentrated on expanding my law office and became more involved in local matters. I only travelled outside the region to attend committee meetings of the bar association and board meetings of Donohue Inc. and the Société générale de financement to which I had been appointed a year earlier.

During that time, Brian Mulroney was beginning his second bid for the leadership of the Conservative party. I played no part in it. The only thing they asked me to do was to solicit funds from my circle of acquaintances, which I did. They certainly did not want me writing speeches — it was still too early for flights of nationalist sentiment. Others penned the words reproaching Joe Clark for having too much sympathy for Québec.

I had been much more active in Mulroney's first leadership bid, in 1976. After a few campaign speeches, I spent the week before the convention at Lake Memphremagog with Mulroney and his advisers. I worked on the French part of his main address. It was not a masterpiece, but the result of our collaboration was certainly less insipid than the speech he gave in Ottawa. I never found out who persuaded Mulroney to drop our joint text for this last-minute effort, which disappointed everyone.

The incident did not alter our friendly relationship in any way. But from 1980 on, we had to put our friendship on ice. Mulroney was on the no side of the referendum and later supported Trudeau's unilateral repatriation of the Constitution. We had remained friends for the good reason that we saw very little of each other during this period.

It was Mulroney, I believe, who resumed contact after he became head of the Conservative party. He called me frequently during the Central Nova by-election. He was gracious enough to invite me for his first appearance in the House of Commons as MP and leader of the Opposition in 1983. In the spring of 1984, I wrote a speech for him describing how much the Trudeau government's adversarial approach was costing the provinces. As the general election drew closer, everything sped up.

Bernard Roy, a university classmate and Mulroney supporter, took charge of the election campaign in Québec. Except in Joliette, represented by Roch La Salle, the Conservatives were starting from scratch. Their first job involved fielding seventy-four candidates.

For a few weeks, Roy badgered me to run in Chicoutimi. Mulroney joined in and even came to Saguenay in the spring. Mila was with him, and she had lunch with my wife to get her agreement. I had a positive talk with Brian, but reserved my decision for later.

For I still had doubts about my credibility as a candidate running under the banner of a federalist party. I had put considerable energy into the cause of Québec sovereignty while it seemed within reach. And, although I had stood on the political sidelines for two years, I had retained my Parti Québécois membership and continued to make regular financial contributions.

When I discussed it with Louis Bernard, his answer gave me pause. "Imagine yourself standing in front of the TV cameras, explaining what part of Brian Mulroney's program persuaded you, a fifteen-year supporter of sovereignty, to carry the banner of a federalist party. You will have to do some fancy footwork. But even if you manage the words very well, you can't deceive the eye of the camera. If you don't feel comfortable with your political choice, it will betray you."

In truth, I saw more and more clearly the need for the people of Québec to overcome their political torpor and break out of English Canada's constitutional ostracism. In spite of what Mulroney was telling me in private, the party had made no formal commitment in this respect. All things considered, I decided not to run. I informed Roy of this at a meeting in Montreal. He was disappointed and told me so.

A few weeks later, however, he called me in Chicoutimi to ask me to participate in the campaign. My role was to remain in constant contact as Québec adviser to our mutual friend, and to prepare speeches for him. After accepting, I attended a meeting with Marcel Masse and some Conservative party organizers at the Ritz in Montreal. My first task would be to draft the party's Québec platform. The organizers gave me a hand, supplying bundles of documents, reports, reviews, and political statements, most of which seemingly originated from national party headquarters in Ottawa.

I set up shop at the Four Seasons in Ottawa and started writing. Then they gave me a downtown office, next to Charlie McMillan, an academic, who was the party leader's economic adviser. Under no illusion about the value of an effort launched in those circumstances, I first drafted a program for Québec, doing my best to harmonize it with the national program, which had been entirely designed by anglophones and had very little relevance for Québec. I spoke regularly with the leader on the campaign trail.

One day, he asked me to write introductory and closing remarks for the leaders' debate in French. With Jean Bazin, McMillan, and Hugh Segal, I was part of a team anticipating questions that might crop up in this debate and the English one after that. Our major concern was to expand the list of answers, attacks, and responses to fit all possible situations. The candidate's lightning visits to Ottawa allowed us to have several sessions with him at Stornoway. We also viewed films of previous debates with him.

The preparations were very professional, excessively so. A deluge of statistical data had to be memorized. Experts gave advice on comportment, gestures, intonations, and camera angles. In the end, Mila Mulroney had the best advice. After most people had left following a rather strenuous session, she said, "Brian, be natural and forget the rest."

He won the two bouts. He was particularly strong in the second one, where he bullied John Turner about the numerous patronage nominations he had inherited from Trudeau. Generally, this sort of debate is won on points. In this case, however, everyone saw Mulroney deliver the knockout punch live.

There was a third debate, this one on women's issues. I made the same preparations, but with a modified team made up of women, like Jocelyne O'Hara, who were knowledgeable about these issues. I accompanied the Conservative leader to Toronto, where the debate took place. No one could have outdone Ed Broadbent, whose claque had taken over the hall, but Brian Mulroney lost no points. He did not expect to do any better than that.

At the end of July, he decided to give a major speech on his economic policies during a trip to Sept-Îles, two weeks later. He gave me the names of two or three economists I should consult and asked for a speech outline. I discovered that economists, like many other people, have a predilection for parties in power. None of those I called was available; they were all working for the Liberals. I called Mulroney and suggested that he speak on the Constitution instead. He agreed.

It seemed a good opportunity to propose to him a new perspective on federal-provincial relations based on a reconciliation allowing Québec to recover the standing it had before the events of 1981–82. A minimal program, capable of appealing to reasonable people, would have to repair the damage inflicted on Québec and restore its place at the constitutional table. It might later be possible to work out a new distribution of powers.

I wrote the speech as if I were delivering it myself, giving free rein to the indignation aroused by Québec's exclusion. I was convinced that it was in our interest to break out of our isolation and throw off the disaffection perpetuating our lethargy. I remembered a report inspired by Senator Arthur Tremblay, whose plea for reform had gone unheeded. When I was putting the final touches to the speech, I checked certain details with Tremblay. I noted in passing the irony of the situation: the ideas proposed by Joe Clark's adviser, discarded during the leadership campaign to win the West for Mulroney, were now surfacing during the election campaign to mobilize Québec voters.

I handed the speech to Mulroney in a hotel room in Chicoutimi. He read it and seemed satisfied. I didn't hear any more about it until that Sunday, August 6, when he spoke in Sept-Îles.

It was a denunciation of the constitutional ostracism Trudeau had inflicted on Québec with his strong-arm tactics of 1982. Insisting on the need to relieve the collective trauma, the speech was a passionate call for reconciliation between Québec and the rest of Canada. The future prime minister proposed changes to the Constitution that would convince Québec to sign it. In the same breath, he reviled "the subterfuges, so close to the hearts of the Liberals, that allow the federal government to interfere furtively with the contents of provincial policies . . . But the Liberals have devised a strategy that, under the guise of uniform pan-Canadian policies, really seeks to invade provincial jurisdiction. The trick is to link financial contributions with management and policy conditions amounting to disguised federal legislation."

The speech raised hopes and was well received. We were cooking with gas. I wrote the speech for election night, September 4. We were already calling it the victory speech. I later found out that McMillan had also been asked to write the same speech. We merged the two into a presentable address.

The leader invited me to spend election evening in his suite at Le Manoir in Baie-Comeau. Even before the results started coming in, euphoria gripped the hotel. The mood was momentarily subdued when Rodrigue Pageau, death in his eyes, was carried in on a stretcher.

Suffering from the cancer that would soon kill him, he wanted to celebrate his last triumph as party organizer for Québec.

In the candidate's bungalow, the atmosphere was tense with expectancy, though tinged with apprehension. I happened to be sitting next to Mulroney, in front of two TV screens, when, shortly before nine, one of them showed a computer projection announcing a Conservative victory. In a fraction of a second, my seatmate on the sofa had become prime minister of Canada. He took me aside and said, "As you know, this is my dream come true. But I need you in Paris, as ambassador." I didn't say a word; I was too stunned to reply.

Then it was the sports centre of Baie-Comeau, the delirious crowd, the winner's slow progress towards the stage, the speech, the return to the hotel, and parties in every suite until the wee hours of the morning. I was awakened with a message: the prime minister–designate wanted a tête-à-tête over breakfast.

I arrived at the appointed time, but had to wait a while. President Reagan was on the phone. As soon as I sat down, my host repeated his proposal of the previous evening. It was no dream; he had not simply given in to some inconsequential impulse. He really wanted to send me to France. I asked for time to think it over.

He then flew to Ottawa, and as usual, I went back to Chicoutimi.

I gave myself a month's holiday in Europe. Towards the end of my stay, I received a telephone call from Bernard Roy, who informed me that the prime minister of France, Laurent Fabius, would be making an official visit to Canada in November. This would be the first trip abroad for Fabius in his new role. Mulroney, who would also be making one of his first appearances on the international stage, was eager to announce the broad outline of his policy to France. He asked me to write the speech he would be giving during a gala reception for his French counterpart on November 7.

It was a tall order. I took the job under one condition: my speech was not to be handed over to the bureaucrats in External Affairs, specialists in banalities. If the prime minister did not like the speech, he could tear it up, but he was not to have it sanitized. Later experience proved what I already knew: bureaucracies are incapable of producing an intelligible and imaginative speech. On the contrary, if you submit the text to them, you can be sure it will come back with the best passages excised and the rest padded with bland gibberish. The problem is not a lack of individual talent. It's that they form a committee, discuss the most daring paragraphs, and finally settle on a compromise that is a pale reflection of the original. The first victims of their censorship are the author's fresh ideas. Bureaucrats are as averse to innovation as the devil is to holy water. It deprives them of the security of routine, the protection of structure, and the comfort of unanimity.

Regarding Ottawa's policy towards France, I knew that the bureaucrats in External Affairs would do everything possible to prevent the prime minister from breaking with orthodoxy: distrust and refusal to base our relations with France on substance.

The least one can say about these relations is that they were in a sorry state. Since General de Gaulle's visit in 1967 and his precipitous departure in the aftermath of his "Vive le Québec libre," relations between the two countries had followed a bumpy course, fraught with tension and discord.

Canadian foreign policy in this matter more than any other is torn between two conflicting attitudes: the official Anglo-Canadian attitude and the unofficial one favoured by diplomats of Québécois backgrounds. For many Anglo-Canadians, France is not a priority partner and, moreover, is not entirely trustworthy. A certain intelligentsia in the Lester B. Pearson Building will readily take up the immemorial rivalries that have opposed the British and their neighbours across the Channel. The collapse of the French army before the German invasion in 1940 helped keep stubborn prejudices alive. Similarly, de Gaulle's own prejudices about Anglo-Saxons did little to repair old attitudes. The closing of NATO bases in France and France's withdrawal from the North Atlantic military alliance seemed to confirm francophobic perceptions.

These factors inspired all of the major decisions Ottawa took concerning France. This was the case when de Gaulle's government wanted to buy Canadian uranium for its nuclear strike force. Ottawa, which had until then supplied the Americans and the British, no questions asked, decided to embargo all sales of uranium used for military purposes.

In June 1965, Lester Pearson announced that to ensure exclusively civilian uses of uranium, exports would be subject to special audits. The new policy was perfectly legitimate, but at the time it seemed to be designed against France. Many believe that de Gaulle never forgave us. Despite all efforts, France never succeeded in penetrating the wall of Canada's distrust in the ultrasensitive field of military cooperation. The Ministry of National Defence turned down French low-altitude radar defence systems in favour of the Swiss Oerlikon company. Aérospatiale's helicopter was rejected by our navy, which preferred a British-Italian model still on the drawing board. The word now is that the cost of the prototype is skyrocketing. As for Oerlikon's system, newspapers reported in 1990 that experts in national defence were not happy with it. Moreover, contrary to earlier indications, the Americans will be acquiring another system altogether. However, Canada escaped the worst: having to buy French equipment.

Federal diplomats of Québec origin, on the other hand, favour close and fruitful relations with France. This group has had many illustrious representatives, such as Pierre Dupuy, Jules Léger, Marcel Cadieux, Jean Désy, Jean Bruchési, Michel Gauvin, René Garneau, Jacques Gignac, and Ghislain and Christian Hardy. But since this group is inescapably in the minority, it is the anglophone hawks who have set the tone for Canadian diplomacy.

Circumstances also played an important part in the conflict. The dynamics were inflamed by the Lesage government's decision to develop an international personality for Québec and first advance it in France. It put the hawks in the right, and they soon organized the resistance.

The first victims were people like Jules Léger and Marcel Cadieux, whose efforts were at best thwarted, and at worst conscripted against France and Québec. Ottawa has always had the ability, in this area as well as others, to arouse some Québécois to foil a Québécois approach.

What could Léger do in Paris, where he was sent as ambassador in 1964, after de Gaulle came to power? He was given letters of credentials that offended the French head of state. After recalling

Canada's accelerated development since 1960, the new ambassador broke with the traditional innocuousness attached to this type of document. He suggested that "these developments" could take place "without France."

The general put aside the reply he had prepared and improvised one on the spot. He followed up with a communiqué containing the following passage:

> In reality, without France, it would be difficult in every respect for Canada to preserve a certain equilibrium . . . Whatever the case may be, France is present in Canada, not only through its own representatives, but because a large number of Canadians are of French blood, of French language, and of French mind. In short they are French, except in that which concerns the domain of sovereignty.

No embassy could start under such inauspicious and unfortunate circumstances. Rejected by the French government and put on the defensive because of French policy towards Québec, Léger found himself, despite his goodwill and personal prestige, reduced to impotence.

In Marcel Cadieux's case, the paradox bordered on personal tragedy. Circumstances compelled this man of talent, a francophile and guru at external affairs, to deploy federal troops in a fight to the death with Paris and Québec.

The government of Québec found in de Gaulle an ally whose zeal exceeded its own. In the end, Premier Daniel Johnson took fright and refused to follow de Gaulle to the limits of his policy exalting Québec. However, as the France-Québec cooperation intensified, it gave rise to endless confrontations with Ottawa. For example, a French-Québécois agreement on culture gave rise to a diplomatic incident. Cadieux had to threaten a break in diplomatic relations with France to force Québec to seek prior authorization from Ottawa.

Some incredible mishaps livened up the guerrilla warfare that raged over symbolic issues between federal diplomats and those Québec was trying to train on the job. The veterans of these backstage hostilities delighted in nocturnal capers, such as stealing or planting flags, changing seating arrangements at official banquets, and so on. It prompted Jean Chrétien, with his usual finesse, to indulge in *joual* ironies concerning conflicts about "*des flags sur le hood.*" And certain francophone diplomats, in Ottawa's pay, shone with anti-Québécois fervour, which earned them fine promotions.

There was one achievement in the midst of it all: the establishment of the Agence de coopération culturelle et technique (ACCT) in Niamey in 1971. Credit goes to the good sense and open-mindedness of people such as Gérard Pelletier, Julien Chouinard, and Claude Morin, who found a way of bringing Québec and Ottawa together within the only international francophone organization in existence. On this foundation, they built the Francophone Summit meetings.

But fifteen years and the arrival of a francophile Irishman in Ottawa were necessary before any meaningful change could take place. Until then, every initiative was poisoned with Ottawa's refusal to organize relations between Canada and France on a triangular basis with a place for Québec. Everybody was a loser: Québec was limited in its influence, Ottawa stood in an awkward position in its relations with a first-rate European partner, France wavered between its interests and its friends, and the world francophone community could not get going so long as Ottawa prevented Québec from joining.

There was no way to end the impasse except by normalizing relations between Canada, France, and Québec. Ottawa had to make a pragmatic move.

I had long been aware that Mulroney loved and admired the French. Their culture and their class impressed him, and he thought France one of the most beautiful countries in the world. As I began writing the speech he had commissioned, I had every reason to believe that he wanted to combine his national policy of reconciliation with a rapprochement as spectacular as possible with the motherland of French-speaking Canadians. It meant settling the triangular quarrel.

So I proposed a speech setting out the framework for an authentic renewal of Canadian diplomacy, at home and abroad, in relation to both Québec and France. The text advocated the explicit and formal recognition, by the prime minister of Canada, that direct and privileged relations between Québec and France were legitimate. There was a safety valve to reassure legal experts, but it was vague enough to preserve the legal consequences of the move: that everything be done within the scope of the Canadian Constitution.

The prime minister accepted the text and even added a commitment concerning economic exchanges between the two countries, a traditionally neglected area. The speech took the French delegation by surprise, most of all Laurent Fabius, whose remarks proposed only words of courtesy. Mulroney himself was ecstatic: nothing pleases him more than surprising people. Paris and Québec understood that something had changed in Ottawa. However, it is not sure that Ottawa understood as much. The veterans of the twenty-year war with Québec probably imagined they could restore common sense to a prime minister carried away with beginner's enthusiasm.

A short time later, while we chatted in his private library at 24 Sussex, Mulroney pointed to a bookshelf lined with Pléiade editions. I looked at the selection of authors and realized there was a link to the speech of November 7, which had ended by alluding to great French writers. Before leaving Ottawa, Fabius had asked ambassador Pierre Cabouat to present the prime minister with the Pléiade editions of the works of all the French authors quoted in the speech.

The speech was well received in Québec, whose government had never been treated so solicitously by federal authorities. It seemed that Ottawa was eager to please Québec. For a while I was de facto liaison between the two heads of government. I brought together their right-hand men, Bernard Roy and Louis Bernard, and introduced them to each other. I remember that Bernard gave his federal counterpart a list of problems requiring urgent attention.

These were the heady days of *le beau risque.*

Mulroney decided he should make the acquaintance of Lévesque, in Québec City. The two had never met. Before the meeting, I saw Lévesque, who quizzed me on his visitor. I drew a portrait and, half serious and half joking, added a word of caution: "Be careful, he will try to seduce you. He is particularly effective in a tête-à-tête." To which Lévesque replied: "It's not because he wants to seduce me that he will. But is he as charming as they say? From a distance, I wouldn't think so." As if he had second thoughts, he added, "Perhaps I haven't been exposed to his charm long enough."

Louis Bernard asked me, some time later, to present informally to Ottawa the list of conditions under which Québec would be willing to resume constitutional discussions. I agreed with Mulroney and Roy: I thought it wiser not to compromise myself in such a weighty issue.

Meanwhile, I continued working with my pen. I would get impromptu calls from Roy: "The prime minister needs a speech for the inauguration of grain elevators in Sept-Îles." Or, "This time, it's for the seventy-fifth anniversary of the Montreal Canadiens."

Mercifully, some topics were more interesting than others. In March 1985, the secretary-general of the United Nations, Javier Pérez de Cuéllar, the prime minister of Canada, and the premier of Québec had all accepted an invitation to speak in Québec City, in March 1985, at the closing banquet of an international conference on minority rights. The triple engagement was the work of Gil Rémillard, who had organized the conference. Again, I was asked to draft Mulroney's contribution. I attended the conference and was in the prime minister's suite when the Americans informed him that Tchernenko had died.

Mulroney left a short while later for the funeral in Moscow, carrying with him documents related to his meeting with Ronald Reagan the following week in Québec City.

No sooner was I back at my law practice in Chicoutimi than I learned from Roy that the prime minister had read the drafts for three or four speeches scheduled for the president's visit. He didn't like any of them and wanted me to write them. The speeches varied in importance, one of them being for the main banquet, another for the airport, and so on. During the week, I worked the day shift practising law for a fee, and the night shift volunteering my services writing about Canadian-American relations. The speeches arrived on time in Ottawa and were apparently satisfactory, since I heard them read in Québec City. During the gala dinner at the Château Frontenac, Mulroney introduced me to Nancy and Ronald Reagan. Never lavish with compliments, he said, with a conniving smile for my benefit, "Please meet Lucien Bouchard, the most eloquent French Canadian I know."

The atmosphere was perfect that evening. Relations between the Canadians and the Americans could best be described as playful camaraderie. Lévesque was present at the dinner and enjoyed himself teasing the Americans. Far from minding, they took pleasure in it and played the game with enthusiasm. I was seated at his table, along with justice secretary Edwin Meese and the president's chief of staff Donald Regan. I asked the latter if he liked his job as chief of staff after having been president of Merrill Lynch in New York. He told me jokingly that he much preferred his first job in Washington as secretary of the Treasury. "I signed the paper bills," he said, taking his wallet from his pocket and extracting a ten-dollar bill bearing his signature, which he circulated around the table. When it reached Lévesque, he pretended to put it in his pocket, drawing pretend indignation from Reagan.

At the next table, the president and the prime minister vied with each other with humour and pleasantries. Brian Mulroney was exuberant. His political honeymoon was not over, and he was enjoying the delights of power and public favour. These were happy days when everything came together: political necessity, loyalty, solidarity, and friendship.

After dinner, everyone gathered in the Grand Théâtre for a show that ended with "When Irish Eyes Are Smiling," rendered by the two descendants of Irish immigrants who had become, respectively, the president of the United States and the prime minister of Canada.

As my wife and I took the seats assigned to us, I realized that Mulroney had not given up his idea of sending me to Paris. All the guests were seated in the orchestra, but all the dignitaries were seated in groups of six in the boxes on each side of the theatre. The president and the prime minister faced each other in the first loges, the second ones being occupied by the two secretaries for External Affairs, and so on. I was surprised to be led to Joe Clark's box. Clark, who didn't know me from Adam, seemed nonplussed by the breach of protocol signalled by Mulroney. It was Mulroney's way of launching my diplomatic career. He was also sending a double signal: reminding me of my forthcoming mission and preparing Clark for my nomination, which had to go through him. In any event, the evening was congenial. As well as Clark and his wife, Maureen McTeer, I met the American ambassador to Ottawa, who had left politics for the diplomatic corps. All the while, I couldn't help thinking that we were seated more or less on the very spot that had been the room where I had lived for four years as a student before the building was torn down.

Since September 1984, I had refused to contemplate a move to Paris. I was reluctant to leave a law practice that had taken me twenty years to build for the sake of a position that was, after all, temporary. The clients I had established assured my professional freedom and my financial security. It would be a leap into the unknown, especially in Paris, where the diplomatic terrain is strewn with obstacles.

Starting in April, Bernard Roy broached the question a few times, saying the prime minister was eager to make changes in France and that he could not wait any longer. I looked at the offer more earnestly and had dinner with the prime minister. At the end of May or the beginning of June, I accepted.

I had arrived at the conclusion that I should take up the challenge, which was really to go beyond what I had achieved in the past. Without being aware of it, my itinerary had prepared me for this role, which called for experience in government and political circles and in negotiating, as well as a knowledge of France. I was eager to normalize and revive diplomatic relations, as the prime minister wanted. There was more to it than simply minding the store and parading at cocktail parties. What was required — and was now possible — fitted the prime minister's national political goals. I knew I could count on his support, an essential condition in such a sensitive post.

I had always been a frequent visitor to France, first through imagination, then through my reading, travel, and friendships. It was the first place I thought of when going on vacation. I knew its history, triumphs, and misfortunes; I have spent most of my spare time in the company of its writers and admired its creative spirit. My three brothers earned their doctorates in France, and my sister married a Frenchman.

Presumptuous or not, I felt ready for the challenge.

The cabinet was meeting in Baie-Comeau when it appointed me Canadian ambassador to France early in July 1985. The announcement came on the same day as Paul Tellier's nomination as clerk of the Privy Council, the official title for the highest position in Canada's public service. It was Mulroney's style to counterbalance the appointment of a sovereigntist with the ultimate promotion of a hard-line federalist who had distinguished himself in the no campaign of 1980 as head of the Information Centre on Canadian Unity.

I had only one more thing to do in Chicoutimi before leaving the country. The law firm I had created and my former associate's firm were now the region's two leading competitors. I informed my old firm that I would like to see a merger. The operation was brisk, and I had the satisfaction of reuniting what I had separated.

My appointment was greeted favourably in Québec. In English Canada, there was an outcry. As I had never been part of the federal scene, and for good reasons, the English-language media did not know me. Outside Québec, they wrote with remarkable unanimity that I was not only an evil separatist but also an incompetent, an object of shameless political favouritism, and an insult to France.

Resisting the temptation to let this pass, I made a firm resolution to make them swallow their inconsiderate and malicious words. I soon realized the best way to achieve this was by succeeding in my mission. My first move was to undergo an intensive program of meetings and preparatory reading. I perused, one after the other, all the files External Affairs sent my way.

I was also given the opportunity of visiting the most important federal ministries and institutions, where, at my request, they briefed me on their activities in France and Europe. I was thus able to meet with most members of the cabinet and many of the top civil servants in government. Afterwards, I toured Canada, from the Maritimes to British Columbia, meeting provincial premiers and businesspeople. I was received with courtesy everywhere.

I will never forget the hospitality of Premier Richard Hatfield, who, in his shirtsleeves, personally opened the door of his modest Fredericton bungalow. After pouring coffee, he spoke of Europe,

France, the Acadians, of Québec and the Canadian problem. He admired Mulroney and wished him success in his goal of reconciliation. He promised me his full support for francophone summits attended by Québec and New Brunswick.

My journey ended in Québec, which I had saved for dessert, since I knew everyone and had free access everywhere. I was full of confidence when I arrived at the Ministry of International Affairs at the end of August. But I was in for a rude shock. They greeted me with haughtiness and a sort of heavyhearted reprobation. They wanted me to liaise with the lower-level Department of French Affairs, whose director was another former classmate from Laval. But I insisted on meeting the deputy minister, my friend Yves Martin, who magnanimously invited me to lunch. But meeting with the minister, Bernard Landry, was out of the question, never mind the premier. In short, they left me out in the cold.

The Paris papers had just printed a statement from Québec's delegate-general, Louise Beaudoin, wondering about my role in France. Obviously, I would not be allowed easily to cross the trenches where the diplomatic war between Québec and Ottawa had bogged down. I took my lumps and went back to Ottawa.

I had barely arrived when I received a phone call from Louis Bernard. He had just found out about the poor reception inflicted on me in Québec and he wanted to assure me that he and Lévesque had nothing to do with it. The premier wanted to meet with me and was inviting me to his forest retreat at Lac-à-l'Épaule.

Located some seventy-five kilometres north of Québec City, this lake figures prominently in the political annals of Québec and is one of the jewels of the Parc des Laurentides. The surrounding mountains form a natural amphitheatre, opening to the south on a clearing with a row of log cabins. On a radiant summer afternoon, I parked my car near the main building. Lévesque was swimming in the lake. Seeing me, he came to shore and invited me into his cabin.

The premier was in a good mood, relaxed and particularly friendly. The conversation was animated, to the point where it was dinnertime without my realizing it. He told me some anecdotes about the Lesage cabinet meeting, in 1962, when it was decided to nationalize

Québec's hydroelectric resources. I was wide-eyed, marvelling at my luck in hearing Lévesque himself describing scenes from that memorable meeting, which had taken place right there: "Jean Lesage was sitting here. Bona Arsenault, furious, was walking up and down the beach, over there. Lesage sent somebody to bring Bona back." And so on.

He teased me about the negative reactions of English Canada to my appointment and gave me full support for the success of my mission. After dinner, he took me for a long walk into the sunset and the mosquitoes. Suddenly, he stopped and said, "Your mission is *la francophonie* (the unification of all French-speaking countries and nations under one umbrella organization). Others have failed in setting up the first francophone summit. Québec, Ottawa, and Paris must have another try at an agreement. You will be in a good position to facilitate matters. As far as I am concerned, I will do everything I can."

Late in the night, I drove back to Québec City. I felt confident, having received the ultimate blessing that would allow me to export *le beau risque* to France.

9

A Mission
of Friendship

There is something enchanting about nighttime Atlantic crossings, ending with the sky illuminated by a premature dawn, followed by the wonder of Paris. But on the morning of September 5, 1985, as the Air Canada Boeing 747 approached the coast of France, many thoughts intruded on the magic of the moment. I thought about the first Bouchard, "little Claude," a craftsman who, 335 years earlier, had travelled in the opposite direction. I thought, too, of my father, who died without ever seeing the old country and who left Québec only twice, once to see the horse races at Saratoga and another time to see Maurice Richard in a Stanley Cup game at the Boston Garden.

My own hockey match would be in Paris. I knew that my father, wherever he might be, if only in the memory of those who loved him, would be watching my moves closely and expecting me to come out the winner.

In any case, the official ceremony greeting me at Roissy was better organized than the one in 1650 honouring my ancestor when he landed in Québec City, carrying his stonecutter's tools. As the plane doors opened, a French protocol representative, along with some of my embassy staff, was already waiting for me, to lead me to the VIP reception room. From there, a cavalcade of limousines took us to my official residence on rue du Faubourg-Saint-Honoré.

A few days later, again in a cavalcade, flags flapping in the wind and motorcycles backfiring, I entered the ceremonial courtyard of the Élysée Palace to present my credentials to President François Mitterrand.

Everyone in Ottawa, Québec City, and at the embassy had helped me grasp the importance of the moment. It is not every day you meet the president of the French republic. For most ambassadors, the first interview is also the last one. It is usually dispatched briskly by a hard-pressed host eager to get through the usual banalities: "Our countries are friends, I have great esteem for your prime minister, welcome to France."

This tête-à-tête is a unique opportunity to send the right message and establish personal contact with a president who is not given to intimate meetings and informal discussions with ambassadors.

I was told that the journalists and cameramen standing guard at the palace gate would derive malicious pleasure from timing my interview. This information would allow them to measure the president's interest in my remarks.

To tell the truth, if my first steps were to be judged in such a superficial way, I was certainly out of luck. The Élysée, which had likely suffered some delay in setting these audiences, had scheduled three others, all before mine. To make matters worse, I was preceded by the new American ambassador, Joe Rogers, a businessman from Nashville, Tennessee, and President Reagan's personal envoy. And all this was taking place as President Mitterrand had his hands full with the *Rainbow Warrior* scandal (the French secret service had sunk the Greenpeace ship in New Zealand, causing the death of a photographer). Political observers even expected him to ask for the resignation of his defence minister, Charles Hernu.

As I walked through the mob of press people, I heard someone shouting at me, "Ambassador Rogers has just come out. The president kept him twenty-five minutes. You'll have a hard time beating that!" The first two visitors hadn't lasted more than five or ten minutes. Cursing my luck, I followed the ushers through the Élysée's deserted halls to the room where the president was expecting me.

He was standing, looking grave. He was without a doubt imposing, his face very pale, as if already carved in marble, animated only by a pair of eyes in a perpetual state of alert. A handshake, the transfer of beribboned credentials, and an official photograph, and I was seated in front of my host.

He opened the discussion by saying, as if it were the most obvious thing in the world, that relations between France and Canada were governed by friendship. Also, it seemed to him that these relations should not have to suffer from the disagreement over fishing rights off the coast of Newfoundland and Saint-Pierre-et-Miquelon. Then, making a discreet allusion to the Québec question, the president expressed his wish to avoid tension and maintain serene relations with Canada.

I reminded him that the Canadian government advocated arbitration of the fisheries dispute. I relayed the prime minister's invitation to come to Canada on an official visit, the first one since de Gaulle's abbreviated trip in 1967.

There followed an exchange about the need to broaden the scope of economic relations between our two countries. The president, without committing himself to an official visit, did not reject the idea. But he returned with insistence to the idea of convening a francophone summit. Stripped of official makeup, the president's message was: "First make sure that I can convene the summit, which neither de Gaulle, nor Pompidou, nor Giscard d'Estaing were able to do. Then we will see about the rest."

Then, changing tone, Mitterrand wanted to know more about me. I recounted the usual facts, mentioning my profession and stressing my Québécois origins. However, he wanted to know more and said with courteous insistence, "Yes, I know all that. But who are you?" None of my summer sessions had prepared me for this question. I went ahead, without adorning facts, and told him about my social and intellectual origins. I stopped from time to time, but he kept asking for more. I had to describe my family background, my education in a classical college (he asked which one it was), my political background, and the friendship I had developed in university with a student of Irish origin, who was also from a family of modest means and who had become prime minister of Canada. I also had to tell him what part of France my forefathers came from. So we talked about Perche and Charente, the regions my Bouchard and Simard ancestors left behind to settle in Canada.

The president talked about the geographical origins of his family. He said a few words about Saintonge, where his mother had been born, and Berry, from which his paternal ancestors had not budged for centuries. After a pause, he said, "In truth, we never come from anywhere except the land of our childhood."

The interview was drawing to an end. Someone entered to tell the president that the minister of defence was waiting. I had obviously exceeded my time. I chose the moment to open one last door: the president's literary activities. I told him I had read most of his books, adding that I was surprised he could find the time to write in spite of the demands of political life.

"For a long time, parliamentary life left me with a great deal of spare time," he replied with a discreet allusion to intervals spent in the political wilderness. "In any case, the pleasure of writing is essential to me." He was writing a long preface for a forthcoming collection of his speeches on foreign affairs.

I had brought along a copy of his book *Ma part de vérité* (My Share of the Truth). I asked if he would autograph it. He gathered his thoughts and wrote on the flyleaf: "For Mr. Ambassador Lucien Bouchard, as a cordial testimony, with my thoughts and my wishes for the success of his mission of friendship with France. September 20, 1985. François Mitterrand."

When I left the small salon, Defence Minister Hernu, a close friend of the president, was pacing the corridor. I learned from the newspapers the next day that he had come to submit his resignation.

Coming out into the courtyard, I saw the satisfied expressions of the embassy personnel waiting with the journalists. "The president kept you for half an hour, which is five minutes more than your American colleague. It is a very good sign," they told me. Personally, I was more impressed with the president himself and his message than with the length of the audience. In spite of how people criticized his haughtiness and lack of interest for anything not concerning his place in history, I found him likeable and even warm, in agreement with the goals of my mission, and ready to make things easier for me.

My heart was happy as I returned to the residence, where many members of the Canadian and Québécois community were waiting for me. Standing in the great wood-panelled reception room, where I could see the garden through the French doors, I proposed my first toast. Everything went well until the conclusion. I intended to end with the traditional words "I raise my glass to the strengthening of the ties between France and Canada," but I heard myself saying Québec instead of Canada.

The malaise that gripped the gathering forced me to improvise, in the same breath, a continuation of my speech. I went on about the presence of Québec in Paris and my determination to work hand in hand with all Québécois and all Canadians.

Nevertheless, I had to admit that this gaffe was not exactly reassuring for the federal diplomats watching me take charge of the embassy. After all, I didn't feel reassured myself.

Diplomacy is basically a question of networking. During the course of their postings, either at the Ministry of Foreign Affairs or abroad, career diplomats never stop establishing ties, first with their Canadian colleagues and then with numerous acquaintances throughout the world, particularly in the areas of politics, business, the media, and the bureaucracy. Thus when the time comes for an ambassadorial appointment, the career diplomat is never disoriented. Landing in an important embassy, such as Paris, he knows he will meet friends and acquaintances with whom he has already worked. There are no surprises either for the embassy staff, who already know the qualities, shortcomings, and working habits of their new mission chief.

My case was the exact opposite. I did not know a single one of the 250 diplomatic personnel and employees at the embassy. To them I might as well have come straight from Mars. Worse still, the editorial comments in the press regarding my appointment would only have filled them with apprehension.

For my part, I had been able, during the summer spent going through my future colleagues' files, to reassure myself of the quality of the team working with me. Two had already been ambassadors: Fred Bild had represented Canada in Thailand and Gilles Duguay in Cameroon and Morocco. The majority of the others were of the same calibre: experienced and well-travelled diplomats, economists, lawyers, military attachés; and specialists in disarmament, international finance, trade relations, immigration, and tourism.

I knew their support was vital to me. My first task was to overcome their reticence and gain their confidence. I lost no time in setting about doing this. First I made the rounds of the offices to meet them all. I readily confessed that I had a lot to learn and needed their help. In return, I promised to spare no effort working as part of the team. My professional activities on behalf of the Québec government had taught me that public servants detest inactivity most of all. When they are given interesting assignments, they jump into action. I used this recipe, but felt compelled first to pay my own dues by starting my days early and ending them late.

After studying embassy files, I held intensive planning sessions with my staff. I held nothing back about my political development, about my acceptance of *le beau risque,* and the reasons behind my presence in Paris.

They immediately saw the opportunity they had been given to participate in the redefining of the strained and quivering policies between France, Québec, and Canada. I assured them no good idea would ever get lost in bureaucratic paper shuffling. The prime minister's keen interest, as well as my personal relations with him, would help us minimize the distance between proposal and decision.

Before doing anything else, however, we had to map out clear objectives and find ways to meet them. We did not need a royal commission to define these objectives, nor did we have to reinvent the wheel. Many political observers and agents had long come to the conclusion that Canada should normalize its relations with France. Defining the means did not require transcendental meditation. The key to success lay in ending the three-way quarrel. Ottawa had been operating on the assumption that it could suppress the triangle by blocking direct contact between Paris and Québec.

Indeed, any Québec initiatives abroad always caused a great deal of nervousness in Ottawa. Gestures asserting Québec's international presence by Jean Lesage, Daniel Johnson, Jean-Jacques Bertrand, or Robert Bourassa had raised the hackles of federal mandarins and politicians. This was especially so when the moves were founded on the constitutional doctrine propounded by Paul Gérin-Lajoie, a convinced federalist who suggested Québec's constitutional jurisdiction should extend internationally. Federal reaction was all the stronger because Québec usually directed its advances to France and French-speaking countries. Witness the extreme agitation of the minister of external affairs over the Johnson government's decision to accept an invitation in 1968 to an international conference of francophone education ministers in Libreville. Not only did Ottawa suspend sending an ambassador to Gabon, it also published two successive white papers to discredit the Gérin-Lajoie doctrine.

There must have been a good dose of legal insecurity behind such a belligerent attitude. The British North America Act does not grant the federal government the express power of international representation, England having originally reserved that right for itself. Even today, to disallow Québec's international claims, federal diplomacy relies on a ruling of the Supreme Court of Canada (the one in 1984 dismissing Newfoundland's case relative to the continental shelf). The need for better constitutional support must have been a pressing one, since federal proposals tabled in the House of Commons on September 24, 1991, called for a constitutional amendment that would cast in stone the federal government's exclusive right to represent the country internationally.

However, from the moment I arrived in Paris, the bureaucracy had to take into account the prime minister's speech during Fabius's visit. So the traditionalists in External Affairs had to recognize the principle of direct relations between Paris and Québec.

My colleagues and I, therefore, had the highest approval to effect a policy of cooperation and reconciliation. But it was not a simple matter of being on neighbourly terms, or of routine social gestures and gracious compliments. Our project required substance, something that would meet national imperatives and represent an extension of internal political realities. The project could only be the establishment of a francophone summit. So the summit topped the embassy agenda.

We then drew up a list of contacts to be established in political, economic, diplomatic, and cultural circles. We also decided to design a specific plan of action, with its own budget, to promote investments and stimulate trade between Canada and France. I later added a tourism campaign designed to double in four years the number of French visitors to Canada. One of my personal objectives was to resolve the dispute on marine territory and fishing limits off Saint-Pierre-et-Miquelon, as well as a new mandate for the Canadian Cultural Centre in Paris.

In addition, it would be difficult to speak of a revival of Franco-Canadian relations without a set of official visits: first, Prime Minister Mulroney's to Paris; next, the French president's to Canada, the first since de Gaulle's tumultuous trip in 1967; and finally, a state visit by the Governor General to France, which could create a precedent in the diplomatic history of the two countries.

I resolved, if need be, to cut through red tape and short-circuit lines of communication. Since my nomination was deemed political, I would be political in the way I did things and the strings I pulled. After all, the decisions required to implement my program were fundamentally political and depended on elected representatives.

In this respect, my situation enabled me to enjoy a measure of freedom unavailable to career diplomats, who must follow the tortuous path of bureaucracy for even the most trivial instructions. Their superiors would never forgive them for going over their heads directly to the responsible minister, or, worse, to the prime minister himself.

To my knowledge, the only one who could get away with it was the former Canadian ambassador to Washington, Derek Burney. To be sure, his was a special case. Even though he was a career civil servant, Burney had agreed to work in the prime minister's office as chief of staff during the critical negotiations of the Free Trade Agreement. He played an important role in the government's recovery from the scandals that had rocked it so badly. He thus forged strong bonds of trust with the prime minister, which earned him his appointment in Washington and direct access to 24 Sussex.

In my case, the prime minister had let people know that dealing with me was pretty close to dealing with him. The French understood this right away; they soon realized that because of my access to decision-makers in Ottawa, responses and solutions were often available within twenty-four hours. The well-guarded gates of the Élysée and Matignon were swung wide open for me.

There is keen competition in Paris among the lobbyists who haunt the antechambers of power, starting with the 140 or so ambassadors and numerous envoys. A reputation for efficiency and promptness helps a lot. I must say that after the first few weeks' initiation, I was never refused an appointment, even at a day's notice.

That having been said, I had to be mindful not to antagonize the heads of External Affairs in Ottawa. Countless dispatches reported on my activities. I inundated them with reports of interviews and work sessions, and I saw to the prompt transmission of administrative reports, planning documents, and follow-ups on decisions. When I thought that some important issues needed political answers, I advised the ministry. After having had a taste of the efficiency of this approach, staff members even asked me to intervene with a minister, or even the prime minister, to speed up some decisions.

On the whole, I was comfortable with ministry personnel. The same went for the minister himself. The situation was not easy for Joe Clark because, technically, I should have reported to no one but the ministry or him. I did nothing to embarrass him or undermine his authority, but it was obvious I was the prime minister's man in Paris, not his. He had the intelligence to see this and the good taste to accept it. We discussed the problem, he and I, before my departure, and he accepted a tripartite relationship that might have annoyed a less easygoing person.

But a divergence opened between us regarding my role in bringing about the francophone summits. Clark and a few deputy ministers wanted to exclude me from the preliminary negotiations with France and other francophone countries. I was told I already had my hands full with my duties as ambassador. Trudeau's failure in 1978 and 1983 to call the first francophone summit had left its mark on External Affairs. Claiming to act out of a spirit of caution, the key players in the Lester B. Pearson building did not want to expose me to any humiliation that might compromise my embassy's success. Also, they planned to give responsibility for the summit to a sort of ambassador to *la francophonie* operating from Ottawa.

Beyond their concern about the success of my mission in France, I could also see another, less altruistic, motive. External Affairs clearly wanted to control the operation. But I believed that its success relied directly on the prime minister. He alone knew the importance of Québec's institutional participation in regular francophone summits for the national reconciliation outlined in the Sept-Îles speech. It consisted of nothing less, for Canada, than restoring a balance by supporting its French component internationally, just as it had supported its anglophone component in the Commonwealth. In a sense, it was the foreign affairs counterpart of the future Meech Lake accord. Only the prime minister could untie the legal knots that had bound the project until now.

Maybe I was rash, but I thought myself the best-placed person for the project. I had one foot in External Affairs, the other in the prime minister's office, and I was Canada's official spokesman in Paris. I also had contacts in the Québec government, with which Ottawa first had to come to an understanding.

I was not going to be stopped by External Affairs' concern about my being identified with failure. If the project aborted, with or without my participation, there wasn't much I could do in France.

Having got wind of a letter Clark was getting ready to send to the prime minister concerning his decision to exclude me, I alerted Bernard Roy, then secretary of the government and Mulroney's chief of staff. I reiterated my views on the matter and insisted that he block the letter before it was sent. Clark's dispatch would have forced me to cause my minister to lose face, something that was at very least hazardous.

I do not know the details, but Clark was persuaded not to send the letter, and I became responsible for representing the prime minister in the discussions leading to the first summit on *la francophonie.*

They told me I would be the prime minister's sherpa, to use the jargon of the trade. Drawn from the vocabulary used for preparing the G7, the annual economic summit of the seven leading industrial countries, the word brought back memories of my adolescence. Very young, I was fascinated by the idea of mountain climbing. At ten, dazzled by Frison-Roche's *Premier de cordée*, I was gripped by mountain fever. Having climbed the hill we called Cran des soeurs (a hundred feet at most) after school one day, I attacked Mount Jacob, which rises above the town of Jonquière but isn't very high either. I rolled off a rock face and knocked myself out on a rock at the bottom. Still dizzy, I took the road home and realized that my mountain-climbing career had also taken a tumble. Nevertheless, the great mountaineers, from Mallory to Messner, Buhl and Demaison (whom I have met), still fascinate me.

Sherpas are the baggage carriers who carry on their shoulders the tons of equipment needed to set up the camp from which the final assault towards the summit begins. I imagined these valorous foils, excluded from the final photograph in which only the official hero appears, holding up a flag on the crest of a snowy peak. The only one of these obscure people whose name has gone down in history is Tenzig, the Tibetan mountaineer photographed in 1951 with Hillary at the top of Mount Everest. In our moments of juvenile delirium, my brothers and I even wondered if he had not perhaps given Hillary a bit of a boost. And I wondered what my brothers would think of my nomination as sherpa.

To start with, the only baggage I had to carry was my own. Until November, I made frequent trips to participate in the negotiations between Ottawa and Québec in order to gain their agreement to take part in a francophone summit.

Because everything depended on that. I had so advised the French ambassador, Jacques Laprette, when he came to see me ten days after I presented my credentials to the president. Clearly, my overtures for a summit had not fallen on deaf ears. Already, in July, Mitterrand had asked this veteran emeritus of the Quai d'Orsay, a specialist in multilateral diplomacy, to explore the possibility of a summit meeting. I reminded Laprette of the difficulties that would have to be resolved back home to enable Québec to attend. I insisted on the need for Ottawa and Québec to make accommodations allowing the premier of Québec to be at the side of the federal prime minister at a conference of heads of state and sovereign governments. In all probability, the conditions agreed upon by both levels of government for their respective participation in a summit meeting would affect its contents, framework, and deliberations. Apart from giving the impression of forcing our hand, France's formal preliminary talks risked compromising our participation and bringing us the sting of yet another setback. The pill would be even harder to swallow because we had been the ones to revive the whole project. I therefore asked my French counterpart to refrain from any agreement with third parties as long as there was no agreement between Québec and Ottawa to guarantee our presence.

The French ambassador's task was not easy. The president had asked him to act quickly. He hoped to convene the heads of state for the following February, only five months away. Otherwise, his heavy agenda would delay the meeting and perhaps postpone it indefinitely, because legislative elections were to take place in March and the outlook for the government was rather poor. As they say in Cape Kennedy, the launching window was narrow.

I assured the ambassador that we would double our efforts to produce an agreement between Québec and Canada. It so happened he was a man of judgement and experience. He accepted my explanations and agreed to stand by.

The negotiations with Québec were begun on August 30.

It is no exaggeration to say that governments operate at two different speeds: slow for matters that are easy or inconsequential; fast for difficult and important questions. The first is the speed of bureaucratic routine. The second usually propels initiatives and their execution to the political level.

This is exactly what happened with the Québec-Ottawa agreement, which was debated and signed in less than three months. True, circumstances were favourable. Still fresh in my memory were Lévesque's remarks at Lac-à-l'Épaule and Mulroney's firm intentions. For all practical purposes, both governments took steps to ensure success. Both sides gave their negotiators the same orders: "Come to an agreement." To ensure compliance, the two heads of government appointed spokesmen able to work directly with them: for the Lévesque government, they were Louis Bernard, secretary of the executive council, and Louis Martin, deputy minister of intergovernment affairs; Bernard Roy and I acted for the Mulroney government. Jean K. Samson assisted the Québec delegation, while Jacques Dupuis and Ernest Hébert, top-level civil servants at External Affairs, advised the federal team.

We began by making a list of precedents. The treaty that had created the ACCT in 1971 already recognized Québec's right to participate in international deliberations on cooperation and culture. Québec acted as a participating government with the designation Canada-Québec. Taking his cue from this precedent, Régis Debray, President Mitterrand's adviser for francophone affairs during the aborted attempt of 1983, suggested another step forward. His idea, which was accepted, was to divide topics for discussion into two sections, one for political and economic matters, and the other for cooperation and culture.

The heart of the problem was the weighting of the role the premier of Québec could play in the discussions of one or the other section. Constitutional limitations resulting from Québec's status as a province within the Canadian federation did not allow it to intervene indiscriminately on all issues under discussion. For example, it could not exercise the same latitude on the Palestinian problem as on bursaries for francophone students.

The parties agreed that Québec would be a fully participating member in all discussions relating to the second section. It would have observer status in matters of the first section. However, Québec obtained a commitment from the federal government that two-thirds of summit deliberations would bear on topics in which Québec could participate actively.

Lévesque wanted to leave approval of the agreement to his successor, Pierre-Marc Johnson. The new premier invited Louise Beaudoin, Québec's delegate-general in Paris since 1982, to join his cabinet. He gave her the portfolio of minister of intergovernment affairs. For the initiated, it was a clear sign that the agreement would not be approved without some changes.

Beaudoin, whom I had met after my arrival in Paris, did not hide her reservations concerning the agreement. She wanted broader powers for Québec in economic matters. Even before her departure from Paris, we had discussed the possibility of adding such a clause. It was a matter of determining, in conjunction with the prime minister, that the premier could speak on economic issues concerning Québec.

A few days after Beaudoin took over Intergovernment Affairs, representatives of the two governments met in Montreal for further negotiations. I was not surprised to see a request for improving the role of the premier of Québec in the discussion on economic issues. I had already informed Bernard Roy of my discussions with Beaudoin. The federal team was thus able to table a text almost identical to the one we had envisaged earlier in Paris. After minor changes, Mulroney and Johnson signed the agreement, on November 7, 1985. Within the next few days, the premier of New Brunswick, Richard Hatfield, signed a similar agreement. Here, too, we used the ACCT as our model. New Brunswick, which recognizes French as an official language, became a participating government along with Québec.

Back in Paris, I joined Claude Roquet, the person responsible for francophone affairs at the Québec delegation, to inform Ambassador Laprette of the success of our negotiations. He could now make official his round of contacts with the other governments. After approaching a first group (Tunisia, Senegal, and Québec), he broadened his circle of consultations to ten countries and received the green light everywhere. Then a first international committee for the preparation of the summit was set up, in which both Québec and Canada took part. The committee drafted the agenda and planned the summit in accordance with the requirements of the Canada-Québec accord of November 7. The committee ordered and published the initial working documents for the first summit meeting of a *francophonie*, eager for action.

The anticipated success (simply holding the meeting was a historical precedent in itself) and the active role we played in it mollified many. I took advantage of the summit to launch a whirlwind tour of meetings not only with ministers and top civil servants but also with personalities in French public life. I talked with many reserve politicians of the republic, including Jacques Chirac, Michel Rocard, and Raymond Barre, as well as numerous businesspeople.

Each time, I described the Canadian political situation, explained the impact of a francophile prime minister, and established the relationship between his desire for a national reconciliation with the referendum defeat of 1980 and the unilateral constitutional repatriation of 1981–82. I reminded them that my mission in France, essentially aimed at relaxing tensions and promoting the economic character of our three-way relationship, was an integral part of Mulroney's internal political objectives.

I always had my political counsellor, Jean-Pierre Juneau, accompany me to take extensive notes, allowing us to file full reports to Ottawa within twenty-four hours. We prepared each conversation with great care: we opened a file on each person's career, his political opinions, his attitudes towards Canada and Québec. I forced myself to follow the meeting plan we had made, which allowed me to meet the two basic requirements I had set for myself: conciseness and frankness.

The first, I immediately noticed, was the rule in French government services. One day, an expert from the Quai d'Orsay presented a fifteen-page report to a committee on which I sat, saying, "Excuse me, but I didn't have time to shorten it." The lesson could apply just as well to the spoken word as the written one. Never did I wait for my host to sneak glances at his watch before taking my leave; half an hour was the limit I had set for a typical interview. When I later became a cabinet minister, I could see for myself what harm a bore can do to his own cause by overstaying his welcome.

My second requirement, frankness, was not exactly a requirement chosen by every diplomat. It is not that diplomats lie, but they live in fear of overstepping their detailed instructions from bureaucrats jealous of their foreign assignment. How can people be forthright without freedom of language? In such circumstances, the diplomat is condemned to circumlocutions, to the word-for-word repetition of Ottawa's instructions, and to the ceremonial flourishes with which less-skilled diplomats caricature others.

Then you report back to the fossils lurking in their offices, cubicles from which you could see the Ottawa River — if there were enough room to put in a window. "Mission accomplished, stop, representations achieved their goal, stop." You tack on a bit of flag-waving about your firmness in defending Canadian interests. This is really meant to convey something like, "And please don't think that we are suffering from *localitis,*" a condition affecting diplomats who have stayed too long abroad and who tend to adopt the views of the host government. Localitis is a terrible affliction. The least suspicion of having caught it is grounds for immediate recall to Ottawa. Returning to Ottawa is the nightmare of all diplomats, except for those who have been posted to Nigeria or Albania.

As I explained, my status as political appointee meant I was free from these constraints. I had come to cherish the label that had stigmatized me at the beginning. It had become a talisman that I wore around my neck as a sort of scapular. Naturally, this did not excuse me from diplomatic courtesies and a certain elevation of language. But speaking frankly is just another way of being brief. It is also a tried and true way of making yourself understood and arousing interest in what you are saying.

I also met the leading mission heads in Paris: the ambassadors of the United States, Great Britain, West Germany, Japan, the Vatican (who thought I was the Spanish ambassador), Israel and many other countries, including the former Soviet Union. A letter or word of introduction often preceded me, from friends such as Ambassador Laprette or acquaintances such as de Montigny Marchand, then on standby for a nomination to the Privy Council. Invitations arrived from everywhere, and people readily accepted mine for luncheons and dinners at my residence.

But the most significant was President Mitterrand's invitation addressed to the prime minister of Canada for an official visit linked to the francophone summit.

There is nothing like a prime minister's visit to revive relations between two countries, consolidate sympathies, and stimulate the operations of an embassy. An imminent visit sends a quiver through apathetic ministries. Files get shuffled to the top of the pile, phones are heard and answered, and political clocks are set to the guest's arrival. Everyone seemed eager to meet this new prime minister, an English-speaking Québécois who, speaking and feeling like a francophone, was staking his political career on the reconciliation of two linguistic communities. Few French officials had actually met him, except for President Mitterrand and Prime Minister Fabius. The latter reportedly fell under the Mulroney charm during his trip to Ottawa the previous year. As for the president, he told me himself that he had been struck, during the Bonn economic summit, by Mulroney's goodwill and open-mindedness.

In more than one respect, the visit proved timely and gave the prime minister maximum visibility. The three-day summit conference would highlight the impetus Canada had given to a decision-oriented *francophonie*. I made sure that Mulroney would be giving an inaugural address at the solemn session at Versailles. He would also open the work of the first section on the international political situation and then, in a second address, report on economic relations between the industrialized countries and the Third World. I anticipated that other countries would support the choice of Québec City for the site of the second francophone summit, in September 1987. We would thus chair the organization committee for the conference. Finally, President Mitterrand officially invited the prime minister to remain in France the day following the conference. He would single him out among his forty colleagues and allow him to share, with his host, the credit for the success of the summit.

I marshalled the embassy staff to make the visit efficient and to give it maximum impact. Our goal was to collect the largest possible number of the conventions of protocol reserved for visiting heads of state in France. But we had a problem: the prime minister of Canada was not a head of state. Consequently, it was not permissible to mark his arrival and departure with the statutory twenty-one gun salute or to fly Canadian flags on the Champs-Élysées and the Esplanade des Invalides. The state dinner at the Élysée was also out. Only presidents and reigning monarchs can receive these centuries-old marks of respect.

But, eager to honour Mulroney, the president made use of all the subtleties of French protocol to give his visit a particular cachet. We were granted a tête-à-tête with the president, an official lunch at the Élysée, a state dinner with Prime Minister Fabius, and a dinner given by the president of the Senate, Alain Poher. We appreciated the efforts of our hosts, not without pointing out that in Canada the head of state, whether it be the Governor General or the Queen, does not have any real power. The prime minister, as long as he has the confidence of the House of Commons, wields quasi-monarchical powers.

Once more, our hosts dipped into their bag of goodies and informed us that Mulroney would be lodged at the Hôtel Marigny, the official residence of heads of state on official visits to France.

We reported our latest diplomatic gain to the staff responsible for the prime minister's travel arrangements. Right after the summit, he would have to leave his hotel, the Plaza-Athénée, for the Hôtel Marigny. But the assistant who received the message immediately phoned one of my colleagues to vent his anger. He heaped a string of coarse remarks on him and said peremptorily, "It's not the French who will be choosing our hotels. We'll stay at the Plaza-Athénée, and that's that. In any case, I've never even heard of the other hotel where they want us to stay." I had to call Fred Doucet, in the prime minister's office, to ask if he could explain to his hotheaded subordinate that he would not find the Marigny listed among the commercial hotels in the *Guide Michelin,* that it was once the residence of the de Marigny noble family but was now used by France to receive foreign heads of state on official visits.

In the midst of these preparations, Gilles Duguay, in charge of public affairs at the embassy, came to see me. This former ambassador to Cameroon and Morocco was full of ideas and put an extraordinary amount of energy into their realization. A father of seven, he had been a disciple of Father Georges-Henri Lévesque in Rwanda and had always been, discreetly, an admirer of Pierre Trudeau and Jeanne Sauvé. I liked him immediately, and I took great pleasure in seeing the sparks that his enthusiasm produced when he was in contact with the bureaucratic machine. It was a question of a difference in speed. Sometimes, I took pity on the machine, which had great trouble applying its usual brakes.

Duguay did not dare approach External Affairs with the product of his most recent brainstorm. He came to me directly. The idea was to attach Canada's name to a new prize to be awarded by the Académie Française. The prize would be announced in the wake of the summit meeting during the prime minister's visit. The problem was the $400,000 Canadian contribution to a fund that would pay the annual prizewinner $100,000. My public affairs minister had even discussed his idea with Maurice Druon of the venerable Académie. I soon found out that everything connected with this august body displays an obsession with duration. Its members are called the Immortals; its chief administrator, Druon himself, had the title of perpetual secretary; and the fund we had in mind would be a permanent one.

Duguay and I left in a whirlwind to meet with the author of *Les Grandes familles* and *Les Rois maudits*. The least one can say about Druon is that he is not banal; he has panache, verve, an insatiable appetite for life. He is an accomplished horseman and a familiar figure in the best circles, a former cabinet minister, a regular guest of the King of Morocco, and a friend of Paul Desmarais. The décor was in keeping with the grandiose scheme: we had lunch at *Drouant,* the restaurant where the jury of the Prix Goncourt comes together to revel and award their prize.

The combined enthusiasm of Druon and Duguay was contagious. By the time I returned to the embassy, everything had been signed, sealed, and delivered: the name of the award (le Grand Prix de la francophonie), when it would be awarded, the criteria (a scientific or literary work by a francophone author, not necessarily French). It was a brilliant idea. All it needed now was an administrator to give it concrete shape. I would be the administrator and would have to find the trifling $400,000 representing Canada's contribution to the fund.

I hardly dare imagine the shrieks among the bureaucrats if I had first passed the business by them. A call to the prime minister put the stamp of approval on the project. I immediately informed Druon. Though he had confidently expected a positive answer, he had not expected it so quickly. He said he was very much impressed with "the remarkable expeditiousness of the Canadian service." Not wanting to be outdone, the French government made a generous donation to the fund, which was also enriched by a joint contribution of $200,000 from Paul Desmarais and Bernard Lamarre, after they had been asked to put some money in the till. Meanwhile, I could not help sympathizing with the unfortunate ministry saddled with the $400,000 bill in Ottawa. Unless I am mistaken, it landed on the desk of Benoît Bouchard, then secretary of state.

However, the young *francophonie* would have another jewel in its crown. I was happy the new prize would take its first steps with the old lady of the Quai de Conti, the Académie, which had tied its fate to the French language. I even thought it might be a guarantee of permanence. The new prize would also demonstrate Canada's determination to promote the francophone project. Finally, it was, as you will see, an invaluable addition to the itinerary of the prime minister.

President and Madame Mitterrand wanted to greet the prime minister in the VIP lounge of Le Bourget airport. At the appointed time, the Boeing 707 parked at the end of the red carpet where I waited. According to protocol, I climbed aboard to greet the prime minister and his wife. They then made their official appearance outside the plane and shook hands with their hosts at the foot of the stairs. While a military band played *O Canada* and *La Marseillaise,* a guard of honour presented arms. It was the beginning of a busy week.

The summit itself went off without a hitch. Most of the important speeches had been written before, the script and the roles of each participant negotiated in minute detail by the sherpas.

The only untoward incident occurred when Premier Robert Bourassa said, as he emerged from a working session, that he had made a proposal for disposing of our surplus agricultural products to the Third World, which was in fact an economic issue. This was a typical Bourassa trick. The premier wanted the press to see him as an independent participant, particularly with regard to the Canadian prime minister. In fact, he had completely fabricated the incident. Inside the conference room, where the press had no access, he had a discussion with Mulroney in which he had agreed (informally, it is true) that he would respect the letter and the spirit of the agreement of November 7, 1985. He must still remember Mulroney's fit of anger over his ploy. The prime minister was walking on eggs because English Canada was not particularly thrilled to see the premier of Québec seated right in the middle of a whole assembly of heads of state. The risk was that Premier Bourassa's words might be interpreted as a provocation and a return to the war of the flags. Finally, everything was sorted out, so that it was possible to arrange with Bourassa the distribution of responsibilities for the organization of the next summit meeting. The forty participating countries had agreed to hold the next conference in Québec City, in the fall of 1987, with Prime Minister Mulroney as chairman.

The next day brought a complete change of play, of stage, and scenery. All lights shone on the leading actor, Brian Mulroney. For two days, Paris was his. Starting from the Hôtel Marigny (no star or fork in the *Guide Michelin,* but still worth a side trip), the limousine travelled alone to the Arc de Triomphe, up the Champs-Élysées, deserted at the cost of mammoth traffic jams in neighbouring streets.

A few minutes later, we were all standing at attention, stiff with cold, protocol, and emotion, while the prime minister placed a wreath on the Tomb of the Unknown Soldier.

I breathed a sigh of relief, thinking back to Premier Jean Lesage's embarrassment when he was ready to make the same symbolic gesture during his visit in 1961. Wanting to lay his offering, he turned towards the delegate-general only to realize, with horror, that the official had completely forgotten about the wreath. Noting the visitor's discomfiture, the French commander of the honour guard, wanting to excuse the negligence, said, "It will be a spiritual offering, Mr. Premier." The word *spiritual* must have triggered a religious reflex in Jean Lesage, who immediately pulled a rosary from his pocket and placed it on top of the tomb.

Everything went off according to the visit's official program, which had been timed to the minute. Someone standing next to me, a French World War I veteran, who must have been close to ninety years old, expressed surprise at the prime minister's youth. He did indeed look young, with an air of bearing cheerfully part of our future. He stood straight and tall in a dark suit, below the vaults with the names of Napoleonic victories, which echoed the last chords of our national anthems.

The next stop was the Élysée. We entered through the Porte de l'Horloge, on the garden side. Mitterrand, bareheaded and wearing a jacket, was waiting for us on the terrace steps at the end of the park. He greeted the prime minister with warmth. The three days of summit meetings seemed to have brought them closer together. We were shown into the president's office, where the spirit of de Gaulle still lingers. On the right, large windows let in light from the garden, still green in spite of the season and the unusual cold. Against the other wall stood a scale model of the future opera house of Place de la Bastille. The president showed it to us and told us that, after one last elimination round, he personally chose the sketches of Carlos Ott, a Toronto architect.

There were six of us in the room, three on one side and three on the other. However, no one interrupted the dialogue between the host and his guest, who seemed to be trying to outcharm each other.

Finally, the serious issues appeared on the table: the relations between the two countries, the shortage of commercial exchanges, the Saint-Pierre-et-Miquelon fisheries dispute, which everyone deplores but no one has the courage, or the rashness, to solve. The two leaders congratulated each other and reiterated the need for constant progress along the newly opened way. Obviously, the president was happy about Canada's contribution, giving the lie to malicious gossip about Canada taking up too big a place within *la francophonie*. Again, Mulroney explained that his commitment to *la francophonie* formed part of his policy of national reconciliation and constitutional reform.

Mitterrand replied that he would follow his visitor's efforts with much interest and sympathy. After mentioning his friendship towards Québec, the president added that he had always thought a federal system would be best for the survival of French culture and language on the North American continent. It was a profession of faith in federalism that seemed to give his visitor great satisfaction.

The conversation soon took a broader, more spontaneous turn. Mulroney had a gift for bringing out the president's verve and the tact to let him speak. He casually asked the president about his decision to invite the Communists to join his government. The president recalled that, on his first visit to Washington, American authorities expressed their concern about the fact that the Communists held four ministerial portfolios. President Reagan and his entourage did not take this sort of thing lightly. "Well, I told them that I was serving democracy and France," said Mitterrand, adding that this circumstantial alliance caused popular communist support to drop from twenty percent to ten percent.

The president lingered on the subject, which he understood perfectly, so well that, for ten minutes, he drew a broad and fascinating picture of the parallel evolution of socialism and communism in the democracies of Europe and Latin America. Before an interested and admiring prime minister, he became even more animated, talking about Gorbachev and the spirit of change he had liberated in the Soviet Union. He said they still wrote personal letters to each other, and he recalled an incident illustrating his independence of mind even before his accession to power. Mitterrand was in the Kremlin, sitting before his host, Brezhnev. It was evening and the meeting had an intimate character, with only a few colleagues present. The conversation concerned the Soviet economy. Brezhnev turned towards his minister of agriculture and asked, "How is our agricultural five-year plan doing?" The answer was swift: "Badly." "What do you mean badly? Why?" "Too many structural constraints." No doubt irritated by such brutal frankness, particularly in front of foreigners, the secretary-general continued to probe: "Well, since when?" The man's name was not yet well-known and he had a strange wine stain on his forehead. He replied with a straight face: "Since 1917."

The anecdote, which showed that Gorbachev had not waited till he was in power to exercise his freedom of thought, made everyone laugh — and reflect. But the spell was broken when someone reminded the president that he and the prime minister were running late for lunch.

The meal was served in the cabinet room. Some thirty guests sat at a long table. The president, with Mila Mulroney to his right, sat across from his wife, who was seated to the prime minister's left. The guest list included Paul and Jackie Desmarais, Bernard Lamarre,

Jacques Attali, and Jean-Louis Bianco. The discussion continued, but in a more relaxed manner. The president was a skilled conversationalist, mixing playfulness with gravity. And he had a lot to contribute. Before making history himself, he had often met it on his way. He enjoyed relating his meeting with de Gaulle in Algiers and the details of his return to occupied France in early 1944 to support the resistance. In Marrakech, a friend put him on board a British military aircraft leaving for London. During the flight, he discovered that the main passenger, treated respectfully by all, was General Montgomery, the future marshal, still resplendent from his victory over Rommel at El Alamein.

Someone at the table saluted the longevity of the president. I made some remark about the skilfulness that both allies and adversaries alike recognize in him. He protested vigorously: "In fact, this reputation originates with an error I committed as a young man." I asked what error. "I was imprudent enough to write a book about Machiavelli!" The most he seemed willing to concede was that in politics "you shouldn't be too clumsy."

In the course of an exchange about Ronald Reagan, the prime minister mentioned that the American president regularly made notes on his mandate at the White House for his memoirs. But Mitterrand replied that he did not do anything as systematic as that. At that point I interjected: "But who knows whether Mr. Attali, like Saint-Simon did Louis XIV, is not observing you, unbeknownst to you, to provide posterity with the picture it will retain of you?" The president frowned and turned towards Attali, and said, "He wouldn't dare." Attali has just published a first volume of recollections of the president's sayings and activities.

The first morning augured well for the rest of the visit. The program unfolded as planned and in a relaxed mood. This was particularly true of the state dinner at the Quai d'Orsay, hosted by Prime Minister Fabius, who brought the political part of the visit to a conclusion. Mulroney's visit to the Maison des étudiants canadiens was particularly friendly, as was his meeting with the artistic community at the Centre cultural canadien.

The visit had been organized in a way to ensure a balance of the various aspects of Franco-Canadian relations.

For example, Mulroney spoke during a luncheon meeting of the prestigious Paris Chamber of Commerce. Besides representing business interests, this institution also owns and manages airports, universities, and professional training schools. Before leading representatives of finance, industry, and commerce, the prime minister gave a speech on which I had worked with some of my colleagues. It was an opportunity for our head of government to set out, within realistic and imaginative parameters, the basic thrust of Canadian trade policy in Europe. I remember spending all of Thursday night putting in the last touches after last-minute consultations with Cy Taylor, then undersecretary of state.

I believe realism dictates anchoring our trade policy on our relationship with the United States. From the triple perspective of the economy, security, and geography, it is inescapable. Perhaps we should even include cultural considerations, since our way of life is so close to that of our neighbour. For example, Ontario's exports to the United States exceed those of Japan. This says a lot when you consider the anxiety resulting from the invasion of Japanese products into that country. It is even truer that only the Americans are able to defend a continent whose geography widely exceeds our means.

However, our legitimate interests require that without rejecting this reality and accepting it wholeheartedly, we superimpose a broader vision.

Mulroney's speech raised the idea of a commercial and political counterweight that only Europe, within the foreseeable future, is able to provide in relation to the United States and the Pacific Rim. External Affairs' fascination with Asia is not without justification. However, it would be a mistake to believe that there are markets to conquer there, over the middle or long term, as profitable as the markets in a Europe without borders — an industrialized consumer, a democratic society located almost next door and so much closer to us culturally. Trudeau had tried to persuade the Pearson Building mandarins, by means of foreign policy of diversification, to open up to Europe. At the time, it was called "the third way," the first two being the United States and the Pacific Rim. But the rebels in External Affairs were ultimately successful, and the whole initiative died a slow death.

Yet the question remains: How can you explain the wait-and-see attitude with which Ottawa's decision-makers viewed Europe's emergence in 1992? Did they perceive it as a threat to their American ally? Did they feel they could not manage all at once the American relationship, the extension of free trade to Mexico, Asian exoticism, and a European opening? Were they afraid of having to give too much importance to our relations with France, given the key role it plays on the European scene? The mystery deepens if you remember that the best days of Canadian diplomacy occurred when the country concerned itself with Europe.

During that luncheon meeting in the magnificent reception room of the chamber of commerce, I was far from despairing of the prospects of our European policy. On the contrary, since Mulroney's speech was well received. It showed how serious we were about intensifying trade and investment relations between France and Canada.

There was also another source of satisfaction that morning. The prime minister had gone to the Académie Française, where he signed the chartering documents of the Grand Prix de la francophonie. Druon had an extremely rare honour in store for him: participating in a working session of the Académie. For more than 350 years, the academicians have been working on a dictionary that peremptorily decrees the admissibility of words. In this instance, the session was working on the word *foresterie*. That day, the word entered into the French language, with the help of the prime minister of another country, where it would prove its usefulness.

That evening, the prime minister informed me that President Mitterrand, in an aside, had accepted in principle the state visit of the Governor General. The next morning, I watched the Boeing taking off, thinking I was now in a position to start working on the substance of the bilateral program.

10

Twenty Years Later

March 1986 was in sight, and so were the first signs of spring, the kind only Paris can display. The summit and the prime minister's visit had proved tremendously successful.

Such was not the case in my personal life. My marriage broke down completely, and my wife of twenty years returned home to Canada, for reasons and circumstances for which I felt myself responsible.

Certain media, mostly anglophone, were bound to find ways of casting a pall on the prime minister's diplomatic successes. Making use of the law on access to information — a parting gift from former prime minister Trudeau, who had never had to reveal the cost of his numerous trips — someone went through the hotel and restaurant bills for Prime Minister Mulroney's Paris visit. There was a great fuss about a $228 lunch for four at a restaurant close to the chancellery where we had meetings with the person responsible for *la francophonie* at the Quai d'Orsay. Others fingered a meal the prime minister had had with his wife and two bodyguards at La Tour d'Argent. The hotel bill at the Plaza-Athénée, for the prime minister and his entourage, made headlines. The Opposition raised the issue in the House of Commons. The prime minister's office became very agitated and the temperature in External Affairs ran close to boiling point. The hunt for scapegoats was on. This is a favourite sport in Ottawa. External Affairs sent a note blaming the embassy. I replied saying I assumed full responsibility for whatever faults may have occurred. As for the Plaza-Athénée, the French government had paid for the prime minister's suite and the five rooms occupied by his staff. Ottawa came back saying we hadn't informed them of this. We referred to a dispatch, prior to the visit and dating back several months, in which we had informed the ministry that the French government would be assuming part of the costs. Just as the uproar seemed to be dying down, one of my closest colleagues at the embassy, a career diplomat with children in school, was ordered to pack up and return to Ottawa immediately. It was a disciplinary recall, a sequel to the expense-account scandal attached to the visit. I called External Affairs and tracked the source of the dispatch to an assistant to the prime minister. I let him know that I would be on the same flight as the scapegoat. The order was retracted within hours.

In short, it was a free-for-all. I came out of it with a few more bruises and a little less naïvety. I was mainly concerned that staff morale might suffer. There was still too much to do to let discouragement take over.

We concentrated on developing an economic program and on the allocation of additional resources for its application. I managed to get supplementary funds for a large-scale operation designed to stimulate economic exchanges with France. We were also involved in discussions to equip the Canadian Navy with a fleet of French submarines with nuclear propulsion.

In this matter as in many others, we were walking on pins and needles. Especially needles when it came to the dispute over Saint-Pierre-et-Miquelon fishing limits. Its numerous instalments and ramifications are too long to be reported here, but suffice it to say the dispute was an emotional roller coaster. The problem trailed me like a ball and chain throughout my mandate in Paris. I had the impression that tensions revived every time an event signalled an improvement in our relations with France.

It was only after I joined the cabinet that the dispute started moving towards arbitration. I managed to get on the cabinet committee in charge of the issue. Uniting our forces, Joe Clark, Derek Burney, and I succeeded in convincing the government to sign an arbitration agreement with France.

Michel Rocard, who was then prime minister of France, knew about the problem, having thoroughly analysed it before taking office. One day, at his request, I met him in his office on boulevard Saint-Germain. A former minister of agriculture whose resignation had kept him from the public eye, he surprised me with his knowledge of the ins and outs of the dispute. I still remember the astonishment of my political organizers at my Alma election headquarters in May 1988 when he called me to get some final action on the file.

People may say whatever they wish about French politicians (they get no better press in their own country than ours do in Canada), but they take their profession seriously. They often know as much about specific issues as do our deputy ministers. They have one advantage over our own politicians, and that is their permanence. They are the professionals of politics, very often graduates of the École nationale d'administration. Politics for them is their career, their public service, and their lifestyle. Some enter politics as others do religion: they devote their lives to it. From one ministry or from one government to another, they have seen and learned everything. They are, therefore, far less dependent on their civil servants than our own ministers are. Ours are ministers today, but yesterday they were lawyers, psychiatrists, accountants, teachers, contractors, and journalists — and to these careers they often return.

I met with many politicians, feeling that I had to build bridges with all sides. The socialists succeeded the Gaullists, and I knew that, some day, others would dislodge them. Diplomats must cultivate their successors, simply because of the permanence of state interests.

I devoted even more attention to my relations with Québec's delegate-general.

Relations between the Canadian embassy and the Québec delegation gave rise to many unexpected turns. The delegation was barely in place when Canadian ambassador Pierre Dupuy told Charles Lussier, future delegate-general, "You are under my authority." Rather timid at first, delegates-general showed more self-confidence with the rise of Québécois nationalism. With Yves Michaud and Louise Beaudoin, Québec's diplomatic presence in Paris had more muscle. With easy access to the most powerful French officials, they practically occupied the whole stage regarding questions of interest to Québec.

For my part, I wanted to maintain the best possible relations with my Québec colleague on rue Pergolèse. I did not perceive the delegate-general as a rival, but as a necessary ally in our common objectives. Québec had everything to gain from the francophone summit, President Mitterrand's visit, and revitalized economic and tourist exchanges between Canada and France. On arriving in Paris, I contacted Madame Beaudoin and then her successor. Contrary to newspaper reports, Jean-Louis Roy and I never let any disagreement disturb our strictly cooperative relationship. I met with him regularly, usually at his apartment, to anticipate and eliminate points of friction, but mostly to articulate joint positions on problems arising from the preparation of summit meetings.

We grew aware of the power our united efforts gave us. I do not remember the embassy and the delegate-general ever losing a single battle with our francophone friends in France or any another country.

Some thought my work was a threat to Québec's place in Paris. The proof, for them, lay in the many visitors who once avoided the embassy and the Canadian residence like the plague. Many of them came for personal reasons, even out of friendship, as was the case with nationalist figures, artists, and writers from Québec. For the péquiste ex-ministers and ex-members of the National Assembly, the example came from high up. Twice, René Lévesque and Corinne Côté attended dinners I gave for them.

It was not an easy situation for a delegate-general who had views diametrically opposed to those of his two immediate predecessors. I also represented a federalist government, but my official views in Paris were in strong contrast to those expressed by Québec's delegate-general. I am thinking in particular of the Bourassa government's amendments, at the beginning of December 1986, to Bill 101, for which the delegate-general had to provide an explanation. French circles were concerned, since they had generally supported the legislation, or at least had always heard the Québec delegation praise its merits. Many people came to me with their misgivings. I reassured them with clippings from *Le Devoir* and *La Presse,* with quotes from Prime Minister Mulroney and Minister of Communications Marcel Masse and headlines such as "Mulroney supports Bill 101" and "The Mulroney government opposes regression of French in Québec."

Who should bear the blame after that if the French officials tended to turn to the ambassador and to tighten francophone cooperation with Ottawa?

In the spring of 1987, I met the person with whom I would be starting a new life. Early one morning, she boarded the plane carrying me to London and took the only seat that was free, the one next to me. We had barely started a conversation high above the English Channel when we arrived in London and went our separate ways, she to Los Angeles and I to Calgary. I only knew that her name was Audrey and that she lived in California. It was several months before we met again, but fate had already begun its work.

Then came May and the French president's official visit to Canada, a key step on the way to normalization.

De Gaulle's "Vive le Québec libre" had done more than galvanize nationalist fervour. It had also sensitized, through shock treatment, international opinion about Québec's aspirations. The cry was such a bold defiance of international propriety that its reverberations in political and diplomatic circles continued to be a source of paralysing malaise. Twenty years went by before Ottawa and Paris could contemplate another visit by a French president. Everyone knew that such a visit would remove the last barriers in the process that had started with the francophone summit and with the removal of Ottawa's interdict on direct contacts between Québec and France.

Fate handed the task to François Mitterrand, who had been de Gaulle's sternest critic for his words of provocation.

Meticulous negotiations preceded the trip. Everyone had particular requirements and preconceptions. Québec wanted to keep the president as long as possible. So did Ottawa, which was planning a heavy agenda: a state dinner and gala reception at Rideau Hall, a speech before the House of Commons, and private discussions with the prime minister. For my part, I wanted to stop the federal government from monopolizing all the time available for the Canadian portion of the presidential visit. It seemed to me important to take the president away from the national capital showpiece and let him discover the real English Canada.

In the end, everybody had a piece of the action, since the French government gave in to our entreaties, extending the visit to five days. It was the first time a French president had gone to Saskatchewan, visited a farm, let some wheat trickle through his fingers, and attended a state dinner given by Premier Grant Devine, in Regina. After a warm welcome in Toronto, he had a conversation in French with Ontario premier David Peterson, who congratulated the French justice system for going ahead with Klaus Barbie's trial in Lyon. Everything went just as smoothly in Montreal, Québec City, and Gaspé.

We toured Canada and Québec, chronometer in hand and eyes on the book of protocol. No one said anything unseemly, and orders were given to the entourage of the premiers (where ninety-nine percent of offensive leaks originate) to speak of the visit in positive terms.

As official reports in External Affairs probably said, the visit met all its objectives, one of which was to avoid making waves.

There was no desire to obliterate de Gaulle's historic words — who could do that? Our purpose was to turn the page, not tear it out. Life had to go on, the life of states and the promotion of their interests, too. Especially as the whole trip would be outlined against the backdrop of the final negotiations leading to the Meech Lake accord.

No one was more aware of the situation than Mitterrand. He decided to borrow the narrow corridor of nonindifference and nonintervention defined, in 1979, by then prime minister Raymond Barre. In tone as in substance, he kept a safe distance from the aspirations for sovereignty. In Ottawa, he did not even say the word *Québec* once. People noticed the omission. The president's active neutrality caused some disappointment. Many in Québec thought the president had not used the leeway at his disposal and had stuck too closely to the nonintervention side of his policy. They would have preferred him to concentrate on the nonindifference side.

The president detected in these reactions, and perhaps also in the reserved crowds along his way, a certain Québécois coolness towards him. He told me so, in so many words, a few months later, during an impromptu conversation on board the *John A. Macdonald,* the Canadian icebreaker on which forty heads of state and government participating in the francophone summit in Québec City sailed around Île d'Orléans: "The Québécois do not really like me. Certainly not the way they loved de Gaulle. They even prefer Chirac's oratorical flights. They are wrong to expect passionate pronouncements from me. I have no right to interfere in their affairs. In any case, the decision is theirs."

What he did not say, and what I thought, was that the unerring Québécois instinct had sensed his predilection for federal systems. There was definitely some merit in his maintaining a certain reserve. In Gaspé, he had to call on all the reasons of state for not giving in to his emotions. On one of those sunny mornings so common in the month of May, the president spoke to a hundred dignitaries and curious onlookers massed around the mound facing the bay, so wide it seemed like the beginning of the ocean. "I say the word *Québec* with love, respect, and hope."

Premier Bourassa was gracious enough to invite René Lévesque to the ceremony. He and I were below the rise where the president and the prime minister were standing. Holding his eternal cigarette, the Parti Québécois founder listened without a word to the French president's statement. The guests then moved to a school, where refreshments were served. People along the way politely applauded President Mitterrand and Premier Bourassa. But they noisily displayed their affection for Lévesque, surrounding him and shaking his hand. He seemed embarrassed by their effusiveness. Maybe he wondered why his fellow citizens, who seemed to love him so much, had refused to support his drive for sovereignty.

If Mitterrand had any questions, he hid them very well behind his customary impassiveness. Having observed him somewhat, I had no doubt he practised self-control the way others practise virtue. He knew from day one that power over others begins with the mastery of the self. If he ever let down his guard, it was in Moncton before five hundred Acadians crowded into an airport hangar to hear him.

The Acadian stopover, as we called it, was a stroke of luck. We were putting the finishing touches on the president's itinerary, at my residence. The closing ceremonies were to be held in Toronto, where the president would take his leave from the Governor General. The meeting was nearly over when a French official casually mentioned that the Concorde had to make a technical stop in St. John's, Newfoundland, before crossing the Atlantic. The plane did not have the range for a direct flight from Toronto to Paris. I seized on the opportunity to suggest a refuelling stop in Moncton rather than St. John's, which would allow the president to meet francophones in New Brunswick and surrounding areas. The matter was easily arranged.

I was aboard the Concorde during its approach to Moncton airport. Instead of landing immediately, the pilot chose to show off the supersonic aircraft, making a long pass over the crowd gathered near the control tower. The huge bird with the droopy beak landed and came to a stop near the onlookers.

While the ground crew refuelled the aircraft, the president entered the hangar where the crowd had gathered. More than 380 years after the foundation of Port-Royal, it was the first time a French head of state had stepped on Acadian land. I had never seen so many people with tears in their eyes. The four Acadian envoys (Gilbert Finn, Léon Richard, Adélard Savoie, and Euclide Daigle) who had been received by de Gaulle in 1968 and who had persuaded him to open the sluices of French cooperation for their compatriots were introduced to the visitor, who was unable to hide his deep emotions. Speaking after Premier Hatfield, the president saluted the audience in France's name, recalled their long struggle, and promised to return.

Mitterrand had certainly discovered within himself a profound empathy for his hosts. He had been carried away by a show in his honour at Rideau Hall with Édith Butler, a pure Acadian. A few months later, he invited her to dine at the Élysée, *en famille*. He also fulfilled his promise to return to Acadia. During the Québec summit, he made a round trip lasting a few hours.

All things considered, and in spite of a belligerent flea-hop to Saint-Pierre-et-Miquelon (always the fisheries dispute), the presidential visit had its anticipated success. Normalization was a fact. It was now possible to move forward.

The Québec summit was on the horizon. Forty francophone countries were putting the final touches to it. However, the bulk of the work was in Paris, where the committees and task forces were at work. Officials of the forty participating countries proceeded, at a conference in Bujumbura, Burundi, with the final revision of the papers and projects that would be submitted in Québec City for deliberation and decisions by heads of state and government.

I returned to Québec City. The whole month of August was spent on final preparations for a meeting that would make the city of Champlain, for three days, the political centre of the French-speaking world.

11

The Summit on Cap Diamant

The game was not over yet, although it was well under way. The international preparations committee had worked efficiently; most of the position papers were ready.

I also chaired the Canada-Québec committee that was in charge of handling the practical aspects of the conference. This committee did not inspire the same confidence as the other. The respective roles of the two governments had been the object of delicate negotiations leading, as usual, to Byzantine arrangements. In each sector (finance, administration, transport, communications, protocol, coordination), federal and Québécois officials and representatives worked side by side like Siamese twins. Some people doubted whether this hybrid organization could even perform.

Already, choosing the dates had caused problems. In 1987, Canada was also hosting a Commonwealth meeting in Vancouver. Their organizing committee was persuaded by Bernard Roy to delay the Vancouver meeting until after the francophone summit. It wasn't easy. Some External Affairs people thought, not unreasonably, that the Commonwealth affair would lose some of its impact. In the same vein, Ottawa was afraid that holding plenary sessions in Québec's National Assembly could marginalize the federal delegation.

All through the long month of August, the composition of the task forces gave rise to some muscling. A five-week test drive was certainly not too long to patch up this Siamese machine. The machine was also somewhat two-headed, because if I was chairman, Jean-Louis Roy, Québec's delegate-general in Paris, had to be vice-chairman. It would have been a serious mistake if I had tried to wield hierarchical authority. Though, by rights, I represented the "inviting power," I knew I was condemned to reach agreement on everything with my Québec counterpart.

While the tourists lounged in the sidewalk cafés of Québec City's Grande Allée or strolled on the Plains of Abraham, discussions and arbitration meetings were going on behind the concrete walls of the "bunker" (the nickname for the Québec premier's office). Harmony between the two partners was achieved through a multitude of small gains and concessions: giving the prime minister of Canada the apartment of the president of the National Assembly; allowing Ontario to raise its flag over a tent on an adjoining lot; rejecting the federal government's idea of flying the Canadian flag on the armoury esplanade, the site for the official welcoming of the heads of state and government; using a federal ship to host an excursion on the St. Lawrence River.

We had to have the prime minister's office step in to break several deadlocks. Only Jean-Claude Rivest could have persuaded officials in Intergovernment Affairs to drop the idea of parading a detachment of the Sûreté du Québec next to an honour guard of the Vandoos.

Security arrangements proved even more troublesome. The two solicitors general had to negotiate a formal agreement to define the lines of authority and determine how the Sûreté and the Mounties could be integrated.

I soon grew very weary of tackling the details of the most trivial problems imaginable. Yet I realized that even one grain of sand could jam the gears of Canada-Québec cooperation. I particularly remember today the example of the francophone games in Marrakech, one of the projects supported by the Québec summit. I was then a federal minister and Prime Minister Mulroney asked me to step in to resolve the conflict between ministers Jean Charest (Ottawa) and Yvon Picotte (Québec) over the participation of Québec athletes in the games. In the end, I had to negotiate with Premier Bourassa himself where and at what height (to the inch) the Québec and Ottawa flags would fly.

As ridiculous as it sounds, the issue behind this peevish haggling was more than a simple question of visibility. There had already been twenty years of unequal struggle, most often between French-speaking Québécois recruited by Ottawa and others mobilized by Québec. These antagonisms left behind considerable bitterness and mistrust.

Relying on its international prerogatives, having powerful means at its disposal (notably Canadian International Development Agency funds), and served by proven diplomats, the federal government had long wanted a francophone summit that would confirm its own constitutional preeminence and confine Québec to a strictly provincial status. Yet it was among francophone countries that Québec had scored its few diplomatic gains. Accordingly, Ottawa was determined to advance its cause within a structure modelled as closely as possible on the Commonwealth conferences. These were attended only by federal heads of state and excluded all provincial premiers. Trudeau once told Yves Michaud that there was no more justification for the participation of the premier of Québec at a summit meeting than there was for a tribal chief from Cameroon.

Obviously, federal intentions have not always been pure. In Trudeau's days, Privy Council analysts must have seen in francophone summits the possibility of a double strategic triumph over France.

France's relationship with its former African colonies is one of hegemony. The price is a stiff one: it maintains military forces in Gabon and other countries, often called upon for "police" operations; underwrites a trade zone in which the Bank of France supports the currency of a dozen African countries; and budgets for expensive cooperation programs. France is also active in an organization called the Franco-African Summit. Ottawa must have toyed with the idea of barging in on this family affair as a counterweight to French preponderance.

Who would believe that the federal government did not welcome the opportunity to break into French-Québec relations as a third party, taking advantage of the close cooperation required of the so-called rich countries?

It is not surprising, then, that Prime Minister Trudeau systematically tried to establish a summit, even without Québec's agreement. Only France's refusal saved Québec from being a wallflower. At times the danger was very real. Trudeau succeeded in finding a valuable ally in President Senghor of Senegal, who counts as one of the fathers of francophone summits. In 1983, at the end of talks with President Mitterrand in Williamsburg, the Canadian prime minister even went so far as to announce unilaterally the convocation of a francophone summit, without informing Lévesque first. The only concession Trudeau had in mind was a two-part summit. The first would take place without Québec. The second would follow, but with a weekend interval. Justifiably, Québec saw the meeting as a split-level summit.

Once more, the French government saved the situation by disassociating itself from Trudeau's announcement.

By the end of August 1987, the day before the forty heads of state and prime ministers arrived, all difficulties had been resolved, thanks to the flexibility shown by Prime Minister Mulroney in the November 7, 1985, accord. But few of my Québec colleagues thought Ottawa had renounced its original objectives.

Beyond the desire to marginalize Québec, Ottawa had much to gain from joining an institutionalized *francophonie*. It would have access to a new network that would be spread over five continents, where it could exert a determining influence. Ottawa had every reason to believe that its relative weight would be infinitely greater there than in the group of seven industrialized nations, where the Canadian prime minister figures as a vassal to the American president. Things would be very different in the francophone summits. As the only significant player facing France, in the midst of a gathering of countries that had little individual influence and were among the poorest in the world, Canada could easily assume a leadership role.

Furthermore, participating in the francophone project also stemmed from Canada's very nature. The logic of federalism requires that Ottawa project its linguistic duality abroad, just as it must recognize it internally. The interests of its anglophone component are well served by intensive activity in the Commonwealth. However, Canada had as yet to find the institutional means to express, in parallel fashion, its francophone reality. It was asymmetric federalism expressed internationally even before the term was coined. Federal participation in francophone summits has corrected the imbalance.

For Québec, more than for any other participant, belonging to a living francophone community, ready to face the future, is a question of survival. Increasingly, international competition and conquest of new markets form the keys to success in a global economy. Our entrepreneurs will have to use other languages, mostly English. The levelling effect of the American and anglophone invasion can only accelerate. This is the age of the American way and of the triumph of its culture in cinema, television, town planning, pop music, and the arts. The English language is taking over the world and is already the language of business, science, and almost all international communications.

Withdrawal is neither possible nor desirable. If we want to live in French, we must do so on the international scene as well as at home.

This is the question: How can we survive and make progress in our language? How can we succeed when our language is threatened, when its protection (at the cost of a law that causes our democracy to be misjudged) is a constant source of anxiety, and when we ourselves speak it rather poorly?

No doubt, Québec's own problems suggest urgent reform of the educational system and collective efforts to improve the quality of spoken and written French. However, the forces at work at the international level require a broader solution, which can only be to establish solidarity throughout the entire French-speaking world.

Language is more than a means of communication. It is also a way of thinking and feeling. It creates a natural community among people who speak it, especially since common use presupposes historical bonds. Québec has long been isolated from the sources of its culture because the means of communication were lacking, and because of indifference and political impediments. In this sense, institutional participation in international *francophonie* will allow

Québec to open a window in the wall that has separated it from the world.

There are those who say that some francophones have been part of federal diplomacy and that, through them, Québec has had access to international activities. While it is true that some francophones had brilliant careers in External Affairs, it does not follow that Québec as such gained a place in international forums. Ottawa's foreign policies are not those of Québec. They are determined by the federal government in the light of pan-Canadian interests. Ottawa's foreign policies do not express Québec's personality. On the contrary, they work against it. Thus Québec has been deprived of true diplomatic experience, because it has been seen as an authority primarily responsible for schools, roads, and hospitals. After that, Québec is fair game for accusations of "provincialism." Ottawa never relented in opposing Québec's timid attempts to take up a little bit of space abroad. By confronting Québec, Ottawa stonewalled francophone summits for ten years.

Nevertheless, common sense should prevail. The six million French-speaking Québécois surrounded by 275 million anglophones joined the community of 150 million francophones living in more than forty countries in four other continents.

We must distinguish between *la francophonie* and francophone summit. One is the dough, the other the yeast. *Francophonie* existed before the summit, but as raw material or potential. Diversity is enriching, it is said. But when it comes to francophone peoples, diversity can easily condemn them to powerlessness. How is it possible to have united action in a community scattered throughout the four corners of the world, split north-south with the haves on one side and the have-nots on the other, juxtaposing Islam, Christianity, and Buddhism, and including former imperialists and their colonies? Even the perception of the common tool differs from one place to the next. For Africans, French is the language of the formerly colonized and of the new dominant class, as well as the only means of communicating with the outside world. For countries like Egypt, French is the prerogative of the élite. In Vietnam and Algeria (a nonparticipant in the summits), French is the abhorrent remains of a tyranny overthrown by revolution. In Canada, it is seen as the obsession of a recalcitrant minority and an obstacle in the osmosis of Canadian values. France expresses its soul and its pride through its language, which, its partners fear, may be used by the mother country as an instrument of cultural hegemony.

Yet, this community can only be articulated on the basis of language, the connecting link with its history and the basis of its unity. The result is that the French language symbolizes, all at once, the strengths and weaknesses of the French-speaking world. It binds in proportion to its vitality. Building the francophone community, above all, means consolidating and revitalizing the language. The fate of one is linked to that of the other.

Two dangers are to be averted: a siege mentality and romanticism.

Struggling on behalf of the French language does not mean beating back an attack. English is not an adversary but a language whose influence shows the dynamism of those who speak it. Defensive attitudes lead nowhere.

Nor do incantations. The scepticism expressed in certain circles about the beginnings of institutional *francophonie* had a lot to do with the nostalgic and ethereal speeches about the past glories of the language. While it should be able to give an account of history, a living language must carry contemporary values and look to the future. Consequently, French-speaking people must act. However, they must first be in a position to make coherent decisions.

A summit is a meeting of decision-makers. Perhaps too many of them. This may be the case with francophone organizations which, over the past twenty-five years, have proliferated everywhere and in every sector. Working at cross-purposes has impaired their effectiveness.

With the establishment of the ACCT, *la francophonie* took steps towards more unified efforts. Although the agency was greeted as the first diplomatic success of the French-speaking community, it was soon bogged down in management problems. In 1986, it allocated seventy percent of its resources to operations but only thirty percent to programs. Member governments proceeded with administrative reforms, under the close supervision of the general assembly. However, the incident reflected internal tension. The secretary-general hired agency personnel on the basis of "geographic patronage." Member countries often fought each other to place their own nationals in the agency's offices on Quai André-Citroën in Paris.

In all fairness, insufficient means impeded the agency's work right from the beginning. On the eve of the Paris summit, its budget was less than twenty million dollars. Wealthy countries were in no rush to make their international cooperation programs multilateral. France and Canada preferred dealing directly with each of the countries receiving their aid. They were reluctant to subordinate their policies, and particularly the size of their financial commitments, to the deliberations of forty insignificant countries.

There were limits to what the agency could achieve. The ministers in the general assembly were responsible solely for francophone affairs within their respective governments, or at most also had charge of international cooperation. They could not commit their governments beyond their own narrow mandates. *La francophonie* desperately needed a forum of true decision-makers, capable of mobilizing their governments from top to bottom and from one ministry to another. There had to be a political body at the head of a harmonious structure, or in other words, summits that would regularly assemble the heads of state and first ministers. A summit meeting could set priorities, allocate resources, and provide directions in a matter of days and in one gulp. The civil servants back home would receive their marching orders. Anyone impeding a project would be defying the orders of the president and the prime minister. No bureaucratic foot-dragging, little or no operational expenses. Only performance. Decisions, action, results.

A leading idea was to use science and technology to modernize and diffuse French culture and language. It was time for action, not translation. The struggle on behalf of the French language should now concentrate on covering all the French-speaking world with networks. So communications were of prime importance.

As expected, the southern countries insisted on the addition of a development and training component. Their attitude was entirely justifiable in light of the hardships affecting their populations and the disastrous state of their infrastructures. Accordingly, the first summit set up four task forces: the first for industry and language, under the direction of a Frenchman, Claude Hagège; the second for research and scientific information, under a Belgian, Hervé Hasquin; the third task force covered culture and communications, headed by a Québécois, Pierre Desroches, and assisted by Jean-Marc Léger on cultural aspects; and the last was on development (energy and agriculture) chaired jointly by a Senegalese, Djibrid Séné, and a Québécois, Christian Latortue.

However, initial discussions revealed divisions on politics and economics, as well as on methods to ensure that summit decisions would go into effect.

Economics did not present any great problems. Many African countries were happy to speak about their debt levels and the low prices paid for their raw materials and agricultural products on international markets. Their interest marked significant progress in relation to the attitude of Léopold Senghor, who thought culture should be at the centre of *la francophonie*'s concerns.

The majority of our partners clearly did not like the idea of debating political issues. Few were eager to open discussions on such thorny problems as disarmament and the Israeli-Arab conflict. France was even hostile and urged us to spare the fragile solidarity of the group, pointing out that there were other forums for these discussions.

Yet, on the basis of its experience within the Commonwealth, Canada saw the summit as an opportunity to form a true political club, to give added weight to its deliberations, and to have the new body take its place among the other international organizations and forums. We also wanted some action on an agreement made with Québec requiring a balance between culture and cooperation on the one hand, and international relations on the other. Otherwise, it wouldn't be worth bringing together the heads of state and the first ministers. With perseverance, we managed to push it through.

The Paris summit adopted a first resolution, a rather spineless one regarding debt loads and trade liberalization, and a second one, much firmer, condemning apartheid in South Africa. The conference was also the scene of a tense exchange between the prime minister of Vanuatu and President Mitterrand about French nuclear testing in the South Pacific.

In Québec City, the summit took a position on the Iran-Iraq conflict and on the Lebanese situation. The meeting also discussed the Palestinian situation. Ironically, Canada, the instigator of this kind of debate, found itself isolated after being the only country to refuse to recognize the Palestinian right to self-determination. In Dakar, the meeting tackled the human-rights problem that Prime Minister Mulroney had broached in Québec City.

There were long and animated debates about who would take charge of the summit's follow-up operations. Many countries wanted to broaden the role of the ACCT and give it the mandate to manage the funds and execute the summit's decisions. Canada, France, and Belgium objected. Resolving this issue took up an inordinate amount of time and energy. It even resulted in a commotion. Without understanding the exact reasons, I noticed that during summit preparations (whether in Paris, Québec City, or Dakar), one had only to conjure up what we squeamishly referred to as the "institutional framework" to set off fireworks and unleash interminable discussions.

The big underwriters distrusted the agency's appetite; they rather preferred the agency to start a diet. In 1986, the Outers report (named after its main author, Lucien Outers, delegate-general in Paris for Belgium's francophone community) commented severely on its administrative deficiencies.

The last thing Canada wanted were summit decisions bogged down in the meanderings of multilateral bureaucracy. We insisted on a direct link, during summit intervals, between national decision-makers and those who implemented projects. We suggested a committee of sherpas, personal representatives of the heads of state, and prime ministers from a dozen countries.

Our solution won in Paris, had a hard time in Québec City, and barely survived in Dakar. From summit to summit, the ACCT made headway. In Québec City, France officially reiterated its confidence and expressed the hope that the agency would eventually become the summit secretariat. Certain countries, Canada among them, accepted allocating multilateral funds to the agency. In Dakar, participants agreed to integrate with the agency the four task forces appointed in Paris. True, the agency made a very positive gesture in devoting thirty percent of its statutory funds to summit projects. The Chaillot Summit in Paris, in November 1991, transferred to the agency the responsibility of a follow-up committee. Consequently, the organization will be getting more funds and will hire more public servants. Have summits reached the age where they are becoming bureaucratic? This would be too bad and contrary to original intentions.

However, the public is not interested in these insider's quarrels. The media ignored them at the Québec summit. The contents of the programs have little that is sensational either. The dry achievements of the summits rarely make headlines. Only certain political questions, such as the condemnation of human-rights violations in Zaïre, manage to attract any attention. Generally speaking, media reports skirt the fundamentals. No doubt, this is why television images — the ones that survive — are concerned mostly with the showy ceremonial side of things: the inaugural session of the first summit in Versailles, the cavalcade of limousines in front of the Manège militaire in Québec City, the entrance to the Élysée Palace, brilliantly illuminated as citizen-president-founder Mobutu entered wearing his leopard hat, accompanied by colleagues in tuxedos.

The Québec summit was assigned an unrewarding role: to act on the promises of the Paris summit. After the first summit, which did not have to do much more than take place, the second one was supposed to deliver the goods. In a sense, the fate of future francophone summits depended on Québec. If it failed, the verdict would drop like a guillotine: a short-lived affair.

To be fair, the Paris summit was more than a media event. It was something for Québec to build on. The broad lines of future action were set. There was a procedure: organized networks for realizing the objectives assigned to each sector of activity. The idea was to set up, beyond the tug-of-war between governments, a purely functional group consisting of people from across the francophone world chosen solely for their competence. This mode of action bore fruit: the Québec summit would verify that a lot of work had been accomplished.

On each of the Paris summit commitments, the Québec summit was able to say, mission accomplished. The four networks? In place. The francophone scholarship program? Functioning. The M.A. program in oil-company management? Already instituted at the University of Montreal. The centre for training agronomists in rural areas? In the process of being set up. The Energy Institute? Founded, with headquarters in Québec City. The French-language pocketbooks? Seven titles published, dozens more to come.

The decisive young *francophonie* already had an impressive number of achievements to its credit. It would be tedious to list them here. Like any good student, it did its homework with diligence and without ostentation.

The Québec summit launched many projects with promising futures: the University of French-speaking Networks, the Remote Training Centre, the Data Bank of Francophone States (a mine of information with 200,000 entries), a program for distributing 110 scientific publications, and a plan for standardizing access to data banks in Canada, France, Europe, and Québec. In each case, the methodology to bring them about and the funding were available. Everywhere, there were concrete moves to be pragmatic and modern: computer training, French-language software, preparation of an energy guide, and so on.

Canada's contribution was significant in every area. Pierre Desroches led a highly effective team within the communications network. I had persuaded Pierre Juneau, president of the Canadian Broadcasting Corporation, to let us borrow this extraordinary operator, peerless negotiator, authentic expert, skilful diplomat, and relentless worker. This Québécois Canadian was the leading architect of TV-5 and many other communications projects.

The most visible achievement of the Québec summit was, no doubt, the extension of TV-5 to North America. The new network has been broadcasting French-language programs since the summer of 1989, including newscasts from Europe. Plans are under way to extend the network to Africa. The Québec summit also announced a bank of television programs and the development of an international radio network.

Admittedly, most of the money comes from Ottawa. Along with France, the Canadian government assumes the financial responsibility for most undertakings. Before the Paris summit, federal support for the different activities of *la francophonie* was about twenty million dollars. At the close of the Québec summit, two years and two summits later, it was close to fifty million dollars, on a par with the Canadian contribution to the Commonwealth.

The itinerary was written to minimize, in public perception, the gap in the contributions of the two host governments. The two first ministers spoke at the inaugural session, Mulroney chairing sessions of the first section and Bourassa sessions of the second. Nothing disrupted the cooperative mood between Québec and Ottawa. Officials on each side and at every level were in a state of alert, ready to intervene in any crisis. Goodwill, diligence, and friendliness prevailed. Everyone seemed aware that this was an inspired and historical moment. The opening speech by the prime minister of Canada set the tone:

> More than two centuries ago, like a branch separated from its trunk, 60,000 French-speaking people were left to face their North American destiny alone. What fate awaited this small band of settlers so abruptly exposed to collective uncertainty and the need to question their own identity? Would the wide open spaces, so appropriate to their disproportionate dreams, imprison them in their isolation and cut them off from the rest of the world? . . . The answer, silent and persistent, could only stretch out in time and space . . . Today, it speaks out vigorously: the French language and the values it represents have survived and will always be alive in America . . . Those 60,000 settlers are now six million people.

Except for the inevitable minor mishaps, the organization and logistics ran flawlessly and with an efficiency that did North American tradition proud. Though the Treasury Board, in Ottawa, was seriously concerned about budget overruns, we were able to return to both governments one million of the seven million dollars allocated to us.

There were just a few snags. Security services showed excessive zeal by doping the pigeons on Parliament Hill for the duration of the summit. They also made the unfortunate decision to blow up a suspicious suitcase at the airport that turned out to belong to an African diplomat. He showed extreme displeasure at seeing his multi-coloured clothes flying in all directions.

The bodyguards of some visitors showed even greater anger on being searched and disarmed by the Mounties. I saw a photograph of revolvers, guns, and weapons of all kinds confiscated at Ancienne-Lorette airport. It was like a cache belonging to conspirators planning a coup. In fact, there was a coup, not at home but in Burundi. It forced the president, Colonel Jean-Baptiste Bagaza, to leave Québec before the end of the summit. But we couldn't be blamed for that.

However, we could not plead innocence when our French friends accused us of taking them by surprise with our announcement that we were wiping out $325 million dollars' worth of African debt to Canada. French officials thought we were trying to outdo them and were hurt by this gesture of facile generosity, and they said so privately. In truth, I had tried, all through the long summit preparations, to have External Affairs make the announcement in Québec City. But they refused because they wanted to keep the scoop for the Common-wealth meeting in Vancouver in December. During the summit, I happened to mention my failed plan to Prime Minister Mulroney, who decided to make the announcement that very day, to the great displeasure of the French and officials in External Affairs. Although my French contacts were too polite to say so, they obviously did not believe my explanations for the incident.

No joy is totally without sorrow. Dozens of members of the summit team were saddened by the absence of their colleague Lucien Outers, who suffered a stroke as he was leaving Brussels for Québec City. This generous man, with a fine cultured mind, a fighter on behalf of *la francophonie,* author of *Le Divorce belge,* had made a valuable contribution to the summit's preparation.

On the whole, the press reports were positive, except in the English-language media. With little to say about the summit itself, they fell like vultures on Mila Mulroney regarding some obscure and unexciting immigration story. She was said to have supported an application by a Lycée Claudel professor to enter Canada. Another journalist, a francophone under special contract with the TVA network, complained in front of all his colleagues about a delay in a press conference I had called. The nature of the grievance and the identity of the journalist caused gales of laughter among the hundreds of reporters present. The plaintiff was the same René Lévesque who had acquired a certain celebrity during his political life for his lack of punctuality with the press.

The last decision of the forty governments present was to adopt the logo the organizing committee had selected as the flag of *la francophonie*. It was a way of letting us know they thought the Québec summit was a success.

The francophone summit was born in Paris. In Québec, all knew it would live.

There was and still remains a lot to do. Though the cost of the Québec summit exceeded a hundred million dollars, the resources allocated to each summit were clearly insufficient. Francophone credibility will soon face an embarrassing disparity between its needs and its resources. Should the situation persist, subsequent summits will run the risk of falling into pious rhetoric, becoming high-society gatherings.

We Québécois have the most to gain from our membership in a large and creative community. It is the only way, for the moment, we can serve an apprenticeship in international relations. Our dependence on the survival of French both as an international language and a contemporary mode of expression is reason enough to join this group. Our collective survival is tied to the fate of the language, itself the object of *la francophonie*'s concern.

La francophonie's international success is vital. Québec should no longer leave it to Ottawa but should pull its weight for the financial load of summit activities. The time is gone when we, in Québec, could rub our hands together with satisfaction and relief on seeing Ottawa assume the costs of culture, the National Film Board, Radio-Canada, and the Canada Council. In the francophone community, as everywhere else, it is important to take charge of one's own affairs. Even federalists should see this as a minimum requirement.

From one end of the francophone world to the other, member countries, particularly in the north, are asked to make a dramatically greater effort. To avoid the division and dispersal of our energy, we must resist the temptation to undertake new projects, and pursue vigorously what we have already assumed. Success comes with perseverance, a virtue that does not naturally come to governments, whose vision seldom extends beyond the next election. Which explains why the support of public opinion is essential. Québec will have that support when we truly understand that promoting the French language also promotes our collective vitality. To this end, we have no other external ally than the solidarity of French-speaking countries.

In any event, I felt that, in Québec City, we had made some headway in the right direction.

Autumn arrived as the tourists were leaving the old capital, in the wake of the heads of state and first ministers who had already left for home. It was hard for me to leave the city. This time, I returned with a pang of anxiety to Paris to don once again my ambassador's hat.

12

The Leap into Politics

My Paris assignment was entering its third year. Time had come for me to take stock of the resolution I had made at the outset to limit my diplomatic excursion to three years. Unlike most of my fellow ambassadors in Paris, I was not at the end of my career (at least I hoped not) and would go back to earning a living in the demanding profession of law.

One more year would be enough for me, a chairman of the follow-up committee, to set in motion the projects approved by the Québec summit and, as ambassador, to complete the program I had set for myself.

My diplomatic agenda lacked only one item to complete the normalization of Canada's relations with France: the Governor General's first official visit to France. After weighing everything carefully, I came to the decision to leave Paris in the summer of 1988.

Once I had set myself this deadline, I had a growing sense that I had started on the downside of my Paris mandate. Two pieces of bad news, coming almost simultaneously, substantiated this feeling. On my arrival at the embassy one November morning I learned of the death of René Lévesque. I ordered the Canadian flag outside the chancellery to be lowered to half-mast. An English-speaking Canadian who was passing by came in to protest. He thought it was indecent to mourn a man "who wanted to destroy Canada." The incident did not go any further, since the prime minister's office had done the same thing in Canada. The whole day was like a wake, with people recalling the ups and downs of the departed one's career, trading anecdotes, and being interviewed by journalists. That evening, I was having dinner at my residence when I received a desperate call from Nicky Guérard. Her husband, Yoland, had collapsed from an embolism while watching TV during the bulletin announcing Lévesque's death. I hurried over to Rueil-Malmaison to find my colleague lifeless and his wife inconsolable.

All the members of the embassy's small community, who had been charmed by Guérard's good nature and irrepressible vitality, sincerely mourned his death. He had lived fully and paid back a hundredfold what he had received. His nomination as head of the Canadian Cultural Centre had displeased the mandarins at External Affairs. Yet he brought to his work an extended and rich experience in show business, a long singing career, and unlimited devotion. Absolutely guileless and convinced that generosity and drive could surmount any obstacle, his fate led him into a crushing encounter with bureaucracy. Nothing had prepared him for power struggles waged with dry and fussy dispatches.

The bureaucrats not only had the director, but also the centre itself in their sights. The government didn't know what to do with it and was endlessly studying the problem. There was talk of getting rid of the building on the esplanade des Invalides and opening a new centre close to Beaubourg or the new opera house at Place de la Bastille. Should they make it a Canada House modelled on the one in London? Or a gallery of modern art, as in New York City? Or a multifunctional hall designed for concerts and experimental theatre? Some thought it would be better to close the place down. This seemed the most likely outcome. The possibility had been raised with me during the summer of 1985. As the result of spending cuts, the consulates in Bordeaux, Strasbourg, and Marseilles had already been closed.

In spite of all my efforts and those of Guérard, it proved impossible to keep the centre going. There were no funds, no motivation, and no ideas. When I left Paris, four months later, the director's job was still vacant. The latest news was that External Affairs had decided to close this window on Canadian culture in France.

I flew to Québec for Lévesque's funeral. Like most of those who knew him were probably doing, I recalled my last meeting with him before his death. It was shortly after the Paris summit, in the lounge of Montreal's Four Seasons Hotel. We were having a drink when two elderly English-speaking women approached him for an autograph. As he graciously signed his name, one of the women said, "We have a great deal of admiration for you, Mr. Lévesque." Handing back the sheet of paper, he said with his inimitable grimace of a smile, "Yes, you admire me now that I no longer frighten you."

The reply led to a conversation about the demoralizing effects of the 1980 referendum. I asked him whether he thought the Québécois had definitely rejected the idea of sovereignty. I can still hear him saying, "In these matters, nothing is definite. You never know. Everything is still possible."

This is what I was thinking when I went with Prime Minister Mulroney to view Lévesque's casket in the Red Chamber of Québec's National Assembly. In spite of changes in fortune and disappointments, Lévesque had never lost faith in his compatriots. And they reciprocated. There was no lack of evidence that day. For instance, when Marc-André Bédard took a taxi to the Red Chamber, the driver refused to be paid, saying, "You are going to view Mr. Lévesque? Then it's free."

I saw the casket carried into the Basilica twenty-eight years after Maurice Duplessis's. Leaving the church to the sounds of Mozart's *Requiem,* I noticed the prime minister stiffening and casting a shocked look at the crowd, which was chanting, *"Le Québec aux Québécois."* Did this intuitive person have a premonition of what would blossom from Lévesque's legacy?

Returning once more to Paris, I started working on the Governor General's visit. French officials were in no hurry to follow through on the agreement with which they had gratified the prime minister. Circumstances had changed. France's president had to come to terms with a prime minister and government that had defeated his own party in the previous elections. Cohabitation, as the French call it, was difficult. And to make matters worse, the people representing the constituencies affected by our cod quotas on the Grand Banks belonged to the same party as Prime Minister Jacques Chirac. The conflict was as virulent as ever.

With his usual fire, kindled by the imminence of presidential elections, Chirac rode the fishing issue for all it was worth and hardened his policies towards us. I thought he was very North American in his attitudes. He was an engaging man, with clear words and forthright manners. At the very time when I was trying to resurrect the Governor General's visit, he summoned me to complain about the treatment we were giving French nationals. I could see his anger was not put on. He believed he had been misled following the expectations aroused by Mulroney's assurances. For the rest, he did not limit himself to outpourings of bile. Many issues suffered from the secondary effects of the fisheries dispute. One was Seagram's acquisition of Cognac Martell. After the minister of finance blocked the transaction, we soon discovered he had done so on instructions from the French prime minister. It took numerous high-level representations to lift the government veto.

I was not surprised to be told, on several occasions, that the Governor General's visit was not one of the French government's priorities. My counterparts seized every opportunity to question me about Jeanne Sauvé's function, her constitutional status, and her relationship with the Queen of England. "Is the Governor General truly the head of the Canadian state?" they kept asking me. I took refuge in subtle legal distinctions to avoid having to confess bluntly that our head of state is indeed the Queen of England when wearing her Canadian crown. This makes the Governor General a viceroy, or a "vice-queen." Accordingly, it is difficult, from a strict point of law, to claim for the Governor General the privileges of protocol usually given a head of state.

Nor could I complain of the fate reserved for Canada, a country for which it would be highly improper to be represented abroad by Elizabeth II, even with the title of Queen of Canada. Hence Ottawa's efforts under Sauvé to Canadianize the function as much as possible.

In truth, we needed a political decision to rescue us, and it had to come from the president. We could not expect any other support. After all, the original overture had been made by the president, who, furthermore, had been rather restrained in his statements on the Saint-Pierre-et-Miquelon affair. After harassing the excellent contacts we had in the president's entourage, we managed to get dates for the trip: January 25 to 29, 1988. The program was set and arrangements were made down to the most minute detail.

The visit could hardly have the same political importance and visibility as Prime Minister Mulroney's. But the French gave it all the protocolary importance they could: the president's presence at Orly, a twenty-one-gun salute, lodgings at Marigny, gala dinner at l'Élysée, escort by the republican guard's cavalry, ceremonies in the Senate, at the Sorbonne, and at the Vimy monument. For the first time, the Canadian flag few on the esplanade des Invalides, along the Champs Élysées, and Place Charles de Gaulle.

But everything seemed to go wrong at the dinner given by Jacques Chirac at the Palais d'Orsay. The French prime minister's toast had the tone of a reprimand to Canada because of our country's attitude in the fisheries dispute. The presence of Deputy Prime Minister Don Mazankowski and Treasury Board Chairman Robert de Cotret, who had to bear the attack in silence, brought tensions to a high point. Many guests were ill at ease, including some of our French friends. Jeanne Sauvé's composure and class saved the day. Without departing from her usual graciousness, she stated the Canadian position with firmness and civility.

Perhaps President Mitterrand was eager to make amends to Jeanne Sauvé. He came to my residence, in spite of a bad cold, to a farewell ceremony I had organized in her honour.

Once the visit was over, I considered that another cycle had ended. I had accomplished the main part of my task.

Québec had to understand that France and Canada (English Canada in this case) have too many interests in common not to maintain close bonds of cooperation. The federal government had even agreed to an exceptional status for Québec in its relations with

France. The latter could now deal with each of its two partners in perfect harmony in the pursuit of its interests and objectives.

All that was left now was to conclude some current business and prepare for my return home. I was planning to go back to law in the fall and was already in contact with a few law firms.

However, politics would soon knock at my door again. The signs were growing. More than one visitor reported the rumours flying around about my being recalled to Ottawa. Some of Mulroney's close associates urged me to become a Conservative candidate. The government, whose first mandate would end in the fall, would normally have to go back to the voters before the end of the year.

Everything fell into place in February 1988. The prime minister wanted to appoint me to the cabinet before I entered the House of Commons. The political outlook did not look rosy for the government, which was still reeling from a string of ministerial resignations and charges of corruption. The prime minister thought it necessary to give convincing evidence that he could rebuild, in Québec, the coalition of Péquistes, old *bleus,* and nationalist Liberals that had brought him to power in 1984. He planned to name me to the cabinet and gamble everything on the outcome of a by-election.

The stakes went beyond mere party interests. They included the fate of the Meech Lake accord and the Canada-U.S. free-trade pact. A Conservative defeat spelled doom for both.

In the Sept-Îles speech, I had supported a policy of national reconciliation in order to later embrace the *beau risque.* The ultimate objective was a redistribution of powers for the benefit of Québec. Before returning to the constitutional bargaining table, from which we had been driven, I thought it imperative to get compensation for the breach of faith and the humiliation of 1981–82. It was also a way of salvaging our honour. I thought, first of all, that Meech did not have sufficient regard for the signature we would be adding to the unilateral act that serves as our Constitution. But it was all we could hope for at the time. As Lévesque had said, "It's no gold mine, but it's better than nothing." The immediate goal was restoration of the right of veto (the one we thought we had) to seal the wide breach of

1982 that left us defenceless against changes in federal institutions. Moreover, the accord of June 3, 1987, made the recognition of Québec as a "distinct society" a basic rule of interpretation of the Constitution and of the Charter of Rights. But I had the impression it was a strict minimum.

I also thought that ratification of the Meech Lake accord would create a climate of goodwill towards Québec's historical claims. It might be possible, in the enthusiasm of reconciliation, for Québec to table a program of constitutional reforms similar in scope to the one that Bourassa's Liberals later put forward in the Allaire Report.

But nothing could be taken for granted before June 23, 1990, the deadline for provincial legislatures to ratify the accord. Without the Mulroney government's reelection, the accord's survival would depend on the Liberals. However, their support was too ambiguous and unreliable, and left little doubt about the outcome: if they were to gain power, the Liberals would have nothing more pressing to do than to sacrifice Meech to the intransigence of Trudeau, Wells, and Carstairs.

The same fate was likely to overtake the free-trade agreement, which had widespread support in Québec. Québécois, who do not harbour the latent anti-Americanism of English-speaking Canadians, wanted to restore the natural flow of trade with their neighbours to the south. Bernard Landry had already published *Commerce sans frontières,* a convincing demonstration that Québec needed to be part of a North American free-trade zone. Québec business and political circles generally shared his views. However, the acrimonious controversy raging in English Canada prevented the government from signing the treaty before it had a new mandate from the voters.

I was told my entry into politics would help the successful resolution of these two issues, equally important for Québec, by improving the government's chances for reelection. I agreed that this was sufficient motive for a commitment that was an extension of *le beau risque.*

However, I was still facing the same dilemma: politics, yes or no? By saying no until then I still had not resolved my ambiguous feelings about political life. We often say no simply to sidestep a decision.

Fascinated yet discouraged by politics, I could neither embrace it nor turn my back on it. For a long time, I had been going over all the paradoxes. Political life is a world that brings out the best and the worst. It brings out leadership. It harbours egos that need inflating. It gives the illusion of power and is a lever of social progress. All that is what politics meant for me.

Everyone has a way of resisting the song of the sirens. But unlike Ulysses, not everyone can have himself tied to the mast of his ship. My more prosaic approach was to immerse myself in the practice of law and take refuge in the upper levels of public service. In 1985, I had opted for the comfortable compromise that allows deputy ministers and ambassadors to fall back on influence rather than pay the price of power. I felt somewhat like a moth who, having long circled a flame and singed its wings, ends up engulfed in the flame.

My thoughts also took into account my personal relationship with Mulroney. We had been exchanging favours for a long time. I like to think, however, that they had not been entered into some fussy balance sheet, for the favours carried no price. I had never thought of my appointment in Paris as a reward, but I know that many commentators at the time thought it was, particularly because of my contribution to the 1984 campaign. Though he may have seen political advantages in it (I was, after all, one of the advocates of the reconciliation), my diplomatic appointment was certainly, in his mind, a gesture of confidence. I was grateful to him for this opportunity in Paris. I could hardly refuse my help in his hour of need.

I concluded that the time had come to settle my old accounts with politics and to pay my debts to Québec society, and also to Brian Mulroney. I decided to answer the call.

In March 1988, the prime minister came to Brussels for a NATO meeting. We met to work out the details of the operation he had in mind. We agreed that the announcement of my nomination would coincide with a cabinet shuffle at the end of the month. As for a ministry, my preference was Justice, with which I had professional affinities. I also said I would like ministerial responsibility for the ratification of the Meech Lake accord.

Finally, I was appointed secretary of state. I knew little about the portfolio but accepted anyway, so great was my inexperience. Later, as I thought about it, I came to the conclusion that as a former professional negotiator, I hadn't played my cards very well. I thought my naïvety more excusable, however, than the irresponsibility of my mentors, who put a prickly nationalist in charge of official languages, Order of Canada appointments, Royal Family visits, and Canada Day celebrations. What a launching for a neophyte who had joined the fray to save Meech and who had to seek his political family's pardon for having embraced *le beau risque.*

The by-election was set for a few weeks after my entry into the cabinet. I had not been promised any riding in particular, though they did mention Chicoutimi. But I needn't worry; my friends would look after these petty details.

I arrived secretly in Ottawa late in the afternoon of March 28, 1988, slept at the house of Bernard and Madeleine Roy, and presented myself the next morning at Rideau Hall to take the oath of office. Coming out, I answered questions from the anglophone press on the anticipated theme: What was a former Péquiste doing in the federal cabinet?

I then returned to Paris to bid farewell and to pack. At the end of a round of receptions, the president wanted to see me privately, even though the second round of the presidential elections was only four days away. I crossed for the last time the office where his watchdog, Jacques Attali, was posted behind his desk (he told me it had once belonged to Napoleon), and entered the president's office. Since he had just ended a long and strenuous campaign, I expected to find him exhausted and strained. He looked as if he had just returned from a holiday. His eyes alive and complexion fresh, at ease in a light suit, he had been calmly waiting for me.

Mitterrand wished me well and talked about the kind of life I would lead, comparing it to an ambassador's life: "People who are elected exist by themselves, ambassadors represent someone else." He added that "politics sometimes brings people into history." I answered that this applied to his own career, but the same could not be said for all politicians. He said: "You know, I am only a provincial who has come to Paris." He told me that when he left for Paris, his mother had given him four letters of introduction to Paris personalities, including François Mauriac. "The two families knew and respected each other," he added.

Looking at him, seated in the chair of the president of the republic, I tried to imagine the young man, towards the end of the 1930s, timidly ringing the doorbell of the author of *Le Noeud de vipères.*

Nothing seemed to disturb my host's serenity. He appeared to have forgotten that in a few days he would find out whether his fellow citizens would renew their confidence in him and give him another seven-year mandate as president of France. I reminded him of this. "Ah, the elections! They tell me one of my opponents is very active." (This was a reference to Chirac, who was crisscrossing France, giving speech after speech.) "He may win," he went on. Then with the ghost of a smile, "But not likely."

I remembered that, at the outset of the campaign, when his opponents were already hard at work, he shut himself up in the Élysée Palace with a dozen Nobel-prize winners from all over the world. For two or three days, before a battery of cameras and microphones, he discussed the fate of the world with his distinguished visitors.

Of course, I would never advise anyone to use this approach anywhere else but in France. There, politics are conducted in short sibylline phrases (only Bourassa does this here, and I am not sure it always serves him well). French voters show a surprising indulgence towards their political leaders, who do not hesitate to abuse the system. Some members of the National Assembly have been caught red-handed breaking election laws? That's all right, we'll change the election law retroactively, which will spare them the inconvenience of a trial and wipe their slates clean. Interviewers always treat ministers with great reverence, and their questions are often submitted in writing in advance. De Gaulle personally chose the questions he thought deserved answers.

I did not see a single journalist blink when Mitterrand, during France's millenary celebrations, sat in a magnificent chair in the choir of the church of Amiens, his back turned on the gathering of notables and leaders, face-to-face with God. Only the count of Paris, head of the House of Orléans, and pretender to the throne of France, had been authorized to sit near the president, but in a less imposing chair. From my seat in the nave, among the diplomatic corps, I was thinking of the jeers that would greet Mulroney if he dared do the same thing in Montreal's Notre-Dame.

My Parisian adventure ended as it had started, with an interview with the president. From the Élysée, I walked to the residence at 135 rue du Faubourg-Saint-Germain, no longer mine, before flying to Ottawa, where another adventure was waiting, an adventure that would not end as it had started.

13

Power and Friendship

The classic career path of a minister goes like this: you're elected to the House of Commons, then become a minister, and later, ambassador. In my case, it was the reverse. I was an ambassador, then entered the cabinet, and later was elected to the House of Commons.

My new cabinet colleagues greeted me with courtesy. However, I was conscious of the vulnerability of my situation. An unelected minister enjoys little credibility. He does not answer to the House of Commons and cannot pretend to be on an equal footing with "real" ministers. I felt like a hockey player warming the bench, a lawyer admitted to the bar without passing its examinations, or a pilot banned from flying. Immediately, I asked for a by-election, and received my first disappointment. There were no available ridings. Contrary to what I had been told, Chicoutimi was not available. Through an oversight, the sitting member of Parliament, André Harvey, had never been informed. Quite legitimately, he was not prepared to give up his seat. I could only blame myself for my naïvety. As a minister without a seat, the only option I had was to beg one from a benevolent MP.

At the same time, a brutal gesture by the Saskatchewan legislature brought the first language crisis to my doorstep. The legislature precipitously abrogated the only law guaranteeing linguistic rights to the French population. It was revenge for a recent Supreme Court decision that had confirmed the constraining power of the law requiring all provincial laws to be available in French. To avoid having to translate all their laws, Grant Devine's government moved to repeal the act. The French community reacted with indignation and asked for federal intervention. Interminable and arduous negotiations between the two governments ensued. Finally, in June, they came to an agreement whereby the secretary of state agreed to spend fifty million dollars, over five years, essentially to allow the recalcitrant province to provide French services to the Fransaskois.

At the peak of the tension, Prime Minister Mulroney wrote a letter to his provincial counterpart condemning the breach of French rights. This letter triggered, a few months later, the first clash between Brian Mulroney and me, one that would cause a split over a Supreme Court decision on Bill 101.

In mid-April, I was still looking for a riding and becoming somewhat impatient. Members of Parliament eager to "accommodate" me were raising their bids. One would be happy with a Senate seat while another had his eye on a Superior Court nomination.

In the midst of the bargaining, the party ordered public-opinion surveys in different constituencies. There were possibilities in Montreal and Lac-Saint-Jean, but the projected margin of victory looked thin. Nevertheless, the prime minister seemed to be in favour of the Lac-Saint-Jean riding. It was a natural choice, apart from Chicoutimi, where I had practised law for twenty-one years, and Jonquière, where I had spent eighteen years of my life. Clément Côté gave up his seat without asking for guarantees. Later, because of good relations between Québec and Ottawa, he became vice-president of La Régie de la construction in Québec City.

Thus I arrived in Alma one cold and rainy April evening and announced I would be a candidate in the by-election called for June 20, 1988.

An election campaign is, above all, an exercise in modesty. Voters assess a politician as though he were a horse on auction. Nothing escapes the critical public eye: his physical appearance, his public speaking, his stamina, his ability to handle crowds, his past, his supposed ambitions, his family, and his friends. The candidate must go out and meet the voters on the street, in restaurants, shopping malls, and garages. He must shake their hands and ask for their votes. To my great consternation most people did not know who I was and were not even aware of a by-election. Some took the opportunity to heap all the unspeakable sins of the Conservatives on my shoulders. Occasionally, I met someone who flatly refused to shake my hand.

While I had expected these lessons in humility, I was not at all prepared for the sorry state of the Conservative organization in the riding. People in Ottawa gave it high marks, but when I got there, I found only chaos and infighting. I did not know which faction to rely on. It took some time to build a highly efficient organization, which I did with competent and committed people who have since become very close friends.

The early stages proved difficult. My chief of staff, Luc Lavoie, took advantage of accumulated leave to stay with me in Alma for the best part of the campaign. Others, sent by the party, joined him, but at the cost of friction with local volunteers.

Three weeks before the vote, the polls showed me trailing my Liberal opponent. A spectre started haunting me: that of Pierre Juneau, who was catapulted into the cabinet and then defeated by a complete stranger when he went to the polls.

Mulroney, accompanied by his daughter, Carolyn, made his first trip to Grande-Baie. He attended an open-air mass as part of the 150th anniversary celebrations of the opening of Saguenay–Lac-Saint-Jean to settlement. For him, the stakes were even higher than they were for me. He returned a few days later, this time with Mila.

My constituency is 160 kilometres long, on the north side of Lac-Saint-Jean and the Saguenay River. It extends west from Falardeau to Saint-Ludger-de-Milot and includes the city of Alma and all the townships to Desbiens. At that time, it also included Chicoutimi-Nord.

After leaving Saint-Fulgence, the prime minister drove out to Alma, stopping in every village to harangue bystanders, always ending with, "I need Lucien in Ottawa. Send him to me."

The next day marked the high point of the tour. My opponents accused me of being an outsider in the riding. I was enraged; after all, my father, my two grandfathers, my two grandmothers, my paternal great-grandmother, and my great-grandfather Sixte were all buried there. My opponents went as far as accusing me of being "the henchman of Chicoutimi's high finance." The visit to the farm where I was born, with noisy media coverage, was probably the turning point of the campaign.

The never-ending presence of the media did not make things any easier. Cameras and microphones trailed me everywhere. For two weeks, there was such a rush of journalists, photographers, and sound technicians that every hotel in Alma posted No Vacancy signs. While I canvassed door-to-door, cameramen occasionally slipped into homes. In a beauty parlour, one filmed a lady with a full head of rollers. That evening, hundreds of thousands of TV viewers saw her desperately trying to hide behind me. At the outset, I consented, rather stupidly, to suicidal experiments. I once toured a shopping mall preceded by a cameraman and wearing a microphone on my belt. Thus transformed into a walking TV and radio studio, I allowed them to record the slightest reactions of the strangers I accosted. For hours, I walked around under the constant fear of being ridiculed or insulted "live."

The most disconcerting thing about the media was how they handled my election commitments. They reported, mostly in English Canada, that I had flooded the riding with money. Some pegged the amount at one billion dollars or more. But I had simply an-nounced a sum of $1.4 million as seed money for new businesses and for a number of studies, notably $80,000 towards the decontamination of the Petite Décharge River. I also made public the reconstruction of the Sainte-Rose wharf, to cost $400,000. The project had been announced so many times in the past that no one in the village would believe it, and they all voted against me. I also promised to advance by one year repairs to the runway of the Alma airport. Finally, I added my voice to the chorus that had been asking, for two decades, for a land link between James Bay and its natural outlet, the Lac-Saint-Jean area.

No matter which way I added up the numbers, I could not get even close to one billion dollars. Finally, I figured out that the media had tacked on to my election promises the amount of $970 million for renewing the agreement for a five-year development plan, already decided on between the two levels of government. It was a regional-development program affecting all of Québec. I found this incredible. More than four years later, I still read stories from time to time saying my by-election was bought at a price of one billion dollars.

I had also introduced a new frontier in campaign financing. The day of my cabinet appointment, the prime minister announced that I would be submitting a report on ethics in the party and on steps to improve political ethics at the federal level. I had not yet presented my recommendations, but I believed I should pay for my campaign with funds gathered through what is known as popular financing. Following Québec's election act, I refused contributions from companies or incorporated organizations. I only accepted contributions from individuals and to a maximum of three thousand dollars per person. As far as I know, this had never been done before at the federal level. My supporters, overwhelmed by the organization of the campaign, balked at the idea of putting so much effort into fund-raising. However, I persisted, mostly with the help of François Gérin, MP for Megantic–Compton, who was actively advocating this method of financing in the Conservative caucus. In addition to his personal contribution, he also dispatched his right-hand man, Jacques Bouchard, who was instrumental in the success of the whole operation. In the end, we had 1,542 personal contributions worth $86,900.

We needed every one of the fifty campaign days to catch up. Sixteen to eighteen hours a day, I covered the riding's twenty-seven municipalities and a large part of the concession roads. Pierre Blais, minister of state for Agriculture, after giving up a trip to North Africa, spared no effort to reassure farmers concerned about the free-trade agreement with the United States.

I faced two formidable opponents, both well-known and experienced. Liberal Pierre Gimaël had represented the riding from 1979 to 1984; NDP flag-bearer Jean Paradis taught computer science at

Alma CÉGEP and he belonged to a family that had left its mark on political life. John Turner, Ed Broadbent, and a slew of party stars came to give them a hand. The campaign was seen as a dress rehearsal for the coming general election. Liberal Jean-Claude Malépart himself came by to give me a little electioneering lesson. "Bouchard, you are always talking about Meech Lake. Well, you had better worry about Lac-Saint-Jean," he said during a rally.

My two opponents thrashed about like devils in holy water. I used to see them at every public ceremony, as well as at picnics and concerts, and in church squares. On the eve of the vote, one hot Sunday in June, we passed each other on the beaches of Lac-Saint-Jean, shaking hands oily with tanning lotion and, in our city shoes, stepping over bathers sunning themselves on the sand.

Bit by bit victory was becoming ours. From the attitude of the people I met during the last days of the campaign, I felt the tide was turning. The telegrams and testimonies of support were piling up from, among others, Corinne Côté-Lévesque, Guy Chevrette, Jacques Brassard, Québec Liberal party president Michel Pagé, and even Robert Bourassa.

On the evening of June 20, I was elected with a majority of 6,200 votes. The Gallup poll, published at the beginning of July, set the number of Québécois who would vote Conservative at forty-two percent, a jump of twenty points compared with early June. Mulroney's gamble had been right.

I was now really in politics. When I returned to Ottawa the next day, I went because I had been sent by my fellow citizens of Lac-Saint-Jean.

* * *

I was not very enthusiastic following my initial contact with the secretariat of state. The federal government deals with a vast range of issues. But apart from External Affairs, which was out of reach, I had no particular wish to handle sectorial responsibilities. For me, the burning issue was the national question, the solution of which depended on Meech. To this end, Québec had twice voted for

My paternal great-grandfather, Sixte, who gave his Christian name to the Bouchard-Sixte branch of the family.

My maternal and paternal grandparents:
above, Évangéline and Xavier Simard;
below, Lydia and Joseph Bouchard.

Philippe Bouchard and Alice Simard on their wedding day at the house on the Decharge concession road, March 29, 1937.

Philippe Bouchard filling up his truck (I can't tell if it's a Ford or an International).

Here I am in Jonquière, 1944, age five.

*With my brothers and sister. From left: Gérard, Claude, Claudette,
Roch, and me during a picnic at Uncle Adélard's
cottage on Lake Kénogami.*

*The family in Jonquière, gathered around Uncle François Bouchard,
a Redemptorist priest, on a visit to the family farm.*

*Great-Uncle Henri Bouchard (centre) on his retirement from
Potvin & Bouchard, Inc., in Jonquière, bidding farewell to his
grand-nephew, Laurent Bouchard (left), with Philippe Bouchard
(right), my father. This was the great-uncle who took pleasure in
grilling his grand-nephews on the exact dimensions of the doors of
St. Peter's Basilica in Rome, which he had measured himself with
his folding rule.*

Editorial staff meeting of the student newspaper Le Cran, *at Collège de Jonquière in 1955. From left: Pierre Tremblay, Yves Villeneuve, Yvon Desbiens, Sauveur Laberge, Normand Simard, and me; Henri Côté and Jean-Pierre Gagnon are front-right.*

Editorial staff of La Presse *in Jonquière (summer 1961). Back to front: Gaston Ouellet, Réal Huot, and me.*

My father giving me my ribbon at graduation,
June 1959, in Jonquière.

Uncle Adélard Bouchard.

Roland Fradette,
Chicoutimi lawyer.

With Robert Cliche in 1971.

Election night in Baie-Comeau, September 4, 1984;
Brian Mulroney has just been elected prime minister of Canada.

With my mother in Paris, 1986.

At the Quebec Summit, Brian Mulroney presenting Robert Bourassa with a reproduction of a portrait of Hector Fabre, who was agent for Québec and Canada in Paris in the 1880s. I am at far left; at far right is Jean-Louis Roy, then delegate-general of Québec in Paris.

January 1988. At the Governor General's official visit to Paris. A friendly meeting at the residence of the ambassador of Canada. From left to right: Simone Veil, then president of European parliament and now a minister in the Balladin government, Lucien Bouchard, François Mitterrand, and Jeanne Sauvé.

(Jean-Bernard Porée)

Election victory in Lac-Saint-Jean, June 20, 1988.

With President Bush at the White House, April 1990,
at an international meeting on the environment.

I am being accosted by the media in the streets of Ottawa after a press conference the day of my resignation. (Laserphoto)

*During a break at the Bélanger-Campeau Commission,
with Jacques Parizeau.* (Laserphoto)

The first caucus of the Bloc Québécois. From left: François Gérin,
Gilles Rocheleau, Louis Plamondon, Jean Lapierre, me,
Nic Leblanc, Gilbert Chartrand (who later resigned),
Gilles Duceppe, Benoît Tremblay. Pierrette Venne,
deputy of Saint-Hubert, joined the group
in August 1991. (Patrick Daigneault)

*In Alma, five days after my resignation, Alexandre Bouchard
(six months), in the arms of his mother (Audrey Best-Bouchard),
prepares to shake a voter's hand. (Laserphoto)*

The baptism of Simon Bouchard, May 9, 1992. Abbé Alfred Simard (my maternal uncle) had also baptized me and Alexandre (right), Simon's brother; on the left is my wife, Audrey.

Mulroney. And it was this issue that ruled political dynamics. My arrival in Ottawa made sense only if I was personally and closely involved in policy-making. Understandably enough, I felt disoriented as head of a department identified with the symbols of the most orthodox federalism. I had not turned down Lévesque in order to be guardian of the crown jewels in Ottawa.

I accepted my stay in the secretariat of state as a period of apprenticeship, a transition to the functions of minister and politician.

It is not my purpose here to discuss policy deliberations by the cabinet or the various ministries for which I was responsible. However, three issues brought to my attention as I arrived at the secretariat taught me the basics of the decision-making process. These issues were improvements in budget allocations for my new ministry, payments indemnifying Japanese Canadians for discrimination during World War II, and a program to combat illiteracy.

It was the treatment of Japanese Canadians that gave me the most trouble. When he was leader of the Opposition, Mulroney had castigated Prime Minister Trudeau for waffling on this particularly scandalous affair. After the Japanese attack on Pearl Harbor, panic swept over the West Coast, both in Canada and in the United States. Hysterical people feared that immigrants of Japanese origin might become a fifth column, committing acts of sabotage and transmitting information to the enemy.

In 1942, without any other legal procedure, the Mackenzie King government ordered the internment of forty-two thousand people, most of whom had resided in Canada for a generation. More than seventeen thousand of them had Canadian citizenship. Men, women, and children were taken from their homes, deprived of their property, and held in concentration camps. Freed after the war, they were unable to recover their homes and farms, which the government had sold to third parties. The proceeds had been used to pay for the camps. A mere decree by cabinet was enough to deport four thousand people, half of them born in Canada, to Japan. I could see in this the proof that there was no political structure in Canada, federal or otherwise, that would be safe from arbitrary decisions and abuses of civil liberties. These things take place in the minds and hearts of people rather than in the organization of democratic institutions.

The inability or refusal, for more than forty years, to recognize and repair the injustice made matters even worse. The survivors had formed an association and never ceased to press for an apology and compensation.

Opponents in Ottawa had a powerful argument: compensation would set a terrifying precedent. The feeling was not without justification. Canadian-Japanese villainy was not the only skeleton in the federal closet. There was the tax on Chinese labour brought to Canada, at the end of the nineteenth century and the beginning of the twentieth, to work on the construction of the transcontinental railway. Then there was the shame of the "preventive" incarceration of Canadians of Ukrainian origin during World War I. If these victims and their descendants were given the precedent of an honourable settlement for the Japanese, how far would it go? And then, in the most secret of federal memories — if not consciences — there was the arrest, without proof, charges, or trial, of 453 Québécois, which a federal law had authorized during the October Crisis. Wouldn't we be stirring up all these people?

The prime minister was eager to meet his commitment to make amends to the Japanese Canadians. He would be unable, during the coming election campaign, to blame his inaction on cabinet reticence. After a few meetings in which I failed to make any headway, I asked for his help. He expressed clearly his intention to remove this blot on Canada's honour. Gerry Weiner, secretary of state for Multiculturalism, conducted negotiations with the victims' representatives with tact and diligence. The talks were arduous: honour does not come cheap. The government had to set aside a fund of $291 million to compensate the victims according to criteria defined in the agreement. The American example helped. In August, the United States announced it would pay $20,000 to each of the 120,000 Japanese Americans who had suffered similar treatment. On September 22, the prime minister signed an agreement with Japanese Canadians just minutes after presenting a formal apology in the name of Canada.

The fight against illiteracy unfolded in a similar way. A report, sponsored by Southam News, showed just how bad the situation was: twenty-five percent of Canadians were functionally illiterate. In other words, they were unable to read a road map or fill in a job application. The secretariat was under heavy pressure to react by financing local groups of volunteers, joint programs with the provinces, and the organization of a national literacy secretariat. The total cost, spread over five years, would reach $140 million, which the ministry did not have and which Finance refused to allocate.

In 1986, the Speech from the Throne expressed a similar commitment. Once again, I put some pressure on the prime minister, who took the matter to heart.

In a parliamentary system, the executive has many of the traits of the monarchy. As long as the prime minister has the confidence of his party, he enjoys a great degree of latitude. So as soon as the PM's entourage sent out the right message, roadblocks fell as if by magic. The program was on track and funds were available. The prime minister and Mila Mulroney announced it in Toronto at an event attended by many children, stressing the necessity and the benefits of reading.

My first discovery was that the cabinet does not really make many decisions. Neither is the prestigious Priorities Committee, which meets every Tuesday, the hard core of the decision-making process. Its agenda and operational decisions are determined by another committee, more select but not as well-known, whose meetings take place every Monday in the discreet Langevin Building. There, no cameras film the comings and goings of the seven or eight members surrounded by a slew of mandarins from Finance and the Privy Council. They deliberate and rule on the "real business" of government: important money grants and legislation, obligatory drug testing in the armed forces, the wearing of turbans by Sikh members of the RCMP, the fund for decontaminating abandoned industrial sites. It is called the Operations Committee — Ops for short. In my time, Don Mazankowski chaired this arm of the Privy Council. It was impossible to get around this politician. Though he was more soft-spoken and had a lower profile and a smoother way of doing things, he was Mulroney's Parizeau and Boivin rolled into one. He was the palace official and the director of the solutions committee, in charge of consoling members of Parliament, of smoothing ruffled feathers, and of keeping an eye on the mandarins. In all matters, he showed honesty and good sense. Ops was the power lever in the hands of Maz, as this one-man band was usually called. Ministers launching a project, putting together a program, or defining a new policy had to appear before Ops. But they had access to this powerful body only by invitation and then only after wearing themselves out getting round the obstacles put in their way by the Privy Council.

Ops distrusts ministers' "terrific ideas," particularly those that cost money. Ministers must submit to the labours of Hercules before the doors of Ops will open. The course is laced with traps nobly baptized "Cabinet Committees," whose secretaries report directly to the Privy Council. Sooner or later, ministers discover that the system is an onion that one never finishes peeling, or a set of Russian dolls with an endless number of dolls.

In fact, the Operations Committee is neither the first nor the last of the onions or the *matriotchka*. I suspect that Mazankowski and Michael Wilson formed the last circle around the prime minister. While the first had greater power, I feared the second more. I could always hope to convince Maz by relying on his good sense and his political judgement. But when Wilson came out against something, there was no way to change his mind. His political vision had only two lenses: deficit and inflation.

Apart from the jumble of committees and the various structures devised by the Privy Council, everything is actually in the hands of the prime minister, who does all he can to lead others to think otherwise.

And that fact was the source of my strength and my weakness. I may have had easy access to the prime minister, but he could only rarely be the *deus ex machina* in my own responsibilities. His latitude was inversely proportional to how often I called on him. I saw this after my first successes; my undersecretary of state and certain colleagues warned me against systematic appeals to his authority. In any case, I soon realized that he hated being the referee between two camps for fear he would seem to favour one side over the other.

At the same time, this early experience made me see the power of the machine, which was more discreet but had longer tentacles than the ministers'. A political leader's credibility is like a bank account: the more you draw on it, the faster you exhaust it. The public service's influence does not suffer from these handicaps. It is diffuse, identified with the system, and equally anonymous.

Yet there is nothing mythical about the federal machine. It even exists in the flesh: a group of very able individuals with unity of purpose and interest borne out of long tradition. It is not enough to say they are federalists. They see federalism only in terms of a centralizing power, the centre being them. At the heart of the system stands the clerk of the Privy Council, who is a clerk in name only. This inoffensive title masks an extraordinary concentration of bureaucratic influence over time and space. Paul Tellier held the title when I was in the cabinet and spent many hours a week, sometimes every day, with the prime minister. The Privy Council clerk acts as a conveyor belt between the political master and the machine, of which the clerk is both product and protector. He maintains its respect. He tames, mobilizes, brakes, and spurs it on. He puts it at the service of the prime minister. Beyond the government, there is the state, towards which he assumes an unwritten responsibility, but completely understood, for the imperatives of rationality and continuity. Governments come and go, but the state must last. The institutional memory, the respect for tradition and ethics, the transition from one government to the next, in these domains the clerk's duties are implicit.

Most of the information supporting the prime minister's thoughts on important decisions passes through the clerk's hands. The clerk also supplies policy alternatives on most topics. He can make and unmake top civil servants. The Privy Council is the breeding ground for talent, which, once tested under the master's watchful eye, moves on to head various ministries, embassies, or Crown corporations.

It would be wrong to see the Paul Telliers of this world as cold and insipid clerks in glasses, drafting reports destined to gather dust. One must view the clerk as a spellbinder whom few politicians can resist, even though they are expert spellbinders themselves. A clerk of the Privy Council needs only a few days to tame a newly elected government, overcome its prejudices, and make himself indispensable by his knowledge of the issues and of the machine.

In this story of spellbound spellbinders, it is easy to mistake the prey for the predator, so close are these lovers of power. Once they have the confidence of those who have chosen the visible aspects of power, these shadowy satraps can gather all the crumbs of power with impunity. Those falling under the prime minister's table can satisfy great appetites. How many decisions come out of the last words whispered in the ear of the prince? Often the confidant does not even have to make a sound to stall a particular project. He merely need hint that only delicacy prevents him from speaking out.

I discovered that the path of a file resembles the moves of the counters in a game of Snakes and Ladders. The Privy Council can push a counter back to square one or push it up ladders to the finishing square.

I have heard many people blame the prime minister for not ridding himself of the top civil servants the Liberals had left behind. In fact, this is something Mulroney could not do. Only this select group could turn the wheels of government. Long years of Liberal power had prevented the development of a neutral public service. Deprived of the diversification normal alternation would have produced, the machine became Liberal. It remained so through a process of ideological rather than partisan osmosis. With a few notable exceptions, such as Derek Burney, the great mandarins of the federal government are the true heirs of Trudeau, whose main ideas they continue to profess: official bilingualism, multiculturalism, modular federalism, centralization of government, protection and promotion of official linguistic minorities, support for the welfare state. More liberal than conservative, Mulroney got along famously with them. It was with his own party that his relationship was askew. There is no other way of explaining the rebellion of western Conservatives and the rise of the Reform party.

Mulroney pursued Liberal policies on official languages to the point of alienating part of his own caucus. A few days after my election, I made my first vote in the House of Commons, in favour of Bill C-72, improving the Trudeau government's Official Languages Act of 1969. I only know about the last skirmishes in a long struggle by francophone MPs to consolidate bilingualism at the federal level. Stormy debates between members, the determined resistance of many anglophones outside Québec, the forceful attempts by reactionary circles in Canada to water down the law, all contributed to the impression that the French language was making important gains.

For the first time, I became conscious of the way life in the glass bubble of Parliament distorts reality. The law certainly strengthened official bilingualism. Its effects would be to favour francophones in the public service. But this perception did not take into account the reaction of the Québécois majority. The awakening was brutal when, among others, Québec Liberal minister Gil Rémillard, Opposition leader Jacques Parizeau, union leaders Fernand Daoust and Gérald Larose expressed serious apprehensions about the effect of the law in Québec. A study commissioned by the Office de la langue française pointed a finger at Article 43, giving the secretary of state the authority to promote bilingualism in private companies, management and union organizations, as well as volunteer associations. The office believed there was a risk that Ottawa would use this clause to favour English and erode the status of French.

Not everyone shared in the self-congratulations of the small world of Ottawa. After Parizeau, my friends and allies Guy Chevrette and Jacques Brassard started attacking me. Gil Rémillard expressed his misgivings in writing. In the midst of my new colleagues' indifference, I tried to extricate myself as best I could from this hornets' nest. But each time I tried to reassure francophones in Québec, the anglophone press issued dire warnings. It reacted very badly to the compromise that Rémillard and I worked out together, which was to harmonize official language policy between the two governments. An exchange of letters on this topic aroused the ire of William Johnson in the *Gazette*.

No one could come out the winner in this business they handed me so soon after entering politics. I resolved that from then on I would wage the struggles of my choice in the camp of my convictions.

General elections were approaching. The Conservatives were afraid the outcome would be affected by the resignations of ministers Côté, La Salle, and Bissonnette, or by the Gravel affair. I was invited to hand in my report on public ethics at the August caucus in Saint-Hyacinthe. I proposed several measures, such as a law on conflict of interest and on popular financing of election expenditures. Québec MPs undertook to refuse corporate contributions and to put a cap of five thousand dollars on individual contributions. However, the party reserved the right to solicit corporate contributions for the national organization. The new policy for constituencies helped the party put on a new face that kept charges of corruption out of the election debates.

The House sat without a break until elections were called for October 1, 1988. I started my second campaign in six months.

Looking to increase my majority, I crisscrossed the riding. I made frequent side trips to Montreal, where I bore the party colours in five debates, notably on the free-trade pact, external affairs, and the environment. Twice, Liberal Jean Lapierre was my opponent. I never imagined that I would be founding a new party with him, two years later.

A few weeks before the vote and the day after the leaders' debate that Turner won, Gallup published the results of a poll that put us twelve points behind the Liberals. Many of our organizers were reeling from the blow. Without minimizing reactions to the debate, I thought free trade was costing us the election. Interviewed by a regional television network, I denounced Ontario's selfishness in seeking to monopolize Canadian-American trade. Without having consulted me, Harvie Andre, Conservative minister from Alberta, made a similar charge out West. The next day, the *Globe and Mail* published our attacks side by side on the front page. Meanwhile, party strategists, comfortably installed in their offices in Montreal, Ottawa, and Toronto, were taken by surprise and panicked. They held a series of meetings to express their concern about our statements and grumble about decisions made "aboard the aircraft," the chartered jet in which the prime minister and his entourage travelled across the country.

Mulroney was the only one to keep his cool. He did not object to my going on the attack again on the same topic, which I did. In fact, Mulrony had thought of a strategic blow that would cause the Ontario vote to shift to the Conservatives. This was to bet everything on a constant of Ontario politics: not to let federal power fall into the hands of others, particularly Québec.

The prime minister concentrated on Québec, taking advantage of its support for free trade. Québec support grew as the idea of Ontario's selfishness gained wider currency. Mulroney put on a great show at Roc Amadour Hall in Québec City. He kept striking with nationalist couplets. He even had me compose new ones. I spent the previous night dipping my pen in the ink of péquiste rhetoric. By showing great strength in Québec, he wanted to send a message to English Canada and particularly to Ontario that massive support from Québec would make the difference. Not wanting a government dominated by Québec, Ontario would jump aboard the Tory bandwagon.

This is exactly what happened. For the second time in a row, the Conservatives formed a majority government. In my riding, my majority went from 6,200 votes to 16,700. I was also ahead in each of the 218 polls.

* * *

The Supreme Court did not let the Conservatives celebrate for long. Less than two weeks after our victory, it announced three decisions invalidating provisions in Bill 101 on unilingual public signs.

The very first day, I had a premonition that this was a crisis that might eventually undermine my solidarity with the cabinet and my relations with Mulroney. Ottawa was expecting Bourassa to modify Bill 101 in the way the Supreme Court had indicated, allowing bilingual public signs. According to supposedly reliable information, Québec was prepared for any contingency.

Things took a turn for the worse when fifty thousand people marched in the street telling Bourassa not to touch Bill 101. All these people belonged to my political family, and even my real family. My mother phoned, full of admiration, to tell me that Catherine, my niece and godchild, whom I had never heard talk politics, had marched in Jonquière in subzero temperatures in defence of the bill. In Québec City, Claude Ryan wavered in his rejection of the notwithstanding clause. The rest is well-known: Bourassa put aside the scenario suggested by the Supreme Court and decided to keep some of the provisions it had declared to be unconstitutional. However, eager to please both sides, he concocted a compromise making a distinction between inside and outside signs, thus managing to antagonize everyone.

There was consternation in Ottawa. The Bourassa solution put the federal government on the spot as protector of minorities and champion of official bilingualism. Everyone in Mulroney's entourage thought he should intervene. They all remembered the angry reprimand he had sent a few months earlier to Grant Devine concerning the Fransaskois. The decision to admonish Bourassa followed from the letter addressed to his Saskatchewan counterpart. Federal logic and equity did not allow treating one differently from the other.

Someone from the Privy Council even prepared a letter for the prime minister's signature. I got wind of it; it was a letter of condemnation addressed to the premier of Québec.

The idea of inside-outside sign regulations did not appeal to me at all, but I could not accept condemning the use of the notwithstanding clause. I told them it was incongruous to compare rescinding linguistic guarantees in Saskatchewan with invoking the notwithstanding clause in a Québec law. The opting-out clause formed part of the 1982 Constitution, which had been imposed on Québec by the very people who blamed Québec for invoking it.

I could do nothing. Bill 178 in Québec had raised the hackles of English Canada and Québec's English-speaking minority.

New drafts of the letter came in one after the other. Each time, the tone became more conciliatory. I could see that efforts were being made to obtain my agreement. In the end, in spite of all the changes, the problem remained the same. The question was whether Ottawa would call the premier of Québec to order or not. No manipulations of the phrasing could possibly answer the question. As far as I was concerned, there should be no letter. My resistance exasperated everyone. The government could no longer hold off. Tension mounted intolerably. Finally, I was told that the prime minister would accept no more delays or changes to the text. I continued voicing my opposition until I was summoned to the prime minister's office.

Politicians hate so-called moments of truth when everything is presented in black and white. I had seen this one coming for some time, but it arrived much sooner than anticipated.

I entered the prime minister's office, a wainscotted room on the southwest corner of the Centre Block. He was alone, seated behind his desk. I sat down facing him, steeling myself against his powers of persuasion. I had been under attack (courteously, but all the more effectively) for several days. I had been a negotiator for too long not to be aware that there are limits to psychological resistance.

The conversation started in a tone of gravity. I could see that our personal paths, converging for so long, were now diverging severely under the pressure of forces beyond our will.

At some point, he read out passages from the letter, trying to convince me that the condemnation was as muffled as he could make it. He concluded, however, that he had to send it. I did not challenge him on that point, recognizing that I should not interfere with what he regarded as his duty as prime minister. But I told him that, in my view, muffled or not, a formal letter of condemnation was unacceptable and consequently I could not support it by staying in his government. I added that my departure would relieve him of a minister who was embarrassing for him and unpopular in English Canada.

The serenity of our conversation was in strange contrast to the feverish agitation surrounding us. In a few minutes, the prime minister would face an aggressive opposition, which, as usual whenever there is a linguistic controversy, smelled blood. Obviously, he wanted to defuse the crisis by making the letter public.

Mulroney got up, walked to a cupboard, and came back holding a photograph. It was that of a white-haired man, handsome and heavyset, standing in the middle of a group. "This photograph was taken during my trip to your riding, during your by-election. I have no idea who this man is. But his resemblance to my father is incredible." He was deeply moved, probably as much as I was. I understood the allusion. This man who never confided, who buried his feelings under loud jokes and under feigned or real anger, could go no further. He was telling me that our divergences were striking at the deepest levels of fidelity. He went back to his seat and said, "I ask you not to attend question period today. Go home and think it over some more."

I left his office and returned to my own, two floors above. I was shaken by the reference to his father. Was I carried away by emotion or by vanity? Did I lack political muscle to deal forcefully with Québec's touchiness?

But the image of his father gave way to mine. While Mulroney had been close to his, he was aware of what my father represented to me. With Robert Cliche, Mulroney had come at the time of my father's death, in 1975, to pay his last respects. I thought that his attachment to the convictions of his own father did not excuse me from my duties towards mine.

I immediately started writing my letter of resignation. Someone knocked at the door. Paul Tellier entered. He came as an emissary, repeating the same arguments. I always got along well with him and had great respect for his judgement and intelligence. I stopped him, saying I was writing my letter of resignation. After he left, I wrote until another visitor appeared. It was Luc Lavoie, my former chief of staff who had recently gone back to the prime minister's office. "Hold it," he said, "The prime minister says he will not be sending a letter to Bourassa."

After the first feelings of relief, I realized that my absence from the House (which the Opposition denounced) and my silence were more than signs of ambiguity concerning my position. I summoned a Canadian Press reporter and stated that one could not blame the National Assembly for resorting to a mechanism provided by the Constitution. I described the notwithstanding clause as an indispensable guarantee for the protection of Québec's identity. These statements, appearing in the press the next day, aroused the prime minister's anger. All the more so because, the previous day, he himself had criticized, with certain qualifications, the recourse to the not-withstanding clause. The clause allows any legislature and the House of Commons to be exempt from certain provisions in the Charter of Rights and Freedoms.

My outburst was seen as a lapse of cabinet solidarity, which brought me a hard time in the Priorities Committee and in the national Conservative caucus. In spite of everything, I resolved not to retract my words. The prime minister, who was in a precarious situation, asked me to stay away from the House of Commons during the three or four days remaining before Christmas. The Opposition was thus prevented from putting me in a position of contradicting the PM. However, it unleashed an attack against me that was not entirely without foundation. In the middle of a language crisis, nothing could justify the absence of the minister responsible for the defence of minorities. Then Jeffrey Simpson published, in January, a devastating column against me in the *Globe and Mail.* Meanwhile, an article by Michel Roy, praising my courage, told me a lot about the schizophrenia hounding French-speaking Québécois in Ottawa.

In fact, 1989 and the new electoral mandate were starting badly for me. The previous December's events had upset me profoundly. I knew that, as proud as he was, the prime minister would not readily forget the retreat I had forced him into with the knowledge of his ministers and principal associates. I drew no satisfaction from the situation. I cursed the circumstances that had forced the showdown and regretted having distressed him. My relations with him had certainly suffered a harsh blow. There was now a gulf between us that could only become wider.

I was downhearted, and angry with myself for being so naïve as to believe that friendship and power could coexist. Mulroney was ignoring me, Bernard Roy had finished his term, my nationalist friends were staying away, and even my family wondered about me.

I am grateful to Derek Burney for doing what he could to restore my courage in these difficult moments. I knew him from Paris, as the number-two man in External Affairs. In our professional relationship, he had always seemed highly gifted and as solid as a rock. His colleague, Fred Bild, plenipotentiary minister at the embassy, often spoke about him, and in very laudatory terms. I had established excellent relations with him when he was Mulroney's chief of staff. He was with Mila and me in the trailer where the prime minister came for a rest from time to time during the first televised debate of the 1988 campaign with Turner and Broadbent.

At the end of December, Burney was preparing to leave for Washington as Canadian ambassador. He noticed the distress resulting from my problems with his former boss and tried to cheer me up. He had enormous influence with the prime minister, whom he had served exceptionally well. His departure, along with that of Roy, left a great void that was never filled and that kept the prime minister and me apart. I always thought that this able civil servant, who owed me nothing, was instrumental in my nomination to Environment Canada.

The prime minister, in fact, decided to take me away from the powder keg of secretary of state and to give me the Environment portfolio. At my request, he also brought me into the Operations Committee. I wanted to be part of the real decisions on the financing of programs in my portfolio.

I was about to congratulate myself on our renewed closeness when an incident occurred that would hardly have made any waves before. It showed the fragility that would characterize our future relations.

As newly appointed Environment minister, I held a press conference in which I described, with overexuberance, the place environmental concerns would have in government policy. Among other things, I announced that no economic project financed out of the public treasury would go ahead without a green light from the environmental committee I chaired. It caused another storm in the prime minister's office. I had to have it out with Tellier and Maz. For weeks, the prime minister looked cross.

I understood our relationship would never again be what it had once been. I came to the conclusion there was only one thing to do: plunge wholeheartedly into the Environment portfolio, and find my redemption there.

14

The Green Plan

My transfer to Environment Canada proceeded, for the most part, from Mulroney's and Burney's concern with restoring my "Canadian" innocence. Ecology is a universal language that knows no borders and transcends ethnic conflicts. They wanted me to fight for virtue, instead of being cast in the role of an unrepentant separatist; to promote what unites rather than what divides.

Although it had ten thousand employees and an annual budget of close to one billion dollars, my new ministry did not count as one of the most important. However, for some time, the public opinion polls had regularly placed the environment at the top of voters' concerns. There was a profusion of ecological groups, which had no difficulty mobilizing public opinion on behalf of any cause, from the protection of baby seals to nuclear bans. The media echoed their interests, in whose service many MPs had already enlisted.

The surge of environmental agitation had placed Environment Canada on a political escalator.

People had not waited for the end of the 1980s to discover the physical world around them. It is our relationship with the environment that has changed. From time immemorial, human beings have had to depend on nature, which they tried to domesticate, for their subsistence. They cut down trees and hunted game. But what they took from nature could never exceed its capacity to replenish itself, because that capacity was endless. The idea of destroying nature never occurred to anyone. In fact, people sought protection *from* nature.

In the nineteenth century, in the wake of the Industrial Revolution, economic development showed the same lack of concern. However, thanks to the explosion of technology and the introduction of new machines and processes, economic activity has multiplied by a factor of twenty. Consumption has grown proportionately, profoundly altering lifestyles. Here is a statistic to show the prodigious leap in Western industrial productivity: the increase alone in world production in 1990 was equal to the entire industrial production of Europe in the 1930s.

Without realizing it, we have gone beyond the ecosystem's margin of tolerance.

The world was shocked at the first signs of deterioration: the discovery of a hole in the ozone layer, deformed sea mammals, fish unfit for consumption because of the toxic levels of poison in them, waterways turning into cesspools, a decrease in oxygen renewal as a result of disappearing forests. Nature had suddenly gone from being almighty and hostile to being vulnerable and damaged. Technological progress had overwhelmed the forests. The oceans were no longer protected by their size. Abuse could wipe out even the most prolific species. The most disturbing revelation was that the human race itself was at risk. Suddenly, we understood its dependence on the balance of nature. Humanity became a predator: wealthy, it always wants more; poor, it destroys forests without being able to replace them and makes do with the most outdated and hence most polluting industrial technology.

Our misgivings obviously have had some positive aspects. At the individual level, we are perhaps taking part in the emergence of a new humanism. At the international level, we are seeing unprecedented solidarity.

Ecological ethics condemns waste and encourages respect for nature. It calls for a type of behaviour once associated with frugality and moderation: energy conservation, recycling, uniformity of packaging, increasing reliance on science to know and protect life.

From an international perspective, the coming revolution will bring nations closer together.

Only a concerted effort can slow down and arrest global warming, save the forests, put an end to the spewing of toxic wastes into the atmosphere, protect the ozone layer, decontaminate transborder lakes and rivers. As the confrontation between two superpowers that has kept half the world pitted against the other half for fifty years comes to an end, there is an opportunity to forge a new alliance between nations, not directed *against* other nations but working *for* the preservation of their habitat. These social and economic mutations, as we can well imagine, are forcing governments to take a new look at themselves.

At first, managing the environment portfolio meant moving from one crisis to another: cleaning up oil spills on beaches, banning fishing in a river contaminated by a pulp-and-paper mill, cancelling the construction permit for a projected dam.

The powerlessness of government authority is due first of all to the insufficient scientific data available to identify the causes and effects of different types of pollution. This leads, for instance, to the question of tolerance levels: At what level does a toxic substance become acceptable to the environment? Where is the borderline between benign and harmful? What is causing the conditions that are decimating the belugas near Tadoussac? Is there a link between the relatively higher incidence of malignant tumours (cancers of the lungs, pancreas, and prostate) and toxic discharges from aluminum plants in the Saguenay–Lac-Saint-Jean area? More exhaustive research is necessary.

Paradoxically, every improvement in detection technology sparks even more questions. The most recent monitoring equipment is so advanced that it can detect infinitesimal quantities of a great many toxic substances. Increasingly aware of the growing risks but unable to assess their importance, people are worried. There is no lack of doomsayers.

How can we know with certainty if the earth is threatened with global warming that, according to some predictions, might cause sea levels to rise one metre over the next fifty years? Scientists themselves are still debating the question.

When in doubt, should governments act preventively against carbon dioxide, the presumed cause of the hothouse effect? Or should they wait for hard evidence?

The obstacles standing in the way of government intervention are not all philosophical. Many politicians believe the environment is a plank for leftists in search of a cause. These politicians distrust the militancy that restricts their authority, if only by subjecting their decisions to prior impact assessments. Is the net effect to put the brakes on economic growth?

This attitude is widespread among classic conservatives for whom every change is suspect, especially if it leads to government intervention. It flourishes in finance. Its top bureaucrats were terror-struck by the large sums of money that would be required from government resources for decontamination work and the social and economic reforms necessary to prevent the repetition of past errors. It is certainly true that the bills for the mess would be arriving at a very inopportune time. Not only was there no money in the till, but debt servicing requiring thirty-three cents out of every tax dollar threatened, and still threatens, to throttle the government.

However, Finance's stranglehold on government operations was no less asphyxiating. Michael Wilson ruled with an iron fist. Anything with social connotations came up against his obsession with the deficit. The Mulroney government had a number of progressive members, such as Joe Clark, Perrin Beatty, and Marcel Masse. But none of them could successfully push his way through the formidable defences of Finance. Wilson could rely on the simple faith of his party. Remember, this is the party that put Felix Holtmann at the head of a parliamentary committee on culture. For those who do not remember, Holtmann was the Conservative member who, as he presided over a meeting of his committee, blamed the CBC for broadcasting foreign music, like Beethoven sonatas. The Conservative creed is expressed in few words: privatize, deregulate, and shrink the government. As the champion of fiscal responsibility, Wilson pleased the hard core of the party. Part of his influence on the prime minister was also based on his strong links with Toronto's financial establishment.

The garrison in Finance was fully prepared for an assault by the new environment minister. But the prime minister reacted differently. He had studied poll results too well to adopt a negative attitude on such widespread and lively concerns. However, aware of Wilson's resistance and of the precarious state of public finances, he took refuge in rhetoric and lamentations about the sad state of the world and the coming catastrophes. He delivered several of his flights of eloquence to international audiences, easily earning a reputation as an environmentalist. But in Canada, the increasingly noisy ecology lobby denounced his vacuous speeches. I fell into the same habit of flights of eloquence — unless it was Mulroney who fell into mine, since I occasionally wrote his speeches.

A key buzzword was *sustainable development.* The concept originated with the Brundtland Commission, named after its chairwoman, the prime minister of Norway. The World Commission on Environment and Development, formed under the auspices of the United Nations, tabled its report in 1987. Refusing to condemn economic growth as such, it opted for a development formula founded on indefinitely renewable resources. Development must allow our children and grandchildren to have access to the same resources we have enjoyed. In other words, each generation, starting with our own, can take advantage of the world's environmental capital on the condition that it can transmit it intact to its successors. This definition gives rise to an ethical view that makes us custodians of the world's heritage. It has a single commandment: Do not undertake and pursue any development that is not sustainable.

It was the expression, more than its contents, that pleased the politicians. It took the form of a profession of faith that sounded good to the public. However, the time for action soon arrived with the fateful question: What does the government propose to do to bind our economy and our institutions to this development model? It was a way of saying we had exhausted the resources of rhetoric and passed beyond the time for lamentations. We had to go into action.

But where to start? I concluded we had to design a plan, set up a timetable, establish priorities, backing all this with assured funding.

The need for a plan stemmed from the very notion of sustainable development. The cohesiveness and synergy of various policy initiatives depended on it. Since our environmental problems resulted from a chain of causes, we can only deal with them by preparing a series of solutions. I saw the wastefulness that resulted from the case-by-case and day-by-day approach. From one crisis to the next, the government was stripped of its credibility, without even getting recognition for what it *had* accomplished. My predecessors had taken many praiseworthy initiatives without changing, in the minds of Canadians, the bad reputation of the Conservatives when it came to the environment. The establishment of five new national parks, an agreement with Québec to decontaminate the St. Lawrence River at a cost of $110 million, the passing of an effective law to protect the environment and its signing of the Montreal Protocol (a great success in the fight against chlorofluorocarbons, the gases that destroy the ozone layer) — these were rarely counted among the government's achievements.

The governing machine professes, at least officially, a predilection for planning. It is always inviting ministers to map out their intentions. What the machine does not like is for these plans to see the light of day, which is why it loses them in the labyrinths of the Privy Council or in the countless committees that grow like mushrooms on Parliament Hill. Thus, the ministers are kept busy and held on a leash. If things go awry, if a plan gets too close to hatching, the next cabinet shuffle assigns the minister to another portfolio. Filing cabinets in every ministry bulge with these fine efforts that are doomed to remain unfinished or have been rejected by a successor, who throws himself into another planning exercise that will meet the same fate.

In truth, nothing displeases the central apparatus more than a series of well-defined measures that have been spread out over time, made public in advance, and prefunded. Because, once such a plan has been accepted, the minister is freed from the cogs of the machine. Happy is the minister who, after the required authorization, can look after the interests of his ministry and realize the larger plan without exhausting himself in endless skirmishes.

The taskmasters do more than verify budget spending and allocations. They also interfere in program contents, cutting here, clipping there, changing one thing or another, and modifying policy directions. Analysts in each ministry have their counterparts in Finance, the Privy Council, or the Treasury Board. Such duplication gives rise to endless power struggles. Without the prime minister's intervention, nothing would ever come out of this hornet's nest. Ministers who understand the rules governing this republic of accountants are mostly content to keep shop.

However, since the environment occupied the political centre stage, the prime minister agreed to a comprehensive planning effort. He seemed sensitive to the argument I presented to everyone I addressed. The public's environmental concerns challenged the Conservative party and the government. Both had the opportunity to redefine and humanize themselves, and to come closer to the preoccupations of ordinary people. I pointed out to the officials in Finance and their minister that even business supported a higher allocation of government resources for environmental improvements. The environmental deficit was having consequences that would be just as ruinous as the budget deficit. It seemed to me that a government determined to press ahead on this issue with concrete and daring measures would be able to mobilize the population and generate collective enthusiasm.

Nevertheless, given the scope of the reforms I had in mind, I had a good idea of the resistance I would encounter. And I did not assume that the prime minister's initial support meant I had won the game.

Like impatient parents, my officials and I christened the baby before it was born. We called it the Green Plan. It was bound to be beautiful, intelligent, courageous, and rousing, and it would make a difference in the world. I did not know that another father would be there at the baby's birth, and that it would not even be the same baby. But, until my resignation, I worked relentlessly for mine.

The first drafts were ambitious. I contemplated a radical reform of government operations so that most decisions would be subject to an environmental veto. The first batch of innovations included an environmental audit for public accounts and revision of existing laws and regulations from the perspective of their ecological impact. The bill was steep: ten billion dollars, based on early estimates. The plan included a "green tax" that would go by statute to the Green Plan.

I can still hear the screams coming from the machine. But reaction was not all negative. I must confess that I benefitted from the interminable discussions in committee and elsewhere that ensued; they allowed us to bring out a more digestible proposal. Colleagues, such as Jake Epp, Perrin Beatty, Joe Clark, Monique Landry, and Frank Oberle, gave me solid support as I ran through the obstacle course of government and caucus processes.

Without turning its back on a regulatory approach, the Brundt-land Commission had insisted primarily on widespread consultations with decision-makers in all sectors. Accordingly, we set up a national environmental forum to bring together ministers from both levels of government, businesspeople, environmentalists, consumer representatives, and so on. I discussed the objectives and the contents of the Green Plan with this remarkable group, which included Jim McNeil, one of the writers of the Brundtland report, Pierre-Marc Johnson, and David Johnston, principal of McGill University, who chaired our discussions with a mixture of brilliance and modesty.

In April 1990, we reached the stage of public consultations. The cabinet authorized the publication of an exploratory document soliciting public reaction to the plan's main proposals.

Setting the question in a planetary perspective, the document listed the policy initiatives for implementing the concept of sustainable development. It insisted on a reform of economic decision-making. Scientific research and partnership agreements topped the list of proposed actions. The plan, however, strongly supported government responsibility. It stressed its role as coordinator, and contained a series of legislative and regulatory measures.

I was eager to prevent the Green Plan from becoming a pretext for inaction. I started work on environmental assessment legislation, draft regulations on pulp-and-paper-mill emissions, transborder shipments of toxic wastes, and gas emissions from motor vehicles. I prompted the appointment of a commission of inquiry into the safety of petroleum transportation off the Pacific coast, and signed several agreements with the provinces, one of them ensuring respect for the environmental jurisdiction of each level of government. With Québec, I concluded agreements on joint decontamination of the

St. Lawrence River, and organized the first operational twinning of a federal and a provincial park. After announcing the establishment of the Saguenay marine park, we were able to sign an agreement with Québec harmonizing the activities of the new park with those of another park Québec already operated onshore. Regarding visitors' instructions, we also managed to work out a compromise between the application of Bill 101 and the requirements of federal official bilingualism.

Things did not work out as smoothly, at first, with Saskatchewan and Alberta. Jurisdictional boundary lines are rather fuzzy in environmental matters. The word does not even appear in the Constitution, so that both Ottawa and the provinces are able to point to various sections of the British North America Act to support their respective initiatives.

Alberta had decided to build several ultramodern paper mills along the Athabaska River and its tributaries. However, a dispute arose between Ottawa and Edmonton over the environmental impact of establishing the first mill near the city of Athabaska. Part of the impact came under federal jurisdiction, particularly regarding fisheries legislation. My department informed the Alberta government that it would not accept Alberta's unilateral assessment and would request participation in order to meet the requirements of federal evaluation procedures.

We were not too happy with this operation. We were forced into proselytizing by a recent federal court decision on the Rafferty-Alameda Dam, under construction in Saskatchewan premier Grant Devine's own riding. The courts had nullified the federal permit granted the previous year on the grounds that Ottawa had failed to conduct the necessary impact studies required under its own jurisdiction. The decision mentioned aquatic fauna, migratory birds, and fluctuations in the flow of the Souris River, which cuts across the North Dakota border and then reenters Manitoba.

The decision had disastrous consequences, since voiding the federal permit halted construction work on the dam.

The court drew the obligations it attributed to the federal government from a directive passed in the last days of the Trudeau government. Contrary to the opinion of legal experts in justice, Judge Cullen said the directive had the force of law. Its provisions, originally thought of as pious wishes, now imposed constraining obligations on federal authorities. Later, similar litigation forced suspension of work on the Oldman River Dam in Alberta as it was nearing completion. In both cases, hundreds of millions of dollars had already been spent.

The result was that federal inaction threatened all projects, provincial ones included, that had impact on the environment, even within a single field of federal jurisdiction. Anyone would be able to obtain an injunction to stop construction.

I spent part of the summer of 1989 in difficult negotiations with then Alberta minister Ralph Klein, former mayor of Calgary, whom I had met in Paris. I wanted to establish with him a mode of federal participation in impact studies. Our discussions, punctuated by denunciations of federal intrusion, led to an agreement on a joint assessment of the project, the pooling of government resources, and shared nominations to the committee in charge of the operation.

Alberta was therefore the first province to bear the brunt of the interventionist policy forced on my ministry as a result of a narrow judicial interpretation. Alberta was not the last province, however. The next skirmish was with Québec and concerned the Grande-Baleine River Dam.

A repercussion of this megaproject was Environment Canada's being called to the scene. After passing through the turbines, the waters of the Great Whale River flowed into Hudson Bay, which is federal territory. In this particular case, no one could challenge Ottawa's obligations to evaluate, in conformation with its directive, the accumulation of toxic mercury in the water caused by flooding the land above the dam. As the water eventually flowed into Hudson Bay, the same considerations applied to the impact of ecological changes on sea mammals in the bay. An important colony of beluga whales had established a habitat there.

A sovereign Québec should come to some agreement with its American and Canadian neighbours on the assessment and mitigation of the impact of these kinds of projects.

From the moment my ministry was obliged to conduct impact

studies for its own areas of jurisdiction and Québec undertook a similar exercise, there were severe risks of incompatibilities and delays. For instance, let's say the federal regulations required public hearings while Québec's Bureau d'audiences publiques sur l'environnement (Bureau of Public Hearings on the Environment) did not. It would be safe to say that, under these conditions, the Québec assessment would not have the credibility of the federal procedure, which is a more transparent one.

I told my counterpart on the Québec side that, in the event of a federal withdrawal, anyone, starting with the Cree and the Inuit, could halt Hydro-Québec's construction work with a mere injunction.

So I offered an agreement similar to the one Alberta had just accepted. But discussions bogged down. There were charges of federal intrusion. The upshot was that precious time was lost. Then there was a breakthrough. Thanks to the efforts of David Cliche, my negotiator, and Hydro-Québec's negotiator, Bernard Roy, everything was eventually settled along the lines of my original offer. It was only a few days before my resignation, so I am not aware of what happened later. All I know is they postponed signing the agreement and there were more delays and mutual recriminations. Finally, at the beginning of 1992, the two parties signed the same agreement that I had proposed two years earlier, without any substantial changes. Had it been signed then, the assessment reports would already have been in, allowing work to resume on the project. An agreement would have been helpful in the economic crisis that followed. The issue gathered mud as it dragged on. The situation opened the door to the propaganda of the Native peoples, to the cancellation of power contracts, and to virulent foreign protests. The harm Québec suffered from delays at Grande-Baleine will not soon be repaired.

In spite of all the difficulties, I found my work absorbing. I was even reconciled to the kind of college life that a minister must lead (the cabinet being the classroom; the caucus, the school; and the House of Commons, the playground). I was travelling more than ever all over Canada.

My most pleasant responsibility was national parks. Like Jean

Chrétien, I saw the Rocky Mountains and I was impressed. There is no doubt that Canada is a beautiful country, blessed with natural resources. Our physical heritage is certainly not lacking in abundance. Parks Canada is one of the federal government's greatest successes. The parks, of which the first — Banff — was established in 1887, are superbly run, staffed, and maintained. The success of the organization rests on personnel with team spirit and a strong tradition of professionalism and commitment. But the national fault line also runs through Parks Canada. Most of the money has been spent outside Québec. The two governments have never been able to agree on a system of property ownership for national parks in Québec. Ottawa insists on outright ownership, which Québec refuses. There are two exceptions, the Saint-Maurice and Forillon parks, which are due to Chrétien and a long-lease formula to which the parties agreed. The Mauricie and Gaspé regions each gained a fine park, providing a lesson in efficiency and aesthetics regarding parks management. As an enthusiastic forest and alpine hiker, I could see the difference between federal and Québec attitudes towards parks. Québec opens parks but does not do enough work on them. I am thinking of parks like Hautes-Gorges in Charlevoix and Bic near Rimouski. There are few signs, groomed paths, service installations, or patrols. I confess I have occasionally been weak enough to wonder why we did not let the federal government spend its money in Québec instead of having it invest the funds elsewhere. After all, Ottawa won't run away with the few mountains, lakes, and forests it might have embellished for our enjoyment.

The money spent by Ottawa on its latest park shows how much we have lost. Just to open the South Moresby Park, in British Columbia, and proceed with the first installations, the federal government has spent $106 million. This budget does not include indemnities to purchase cutting rights already granted to private enterprise.

The decision was made a short time before I took over the ministry. Implementing it gave rise to one of the problems I had to solve. The new park's land is claimed by the Haida nation, which lives on parts of it. Parks Canada was unable to open the park: the Haidas, who do not consider themselves Canadians and have never signed a treaty with anyone, intended to behave as a sovereign nation on their island. They refused access to tourists and vacationers, even those with Canadian passports. The only passport the Haidas recognized was their own, and they would deliver one for a fee. They also prevented Parks Canada from undertaking any maintenance work on the island. Worst of all, they refused to negotiate.

I decided to go there to persuade them to negotiate an agreement that, without prejudice to their claims, would allow park operations. The land of the Haida is at the end of the world, way up north, close to Alaska. A helicopter set me down in the village. I was taken to the longhouse, a communal structure where the elders meet, sitting on benches along the walls. There was absolute silence. In the centre, in a sunken area, stood a long table. I was asked to sit at the end of it, facing Miles Richardson, the young chief who had just graduated from university. The elders, sitting on the benches against the walls, observed me and waited for me to begin. I explained the purpose of my visit. After a while, some of the elders drifted down one by one to the table. The most senior of the group started speaking, enumerating his people's grievances. Negotiations had started.

Before leaving the village, I presented Richardson with a sacrificial Haida plate sculpted in wood. The federal government had acquired the two-metre-long plate from a museum in New York City, where it had been on show for decades. It dated from the late nineteenth century and was from South Moresby. From the emotion they showed on receiving the plate, I gathered that my hosts appreciated the symbolic gesture I made in the name of the Canadian government. This did not stop them from driving a hard bargain during the long months ahead. Richardson, who must have studied negotiating at university, gave us a rough time. We reached an agreement in principle before my resignation. The Haidas approved it in a referendum.

I had a similar experience with another group, the Attikamek-Montagnais of the lower north shore of the St. Lawrence River. In this case, I signed the agreement myself. Some time before, at the francophone summit in Dakar, Prime Minister Mulroney opened the conference in Ouoloff, one of the Senegalese languages. I wanted to imitate him and learned by heart in Montagnais the first few sentences of my speech. The audience was tactful enough to applaud me, pretending they understood what I had said.

On these two occasions I was accompanied by Audrey, who had become my wife. We had a travelling companion nine months after our wedding. This was Alexandre, who, until the birth of his brother Simon, travelled with us to Europe, California, Washington, Toronto, and Vancouver. I flew for the first time when I was twenty-six. By his first birthday, Alexandre had made his twenty-fifth flight. I think this is what they call a generation gap.

Environmental problems are international in scope. Each country pays the price of others' carelessness. Most are aware they must combine their efforts to prevent global warming, protect the ozone layer, and prohibit the transport of toxic wastes. Environment Canada spends a good part of its time in international meetings, negotiating common policies. I enjoyed this type of activity, which allowed me to make use of my experience as a negotiator and diplomat. It was a hectic life. One day I would be speaking before the United Nations in New York, the next before a committee of the Bundestag in Bonn. Then there would be a ministerial meeting in London, a speech to make in Washington, followed by one in Paris before the French Senate.

I had the impression that my relations with the prime minister had recovered. After we announced Alexandre's birth to Audrey's family and to mine, Mulroney was the first person I called in the early hours of the morning, at the end of November 1989. Audrey and I were touched by Mila's visit to the hospital.

In fact, everything was going well. I had developed close alliances and friendly ties with several cabinet colleagues. English Canada seemed more receptive to me. My performance as minister got an *A* on several occasions from the English-language press. My Green Plan was gathering support in the cabinet and the public service. The prime minister promised financial support at the rate of $5 billion over a period of five years.

He had been right: environment was the right spot for me.

However, the real issue, the one which had drawn me into federal politics, was the Meech Lake accord. It was not doing well at all. It clamoured for attention, in spite of my environmental enthusiasm. Even Alexandre's arrival did not distract me for long from the agony surrounding the accord. In English Canada, the latest polls indicated rejection. New Brunswick and Manitoba were stiffening their resistance. Québec was becoming impatient. The decibel level was rising everywhere.

In the new year, everyone realized with apprehension that we were on the last stretch, that the countdown was no longer in years but in months, and soon in weeks and then in days. As time ran out, more urgent questions would emerge. What was in store for us at the end of this sprint? The desired revival or defeat? Solidarity or dissension? If defeated, what would happen to government cohesion, Québec's aspirations, personal destinies, friendship, loyalty? Loyalty to whom and to what?

15

The Break

I knew right from the start that Meech would not be easy.

In May 1987, on the eve of Mitterrand's visit, Pierre Trudeau had lashed out against the accord, signed on April 30. He accused Brian Mulroney of being a coward. In September 1987, Frank McKenna was elected premier of New Brunswick on a promise of blocking ratification of the accord, sending Richard Hatfield into oblivion. Eight months later, Manitoba voters fired Howard Pawley, replacing him with Gary Filmon. It was as if the signers of the accord were under a curse, like the ill-fated archaeologists in Tintin's *Seven Balls of Crystal* after their digs desecrated the land of the Incas.

In spite of everything, it was still realistic to expect that common sense would triumph. How could one imagine that English Canada would pass up the opportunity of obtaining — so cheaply — Québec's assent to the Constitution of 1982? After all, the accord had the signature of eleven first ministers and the official support of three national parties. Gary Filmon himself, in November 1988, had promised he would ratify it.

Beau or not, the *risque* was mine, and I intended to go through with it. At no point in my environmental proselytizing did I stop worrying about the fate of Meech. Starting in the winter of 1989, I gave some twenty speeches, all in Québec, on the beginnings and the development of the current situation. I explained the meaning of the course followed by Québec Conservatives under the leadership of Mulroney and the opportunity being offered English Canada. The speeches were generally improvised, but I refined them from one time to the next. In November 1989, I got a transcript of a speech I had just given at Val-d'Or to a crowd that had been particularly enthusiastic. It was later distributed to members of the Québec caucus. On rereading it, I recognize many elements of my comments in this book:

> Next June, our course will bring us closer to our fault line. Everyone must understand this and be prepared to accept the consequences of their decision. Let no one assume that Québec's spirit is broken. We have always lived upright, with self-respect and the knowledge of who we are. Whatever happens, Québec will continue living according to its aspirations.

These statements never earned me any disapproval. In fact, they represented the party line: Meech could not be modified, and its rejection would provoke readjustments that would prove painful but still form part of Québécois continuity.

I could see, once ratification could be taken for granted in Québec, that it was more logical to address my plea to English Canada. Yet I could not help noticing that the accord's unpopularity was paralysing my English-speaking cabinet colleagues. Few of them were willing to go out and sell the accord to their fellow citizens. And if they did, it was only with a few phrases here and there in their speeches. Though I was not the most suitable spokesman, I began, for lack of other volunteers, to address English-speaking Canadians towards the middle of 1989.

In Ontario and several western provinces, I developed similar arguments and described Québec's drive for its own economic and political development. At public meetings, on television and radio, it was always the same conclusion: Meech must be ratified *as is*. Apart from the prime minister, no one in the cabinet was as intensely committed as I was to promoting Meech as much in English Canada as in Québec.

Because of the way the situation was evolving, I thought I should emphasize defence of the accord in English Canada. I was seriously worried about certain rumours going around. Officially, Lowell Murray was in charge of constitutional matters. But in practice, the prime minister had shifted the responsibility to a small group that included, apart from Senator Murray, Norman Spector and Paul Tellier. Everything was considered, contemplated, and decided behind closed doors. No francophone minister was involved, and I don't think any of my English-speaking colleagues — except, perhaps, Don Mazankowski — were called upon to contribute to the government's strategy.

It was not necessary to be particularly prescient to be aware that firmness in certain areas was actually going soft. I felt that the integrity of the original accord was in jeopardy. From all over English Canada, the prime minister was being accused of inflexibility and lack of imagination. People said he was intransigent for not reopening the accord of June 1987. I suspected government insiders of seeking some accommodation to overcome opponents' preconceptions.

In November, I applied myself to preparing two speeches that I later delivered in Ontario and New Brunswick. In Moncton, I pointed to the fact that Québec had little room to manoeuvre:

> Québec's position, which is that of all the signatories, far from being extreme, is minimal. And Premier Bourassa, in the name of Québec's historical interests, is bound by the actual contents of the accord. In other words, we must exclude the possibility of reopening the accord.

In Toronto, I hammered home the same point, pointing to the minimal character of Québec's five conditions for accepting the Constitution. With calculated sobriety, I drew attention to the consequences of failure:

> I do not know if the failure of the Meech Lake accord would result in political rupture. I do not know if Canada would recover. But I am sure it would provoke a psychological break, and I ask opponents of the Meech Lake accord to think it over. Québec could promote its distinc-

tiveness by indifference towards the rest of Canada. It will not withdraw within itself, nor will it build barriers against the rest of Canada. On the contrary, Québec will want to be open to the whole world. But it will also want to be as autonomous as possible.

In mid-January 1990, I resolved to intensify my campaign in English Canada, where only anti-Meech voices were heard. At certain times, the debate seemed to be mired in stupidity: some people claimed the accord would force women to have babies. I offered to work with some of the prime minister's staff on a hard-hitting speech he would deliver in English Canada to promote Meech. Without actually being turned down, my proposal met with the indifference of certain members of the prime minister's entourage; they had decided, I was told, to speak instead about competitiveness.

At the beginning of February, *Le Devoir* held a ceremony in its offices to unveil a plaque in memory of its founder, Henri Bourassa. I took advantage of the occasion to reaffirm the inviolable nature of the accord signed by the first ministers. I also gave an idea of what Canada could expect without ratification.

Very few people will understand why the rest of Canada could reject Québec's outstretched hand. Even fewer Québécois would take it lightly that they were being sent back to the solitude to which the ostracism of 1982 had originally confined them. Solitude, when it is imposed by others and shared by many, has a way of changing into solidarity. This is precisely one of the first effects — a beneficial one — of the present debate: for the first time in a long time, a consensus is taking shape in Québec on the essentials. It is expressed in a refusal to dilute the compromise already negotiated and a demand that all signatures at the bottom of the agreement reached on June 3, 1987, be honoured. The consensus also takes the form of a determination to contemplate the consequences with firmness, dignity, and confidence.

Finally, because Bourassa had turned down an invitation to speak before the Empire Club in Toronto, I was the one to address this distinguished assembly. I did not suspect that such a trip could generate so much tension and anxiety in Ottawa. I completed the draft of my speech during the night of February 14, so that the prime minister's office was not able to read it before morning. The telephone assailed my assistant and me just as we were about to fly to Toronto. They were asking for dozens of changes. I dictated several during the trip. The calls resumed when we arrived at the hotel. After hastily scribbling more changes, I ran to the elevator to meet my audience. I was still waiting for a clean version of my speech when the president of the club started introducing me. The text arrived practically as I was walking to the microphone.

I delivered a moderate message, refuting some of the classic objections to the accord. But I repeated to my audience that "the accord is the ultimate compromise, the product of a long and difficult process during which Québec never stopped making concessions." I also criticized the unilateral repatriation of 1982, concluding that

> even in their moments of greatest mistrust, the Québécois never imagined that the pact of 1867 could ever be changed without their consent. Hence the impression they had in 1982 of a breach of trust, of a violation of the national bond's integrity. The descendants of Georges-Étienne Cartier did not expect this from the descendants of John A. Macdonald. Perceived as trickery in Québec, the repatriation of 1982 has placed a time bomb in the political dynamics of this country.

The people at the Langevin Building had got into a lather over nothing. The speech, possibly because it had been so emasculated, fell flat and received no coverage. Whatever the reason, I decided I would never again let anyone reduce my speeches to platitudes, particularly when the speeches set out government policy in very orthodox fashion.

It took me a while to understand that, in fact, government policy was about to change direction. Subsequent events told me why the prime minister and his secret advisers had been so nervous about my defence of Meech *as is* in Toronto.

To begin with, they needed someone in Québec to vouch for them: it would be me. On February 23, I was named minister responsible for Québec, which was a good way of tying my hands. At first, I interpreted it as a gesture of convenience, relations between my predecessor Marcel Masse and the prime minister having been notoriously bad.

I should have known, however, to beware the ides of March. That fateful time set in motion the events leading to my resignation.

The preliminary signs of an about-face on the irreversible character of Meech appeared one by one. With growing frequency, I heard the words *flexibility* and *opening,* as well as certain expressions, such as *to move the furniture around.* I reiterated my opposition to any renegotiation.

Similar rumours must have come to members of Parliament, since the Québec caucus soon showed signs of agitation. Its chairman, André Harvey, convened a special meeting at Meech Lake. It was held on March 13, in the very room where the eleven first ministers had signed the accord. One by one the MPs rose to take stock of the situation. Without revealing any names or details, I can say that many of them experienced pangs of conscience and were on the verge of radical decisions in case the accord was rejected. I confess I shared their agony. Nevertheless, I called on their solidarity until June 23, so that we might use every means to win ratification of Meech *as is.* Until then, we would stick together. This is what we announced at the close of the meeting.

For me, more than ever, *as is* was a rallying cry. But without being aware of it, we were fighting a rearguard action. No one could stop the revisionist surge or put an end to the manoeuvres being hatched without our knowledge in the Langevin Building. Innocent Québec caucus! How many meetings it had called to protest, show its indignation, bare its teeth, only to learn later that the abhorred decision had already been made.

The day after our Meech Lake meeting, Southam News carried a story showing a discrepancy between my position and that of Mazankowski. The latter had said recently that Senate reform was the key to saving Meech. Of course, when westerners speak of Senate reform, they really mean watering down Québec's influence. This did not augur well.

At about the same time, Québec sources told me that a special envoy from Lowell Murray had tried to persuade Québec minister Gil Rémillard, or some of his advisers, to insert in the Meech accord some limitations on the use of the notwithstanding clause. I immediately informed the prime minister of this initiative, voicing my disapproval. The news seemed to surprise him. I was only half-reassured.

A short while later, environmental business took me to Vancouver. There I learned about the McKenna resolution, which had been published in Fredericton and which the prime minister intended to have tabled in the House of Commons for study by a parliamentary committee. The next evening, in Vancouver, I heard his televised address to the nation when he announced the formation of the committee.

No one had told me anything about this before I left Ottawa.

On obtaining a copy of the resolution, I saw that it altered the substance of Meech. It added a dozen new elements, the most significant being a broader federal role regarding linguistic duality. While the accord said it was the federal government's responsibility to *protect* linguistic duality, the McKenna resolution assigned it the additional task of *promoting* that duality. There could be no doubt: the resolution would destroy the fragile equilibrium of 1987.

Murray hastened to say that the resolution was promising. The prime minister said it offered a good basis for discussion. I was asking myself some serious questions. When Benoît Bouchard phoned me, I told him I was both perplexed and anxious. He felt as if the sky had fallen, and said so publicly the next day on the radio. He apologized in a press release later that afternoon before leaving for Florida.

I was puzzled by the haste with which Murray and the prime minister had thrown themselves on the McKenna resolution. In spite of denials of collusion, I could not help wondering about the superb coordination between Ottawa and McKenna, who was the first to plunge his dagger into Meech. At least I could admire the orderliness of the internal sequence. On March 20, 1990, Trudeau published his book, *Les Années Trudeau,* and launched his own fight against Meech. At the same time, Newfoundland's House of Assembly started a new debate on the ratification it had already voted for. On March 21, the

McKenna resolution leaped out of the hat. The next day, in a televised address, Prime Minister Mulroney welcomed this great contribution to Meech's rescue. On March 23, he tabled the resolution in the House of Commons for federal study. It was a brilliant improvization, neutralizing Trudeau's brutal attack, transforming Clyde Wells into a quarrelsome politician, and putting the renegotiation of Meech on the rails.

Once again, I was in a bind and felt I was being manipulated. I could not possibly support the McKenna resolution.

I could see I was being dragged into proceedings that were already a *fait accompli*. At this pace, would they gradually wear down my defence of the accord's unalterable character? Battles like these are waged every day; they do not stand out with the clarity of St. George's combat with the dragon. Within the closed world of politics, courage and compromise are equally valued. Far from being mutually exclusive, the two are indispensable. The second must be employed when the first fails. But it takes a shrewd person to know, at every stage of a blind fight that lasts days and weeks, where the distinction between them lies. Errors of judgement are costly. They lead to one of two extremes to be avoided: intransigence, if the pursuit of compromise is interrupted too soon; cowardice, if it is interrupted too late. Even shunning cowardice may carry a risk: some people call it treason. This is the choice confronting you: to be a traitor in the eyes of your accusers or a coward in your own.

In a normal situation, a political leader or negotiator learns to protect himself from excesses by draping a safety net around the hard core of his principles or his objectives. It gives him room to manoeuvre. By means of successive concessions, traded for corresponding gains, he can practise the art of compromise without sacrificing any of the essentials.

However, in the case of the accord of June 1987, Québec MPs and ministers in Ottawa were in the worst possible situation. The negotiations had already taken place, the compromises had already been made, and the point of equilibrium had been determined. Wherever Bourassa had been, there was nothing left to concede — he had picked everything to the bone. Therefore, from the moment that English Canada managed to restart the negotiations, we were condemned either to intransigence or to treason.

We had not yet reached that point, but I could see more and more clearly how we would soon be confronted with this Manichaean choice. I was told that the whole process was aimed at restoring dialogue and preserving the substance of Meech. In other words, I was not asked to jump into the meat grinder but just to insert a little bit of my tie. Who wants to resign for the tip of his tie? Who doesn't imagine he won't be able to prevent the rest from following?

In the meantime, passing through Toronto, the prime minister kept his distance from the resolution, saying the government was not bound by its contents.

Reluctantly, I made my submission, vowing never again to be taken in. I said I agreed with the creation of a special House committee as an instrument of dialogue, but that, all things considered, Meech had to be approved *as is.*

That was the position I took before the Québec Conservative caucus at its meeting of March 27. Its members were torn. Resignation rumours were running all over Parliament Hill. I reminded them we had agreed to stay together until June 23, the deadline for the ratification of Meech. We all felt that we could stick with our resolve only as long as Meech was intact. Accordingly, I expressly warned them that the special committee's report might derail Meech altogether. I explicitly mentioned the changes proposed in the McKenna resolution, which Senator Arthur Tremblay had analysed during the meeting, comparing its content with the provisions of the accord of June 3, 1987. If it departed from Meech, the report could bring everything into question before the fatal deadline of June 23. This is why, as I came out of the caucus, I repeated that the special committee should not prevent the ratification of the accord *as is* — that no accompanying resolution should affect its essential elements.

Organized at the end of March, the special committee began its work under the chairmanship of Jean Charest, a trusted protégé of the prime minister. Mulroney and I agreed that this brilliant young lawyer from Sherbrooke, one of the few perfectly bilingual people in the House, was the ideal choice. When I approached him on behalf of the prime minister, he readily accepted. He showed so little surprise that I have always wondered if he had been tipped off. Or maybe I imagined it. In any case, the cavalier way I had been shifted aside on this issue had left me with few illusions about my relationship with the prime minister.

The spring was being wound ever tighter, and the gulf between Québec and English Canada was widening. On April 5, Liberals and Péquistes in the National Assembly in Québec voted to reject the McKenna resolution and assert the inviolable character of the Meech Lake accord. Two days later, there was a clap of thunder: former premier Brian Peckford's resolution ratifying the accord was revoked by members of Newfoundland's House of Assembly led by newly elected Clyde Wells. The machinery, which had been set in motion in March, was now completely out of control. Everything was tumbling down in an unstoppable landslide.

I learned of Newfoundland's revocation on a bright Friday morning at the Château Frontenac in Québec City. Rémillard and I met that day to sign the negotiated agreement for the Saguenay marine park with its management integrated with the adjoining provincial park. It was a minor and amicable example of cooperation between Ottawa and the provinces. However, the peaceful scenario was shattered into a thousand pieces before the bewildered guests, who witnessed the most extraordinary release of pent-up emotions. The ink at the bottom of the document was not even dry when reporters started peppering us with questions about the latest news from Newfoundland.

Rémillard, usually so calm, and I were practically competing to display the most aggressive reaction. Knowing that Newfoundland's blow would aggravate the revisionist pressures that the McKenna resolution was bringing to bear on the accord, I gave way to indignation. I accused Wells of having torn out a page from the legislative annals of his province, and I denounced his unreasonable gesture. Then I issued the warning that set off the powder keg: "English Canada will have to choose between Newfoundland and Québec."

Anglophone media swooped down on me. In minutes I had expended the small political capital that I had laboriously accumulated in English Canada over fifteen months of demanding work at Environment Canada.

The following Tuesday, Brian Tobin, MP from Newfoundland, launched a violent attack in the House, daring me to repeat my admonishments. I took the advice of my colleagues around me and turned a deaf ear. Tobin then shouted out that I was spineless, a coward.

I jumped up and said I was ready to repeat everything the media had reported. "I will never accept that Québec be made to feel guilty for seeking ratification of the Meech Lake accord, which has already been approved by this House," I said. And then I added that I did not see "why I should repudiate an agreement approved by ten provincial premiers two years ago, even though some of them are rejecting it now." The whole thing degenerated into a tavern brawl; Tobin shouted that I was inept for a federal role, and I invited him to step outside.

It wasn't over yet. Ten days later, John Nunziata, an Ontario MP, took up the charge. This candidate for the Liberal leadership was taking part in a debate with his opponents in Halifax. He thought he'd please his audience by calling Québec separatists "traitors" and "racists." A group of Québec Conservatives raised a question of privilege to which Nunziata would respond on April 25. I wanted to take part in the debate and informed the prime minister, who vetoed the idea. He reiterated his interdiction publicly, before the members of the national caucus. I went to the hearing where the Liberal representative was expected to retract his insults. Instead of limiting himself to an apology, Nunziata went into a series of verbal contortions about the definition of treason and ended with an allusion to cabinet members who "ask Canadians to choose between Newfoundland and Québec." Obviously, he was referring to me.

The prime minister, I now realize, must have thought that my public flareups on the respect due to the terms of the accord were harming the "flexible" policy he had in mind. Someone had to set things right, for the memory of Lévesque and the democratic ideal of his approach. I said in the House:

I knew Mr. Lévesque personally. Mr. Lévesque was a great democrat, a man whose democratic and peaceful character all Canada should appreciate, a man who led a very difficult debate in an extremely unsettled situation and brought it to a democratic conclusion with the verdict that we know. I believe we owe this man and those who supported him the respect of this House, at the very least.

Addressing the Opposition, I continued:

Do not ask us to forget that we are Québécois. Do not ask us to forget that we belong to a society that owes its survival solely to a perpetual struggle.

In passing, I reproached Chrétien who, when asked by a reporter to distance himself from his colleague's statement, had nothing better to say in defence of the "separatists" than that they were "not all criminals and racists."

My final words were addressed to those who wanted to scrap Meech:

The Meech Lake accord is the road along which the prime minister is leading the country, by virtue of a commitment made in 1984 and that he has respected, a road that all heads of government in Canada, in 1987, have agreed to travel. . . . I hope, Mr. Speaker, that everyone will avoid the kind of statement that revives memories unfortunately too close to us, memories that risk reviving embers that only a true reconciliation can extinguish. A reconciliation with honour and enthusiasm. With honour — yes, honour! — because a nation demands respect! Yes, and enthusiasm because a nation needs hope.

In the midst of this political storm, my advisers and I were nervously preparing for the important Bergen Conference in Norway, where some fifty countries, including the Soviet Union, would be asked to set a goal to reduce carbon dioxide emissions, the leading cause of global warming. The conference, scheduled to start May 7, would unfold in two steps. During the first week, various organizations (young people, environmentalists, businesspeople, scientists, and so on) would prepare their statements and their recommendations. During the next four days, ministers from the participating countries would deliberate and make decisions. Canada's delegation was strong in numbers and quality. Pierre-Marc Johnson was to be general reporter of the conference, which had been the product of a year's intensive international preparation.

Audrey was already in Paris with Alexandre at his Parisian grandmother's place. I was to meet them Wednesday, May 16, after Bergen, and fly home to Montreal with them on the weekend.

The Charest committee was scheduled to table its report on Wednesday, May 18. I expected to be in Ottawa in time to read it and determine with my colleagues what attitude we should take.

I was not expecting the committee to put aside the whole of the McKenna resolution, but I had reason to believe it would not propose any change in the substance of the Meech Lake accord.

Indeed, two or three weeks earlier, towards the end of April, as I listened to the House of Commons debates, Charest sat down next to me. From this conversation, I remembered that the committee would be making proposals compatible with the essential elements of Meech. However, we had to be prepared to make concessions to Native peoples, there being tremendous pressure from this direction. In a word, things seemed to be going well.

I communicated whatever anxieties I still had to the prime minister in one or two telephone conversations. They touched less on the Charest report than on the slippage to which he would be exposed on the homestretch by virtue of his conditioning as a negotiator. A professional negotiator will occasionally want a settlement for its own sake. To achieve this he desperately needs room to manoeuvre. I only had to recall my own experience to understand the temptations facing the prime minister. Since those needing to be mollified were Wells, Filmon, McKenna, and Carstairs, any classical bargaining strategy would necessarily have to be at Québec's expense. I spoke even more clearly of my misgivings during our last telephone conversation before my departure the morning of May 10 or 11, just before Mulroney himself flew to Toronto. Nothing he told me indicated that the grand design was already being executed. We agreed to talk about it on my return.

On the morning of May 11, Tellier called, asking to see me. As usual he offered to come by. I told him I would drop by his office on my way to Mirabel later in the morning. If I remember correctly, he had also called Benoît Bouchard. Since Bouchard could not make it, the meeting was a tête-à-tête.

The clerk of the Privy Council summed up the political situation and came right to the point. The opposition to Meech was coming from the Liberals in Newfoundland, New Brunswick, and indirectly, Manitoba, where Carstairs had paralysed Premier Filmon. It would be possible to stop these recalcitrants if they did not have the green light from Chrétien. Tellier already knew the price of this alliance: federal responsibility for the promotion of linguistic duality as part of the Canadian Constitution.

I could hardly believe my ears. Five minutes before leaving for the airport, my suitcases in the car waiting for me, my staff already in Bergen, after months of hide-and-seek and soothing reassurances, they were letting the cat out of the bag: we had to make a deal with Chrétien, who represented everything I abhorred about politics. Our alliance with him would be sealed by the dilution of Meech. For two years now, I had been campaigning for Meech *as is,* according to government policy and the party line. Were they really asking me to help Chrétien collapse the floor into the basement?

That was precisely what they were asking. Could I sell this reversal to the Québec caucus? "No," I answered. "Why not?" Tellier wanted to know. "Because I can't even sell it to myself," I said. He quoted the law on official languages in which article 43 gives the secretary of state a certain role in the promotion of official bilingualism. I drew his attention to the fundamental difference between a simple parliamentary law and an obligation inscribed in the Constitution. Not to mention the fact, as I told him, that in spite of their limited application, the provisions of the Official Languages Act had drawn

stormy protests from Québec. The uproar had come to an end only
after Ottawa undertook to apply them in harmony with the government of Québec.

This conversation with Tellier certainly must have taken place at
the instigation of the prime minister, alarmed by my apprehension.
I had no doubt, either, that he would learn about my refusal to reopen
Meech and make a deal with Chrétien, his newfound ally. Thinking
about the matter on my way to Mirabel, I found encouragement in
the fact that, before going ahead, he had felt the need to consult me.
In spite of everything, I remained convinced my opposition would
lead him to stick to the negotiated accord and not compromise
himself with Chrétien.

The Bergen discussions, lively at the beginning, soon hardened,
putting Canada on the spot. We found ourselves opposing the Americans, who confirmed the hesitation they had expressed a few months
earlier in Washington about further cuts in carbon dioxide emissions.
They refused to set a ceiling that would reduce, by the year 2000,
emissions to their 1990 levels. Canada had allies, but their numbers
were dropping day by day. But we held out until the last night. In the
early morning we agreed on a wording that met our objectives.

As planned, on Wednesday evening I joined my family in Paris.
We stayed with Patricia and Marc Lortie, who had been kind enough
to invite us. Recently posted to the Canadian Embassy, Lortie had
been the prime minister's spokesman. During that period, I had
forged with him professional and personal ties. Along with Bob
Fowler, he had been one of the first to assist me with his diplomatic
experience.

Camille Guilbault, an assistant to the prime minister, had left a
message to call her. When I did, I learned that the Charest report
would be coming out the next day and that it contained certain
"delicate" elements. She suggested I avoid all public statements before
my return, to which I agreed. The next day I had the report faxed to
me and read it in the peace and quiet of the apartment on rue
Saint-Dominique.

I could not believe my eyes. The Conservatives had agreed with
the Liberals and the New Democrats on the modification of at least

two essential points in the accord: the federal government's role in the promotion of linguistic duality, and the subordination of Québec's distinct character to the Charter of Rights. Many of the twenty-one other recommendations represented setbacks for us, such as the establishment of new provinces without Québec's assent and, as regards Senate reform, the replacement after three years of the rule of unanimity by a less constraining form of veto.

The veil had fallen: Tellier's words the preceding Friday had nothing exploratory about them. The alliance with Chrétien had already been consummated, or was on the point of being so. The strategy and positioning of the government of which I had been a part for more than two years had finally been revealed to me: the 1987 accord had been downgraded to nothing more than a negotiation paper accommodating the shopping list of each of the other provinces, as set out in the Charest report. In the end, Chrétien had triumphed over the prime minister's closest friends.

Benoît Bouchard and Charest were trying to reach me by phone. I wasn't taken in by their behaviour, which consisted of speaking to me only after the Charest report had been tabled. They had made their bed. I did not need them to understand what had happened and I could guess the rest. All I had to do was decide if I would participate in the outcome.

I remembered a telegram I had to send. A few weeks earlier, the Parti Québécois had invited me to a meeting of its national council that would be held May 19 in Alma. I wanted to show up, if only as a matter of courtesy. After all, the meeting was taking place in my riding. I had many friends in the party who had put us all in Ottawa, Mulroney included. Knowing I could not attend because of my trip to Europe, I thought of sending a telegram. I had had no time to prepare it before leaving for Bergen. I had put the invitation in my briefcase, intending to wire from Bergen. During one of the sessions, I worked out a rough draft, which got lost among my papers. In Paris, on Thursday morning, I suddenly realized how urgent the matter was. I can see now that the Charest report had put me in such a mood that I was writing with a rather heavy hand. The lost Bergen draft had been more wooden than the version sent from Paris:

Dear compatriots from all over Québec,

Alma welcomes you with open arms and warm hospitality. I heartily join my colleague, the provincial member for Lac-Saint-Jean in Québec, Jacques Brassard, to wish Mr. Jacques Parizeau and all of you the most fruitful stay among us in what is also our federal riding of Lac-Saint-Jean.

During the council meeting, you will be discussing, among other things, the problem of the environment. The future of nations and of our planet is largely tied to the success of the fight against pollution. You understand how high the stakes are. We support your commitment and your determination to preserve our national heritage.

Your meeting will also celebrate the tenth anniversary of one of the high points of Québec's history.

The referendum concerns us all as Québécois. Its commemoration offers another opportunity to recall the sincerity, the pride, and the generosity of the yes we defended at the time, around René Lévesque and his team.

René Lévesque's memory will unite us all this weekend. He was the one who led Québécois to realize they had the inalienable right to decide their own destiny.

Even today, as I read this text again, I have trouble understanding why the reference to Lévesque and the right to self-determination so shocked English Canada. There are so many Conservative ministers and MPs who supported the yes side during the referendum campaign in 1980. Are they expected to repent publicly for doing so? I am convinced they are all proud of it and that many will remember it in the next referendum.

I had made arrangements for getting the telegram to the meeting. David Cliche, a true Péquiste, planned to attend, and we had agreed that I would address my telegram to him so that he would hand it over to the meeting's organizers. My press officer, Micheline Fortin, who was with me in Europe, typed the text and sent it to Cliche. I admit that for a moment I dwelt on the thought that the message bearer was the son of Robert Cliche.

However, the Charest report was uppermost in my mind. I saw they expected moral support from me, if only through my silence. I would have to take back everything I had said in the last two years about the inviolable nature of the accord. My statement about a reconciliation "with honour and enthusiasm" was coming back to haunt me. I could think of nothing else as I walked the streets of Paris and strolled through the halls of the Marmottan Museum and the gardens of Giverny. One afternoon, ambling along the Seine with Audrey, Alexandre in his stroller, the memory of an article, published in the *Toronto Star* on the eve of my departure for Bergen, suddenly intruded on my thoughts. The author had speculated on possible resignations by Québec Conservatives if Meech failed. He analysed the cases of ministers Monique Vézina, Benoît Bouchard, Marcel Masse, ending with my own. He then reported the confidence of a Québec Conservative organizer: "You must always remember that when there is a conflict between a principle and a limousine, it is usually the limousine that wins." Was this the measure of respect given Québec ministers in Ottawa? In any event, I tried to keep my mind off the black Crown Victoria Ford waiting for me at Mirabel.

Towards midnight on Saturday, the eve of my return to Montreal, the phone got me out of the shower. It was Tellier. Speaking in solemn tones, he kept repeating the word *telegram* in every sentence: "reaction to the telegram," "the telegram badly received . . ." The monologue was surrealistic: he kept talking about the telegram, I kept thinking of the Charest report. I was wrapped in a bath towel and dripping water all over Marc Lortie's kitchen floor. I can still hear myself shouting, "I don't give a damn about the telegram. The Charest report, that's the problem. You knew I could not accept these changes. Wait till Monday, things will be happening."

The next day, on the plane at ten thousand metres above the Atlantic, I came across Marc Lalonde, who said he found the Charest report to his taste. Coming from him, that approval didn't help me one bit.

When I arrived at Mirabel, there was a call from Luc Lavoie, who was then in the prime minister's office. He wanted to see me that evening in Ottawa. We had a long and painful conversation. I told

Lavoie frankly that it was impossible for me stay in the cabinet and in the Conservative party. They had used me and then presented me with a *fait accompli*. The prime minister knew I would abhor the Charest report, which is why he had been wheeling and dealing with Chrétien. He had gambled on our thirty years of friendship, on my weakness in accepting to play the game on the McKenna resolution, on my attachment to Environment Canada, on the five billion dollars he had promised me for the Green Plan, and on the difficulty of breaking with a party and a whole group of friends. He was wrong, that's all.

Lavoie left me, probably to report to the interested party. As for the rest, I had already discussed the problem with Audrey in case I stayed in politics as member of Parliament. After discussing the changed lifestyle and the financial consequences, she said, "I met an ambassador, I married a minister, and tomorrow I will live with a member of Parliament." She added with a smile, "What is the next stage?"

For the first time in my life, I was a father. I cared about what Alexandre might think of a fifty-one-year-old man who sacrificed his dignity. I wanted him to be as proud of his father as I was of mine and as my father was of my grandfather. I did not want this chain of pride and love to be broken.

However, my future judge seemed content with his bottle. After feeding him at five o'clock in the morning, I could not go back to sleep, though I was still jet-lagged. I sat down at the dining-room table to draft my letter of resignation. At eight o'clock, Pierre de Bané called, advising me to soften the impact of my telegram. I was touched, but I replied that I had gone beyond that stage: the die was cast and I was going to leave the cabinet.

On Monday, May 21, Ottawa was celebrating the Queen's birthday, while Québec fêted Dollard des Ormeaux. It is a strange country that can't even agree on its celebrations. The joy of one is balanced by the indifference of the other.

At eleven, I called in a typist to copy the first draft of the letter. I spent a large part of the afternoon correcting it and polishing successive versions. Many phone calls and visits, attempts to dissuade me from burning my bridges, interrupted my work.

Tellier asked to see me. I crossed Wellington Street and went up to his office.

After going over the sequence of events, I told him I would be resigning that very day. He pleaded with me and finally invoked my friendship with the prime minister and the blow it would cause him.

The ensuing discussion was rather long. No one, I pointed out, could deny the facts: specifically, transforming the Charest report into a basis for renegotiating Meech, which was decided without my knowledge and despite what they knew was my position. The prime minister would have to take the turn he had planned by himself and he would have to be happy with his new fellow traveller, Chrétien. The turn was too sharp; centrifugal force was ejecting me from the vehicle. I persisted in thinking that the best policy would be to stay the course, brandishing the signed accord. There was neither honour nor enthusiasm at the end of the tortuous road the government was letting itself be pushed into taking: wheeling and dealing behind closed doors and last-minute swaps conjured up by exhausted negotiators in front of urinals.

I did not hide the fact that the rupture in personal relations would be extremely painful. But the circumstances had gone beyond a debt two friends owed each other. They had gone beyond personal ambitions and the squaring of accounts. Even reduced to this level, the friendship of one had not been less than that of the other. Our disagreement touched on the interests and the honour of Québec, the respect for one's commitments and for oneself.

This is the essence of what I explained to Paul.

Silence filled the room. He stood up and said, "Bernard Roy is downstairs. I'll go get him." He was a while coming back, probably because he was informing Roy and the prime minister of our conversation. Walking around the office to stretch my legs, I saw an engraved plaque of the type awarded in bowling tournaments. The inscription expressed to Tellier the gratitude and admiration of the staff of the Information Centre on Canadian Unity. It was that organization's machinations, under Tellier's leadership, that had produced the federal victory over the sovereigntists in 1980. It was an opportune reminder of the true allegiances of the camp I had joined. How could

I be surprised by the pro-Chrétien turnaround of these circumstantial allies? On second thought, it was less a change of path than a return to the fold. After all, hadn't Mulroney himself supported the unilateral constitutional repatriation of 1982?

My determination was stronger than ever. A good thing, too, because I was about to undergo the strongest attack of all. That day, Roy was not in Ottawa by chance. The prime minister was playing the ultimate card. I liked Roy for his sincerity and his sensitivity. Had he still been in the prime minister's office, they could never have played such a game of hide-and-seek with me. His frankness would no doubt have led to a clash, but at least everything would have been in the open. And I would have had a chance to block the manoeuvre.

Within the first minutes of a very intimate conversation, Roy saw, I believe, the irrevocable nature of my decision. Of all the wounds inflicted by my resignation, his were the deepest and most sincere. For my part, I felt he would never understand and that the rupture would extend to him. It saddened me but did not surprise me, so well did I know his quasi-unconditional veneration for Mulroney. The tension rose a notch when he asked if I was ready to see the prime minister. I answered that I did not think it was necessary. Hadn't Mulroney ignored me for the last ten days, preferring to dispatch messengers? Bernard took it badly. "You mean you would go without meeting him?" he asked. I replied: "I won't refuse to see him, if he wants. But, if he thinks he can dissuade me, I wouldn't advise it. I will not change my mind."

Back on Parliament Hill, I had a call from Tellier summoning me to 24 Sussex. "He" wanted to see me. I put my letter of resignation in my pocket and went.

Mulroney met me in his study on the ground floor. He said, "Whatever happens, we won't erase thirty years of friendship." Then, referring to notes on his lap, he broached the subject of the telegram, saying things like, "As prime minister, I can't accept that a minister . . ." I saw that he wanted to represent my departure as a disciplinary measure justified by my behaviour. I wasn't leaving; he was throwing me out. I refused to let this diversion sidetrack me, and I pointed out that the telegram had nothing to do with the fundamental issue. Returning to the Charest report, I said I could not accept it and that this was the reason for my resignation. He replied that there were no serious grounds for my resignation. I stuck to my guns and handed him the letter. He read it attentively, then made two requests: He wanted me to wait until the next day before officially tabling the letter and remove a passage that seemed to annoy him particularly. I had mentioned Trudeau in the letter, recalling that when he was remodelling the Constitution to suit himself, in 1981, he had not dared include the clause on the promotion of bilingualism, yet Mulroney was ready to do so in the wake of the Charest report. I agreed to both requests.

We shook hands on the porch. Then, like someone who has just had a sudden idea, he stopped and said, "Why not simply leave the cabinet but stay in the caucus?" Tension, fatigue, and lack of sleep almost caused me to fall into the trap of saying yes. I hesitated. I said I would think it over and call him back. In my car, I realized that by staying on as a Conservative member of the House, I would be substantiating the prime minister's initial spin, which was that I was being cast out for sending a subversive telegram. His entourage would rush to inform media relations under the courageous cover of ano-nymity that the prime minister had severely censured Bouchard for his seditious telegram; yes, he was fired. The Charest report would disappear in the fog while they railed against the ill-advised scribbler of telegrams. I could see the headlines: "Mulroney cracks the whip. Bouchard fired."

From my office, I called the prime minister to confirm that I was leaving both the cabinet and the caucus. We have not spoken to each other since. The next day, I sent him the final draft of my letter of resignation. It speaks for itself:

Mr. Prime Minister,

When, answering your call a little more than two years ago, I entered political life, all the heads of government in the country had agreed to follow you on the road to national reconciliation. At the time, they all understood that the whole country had to make a gesture of reconciliation towards Québec, which had been ostracized by Mr. Pierre Elliott Trudeau's power move.

Following arduous negotiations, the Meech Lake accord determined the conditions under which Québec would accept the Constitution. Many people in Québec thought the conditions were rather inadequate. Some said Québec was too generous in wiping out the villainy of 1982. However, in their hearts, Québécois wanted to hold out their hands to their fellow citizens and spare themselves the trauma of another constitutional crisis. They wanted the future of the country to rest on an open and generous form of federalism, different from the present one in which Québécois feel excluded and misunderstood.

Once again, armed with patience and ready to give their trust, they supported Premier Bourassa when he cut to the bone the price of Québec's pardon and its return to the constitutional family. This was also the way I saw the situation, and it inspired me to enter politics. In less than six months, I waged two election campaigns — both based on ratification of the Meech Lake accord and the signing of the free-trade agreement.

I assumed that the signatures newly affixed to the Meech Lake accord would be respected.

Like other Québécois, I noted, with growing consternation and sadness, English Canada's reactions against the accord. Instead of the expected show of generosity and respect for Québec, the accord emphasized the division in the country and provoked a fresh outbreak of prejudice and emotions that did no one honour. Québec, whose forgiveness was being sought, was being called on the carpet.

Francophones across the country witnessed new displays of intolerance. While the Québec flag was being trampled, supporters of the yes side in the referendum were accused of racism and treason. Like many others, I was surprised to see that those who exalt freedom of expression will not allow a federal minister, ten years after the fact, to recall the altruism, nobility, and pride of René Lévesque and yes supporters. Even the mere mention of self-determination gives them hives.

The height of the irony came when other provinces repudiated the signatures of their premiers (one province particularly distinguished itself by tearing up the act of ratification it had already approved) and then came up with their own demands, their own "shopping lists."

Many of these demands modify essential elements of the accord.

All this is accompanied with incantatory exhortations about flexibility and negotiations. Québec is generally blamed for its lack of flexibility, its refusal to dilute the five meagre conditions it timidly advanced for its constitutional reintegration. I have nothing against the idea of launching another discussion leading to other constitutional changes, such as the equality of the sexes and more secure guarantees for Native peoples. However, I cannot and will not subscribe to a procedure, whatever it might be, that alters the accord itself. This is why I supported the convocation of the Special Committee with the proviso that the Meech Lake accord be accepted as is, without any modifications, at the time or subsequently. Also, on several occasions, I said I could never accept any committee recommendations that might alter the fragile equilibrium established by the accord.

I was astonished last week in Europe to learn that the report proposed twenty-three modifications as a basis for discussion at a future conference of first ministers. Several affect the essential nature of the accord. I am thinking of the levelling of Québec society's distinctive character by inserting in the same clause the equality of New Brunswick's anglophone and francophone communities. I am thinking of the dilution resulting from the joint application of the Charter of Rights and Freedoms. I am also concerned about the recommended suppression of the rule of unanimity for Senate reform and about the risks for Québec's veto inherent in the ambiguous formula of "regional approval."

Above all, I consider totally unacceptable the recommendation giving Parliament and the federal government not only the responsibility for protecting linguistic duality, as stipulated in the Meech Lake accord, but also for promoting it.

The National Assembly of Québec has already expressed, clearly and almost unanimously, its determination to reject any modification to the Meech Lake accord. We already know the fate of a federal-provincial conference in which the prime minister of Canada would submit the sum of the Special Committee's proposals to the provincial premiers. The federal government has to do more than state that it will not undercut what Québec already has. Once it is our official policy not to isolate Québec and to ratify Meech as is, it is contradictory and eminently dangerous to submit for discussions any proposal modifying that accord.

The government of Québec will be unable to subscribe to these proposals. I am sure of it as much as I hope so. Once again, Québec will be isolated. This is what had to be avoided at any cost. The role of victim that was handed Québec in 1982 is not so glorious that Québec should now, in 1990, play the part of guilty party. Because of a hypocritical diversion of the operation's initial concept, certain historians will feel they have authority to blame Québec for scuttling, in 1990, your efforts at national reconciliation. These are the consequences of the dynamics unleashed after tabling the Special Committee's report. This report, I must say, Mr. Prime Minister, seems to me the report of the opponents of the Meech Lake accord. It is not surprising they are so happy with it. I imagine many must be jubilant, Jean Chrétien first among them.

I reject this report and I also refuse to support it with my silence.

I feel a moral obligation to withdraw from your government. I ask you to release me from my ministerial responsibilities and from my responsibilities for Québec.

I wish my successor at Environment Canada all the best and assure him of my support. I hope particularly that you will give him the same support you have given me. I am torn by having to leave this portfolio, knowing the crucial importance of the struggle that must be waged in this realm.

Please transmit to my colleagues in the cabinet and the caucus all my respect and my best wishes. I am honoured to have served with them.

I will not dwell too long on the difficult decision I am communicating to you today. It wounds a very old friendship, one that has stood the test of time. But once a question of principles arises, there is no other choice.

One of the first veterans of sovereignty, I ran the *beau risque,* so well named, and legitimized, by Mr. René Lévesque. No one has done so with as much loyalty as I have.

You must know that I appreciate to the highest degree the qualities of heart and mind you have placed at the service of the country. I would have hoped to be able to help you longer. We have travelled together the same long stretches of road. There had already been some disagreements in our views on the future of the country, but never in the feelings of respect and friendship that we kept alive.

I am all the sadder at what has come between us because I feel a great admiration for the courage and lucidity with which you launched your work of reconciliation.

In any event, my departure will bring relief to those who believe that Québec's representatives in Ottawa should cling unconditionally, if not sacramentally, to the present federal formula.

I will keep my seat as member for Lac-Saint-Jean. After twice electing me to represent them in Ottawa, my fellow citizens have given me the greatest imaginable testimony of their confidence.

I will remain in federal politics, at least for a certain period of reflection and particularly to consult with the people in my riding. I will sit as an Independent in the House of Commons. I will make use of my freedom of speech, fully recovered, in the interests of Québec and of Canada.

I have the profound conviction we must rethink this country. It is necessary to stop trying to fit Québec into the mould of a province like the others. Beyond the legal arguments, there is also a compelling reason: Québécois do not accept that mould. Their reality has an explosive effect on it.

Québécois, in particular, must redefine the degree, the structures, and the conditions of their participation in the Canadian system. To me, it does not matter whether we call it associative, confederative, or anything else. However, it will require another round of negotiations: a true one this time, one concerned with fundamental issues. The negotiations will be genuine because the motivations that govern its dynamic force will be genuine. In other words, it will be necessary to negotiate from a position of strength. Only a Québécois state with a clear mandate based on the recovery of its full attributes will have the proper political authority to negotiate the Canadian association of tomorrow.

As the tribulations of the Meech Lake accord show, English Canada has not taken Québec very seriously with its minimal demands. He who starts negotiations on his knees will end them flat on the ground.

For the time being, the accord must be concluded in its initial form. We must not deviate from it, even at the risk it might fail. That way everybody will be able to identify the wreckers, who otherwise would take on the airs of saviours who have been thwarted in their noble enterprise. I profoundly regret that the Conservative members of the Special Committee formed an alliance with the Liberals of Messrs. Trudeau and Chrétien, and the New Democrats of Ms. MacLaughlin. It was too high a price for unanimity. I would hate that it could be said that the supporters of the Trudeau brand of federalism requested a higher price for their signature than Québec received for its. I also dissociate myself from the equivocal attitude the federal government adopted on the Special Committee's recommendations, which drained Québec's demands of their sense.

In the end, it is better to have honour in disagreement than agreement in dishonour. In any event, nothing could ever be worse than dishonour in disagreement, a fate reserved for those who would attempt, in vain, I hope, to convince Québec to attend another booby-trapped conference with the idea of snatching back ultimate concessions that could be nothing but humiliating.

It pains me to say all these things, particularly to you. They are probably even harder to hear. But I had to do it.

I know you are true to your dreams and to the commitments of your youth. You will accept, I am sure, that I remain true to mine.

Please accept my respects and my gratitude for everything you have done and will do for Québec and Canada.

I then drafted a speech, which I gave that afternoon in the House of Commons from my minister's seat.

It was all over. All that remained was for me to bear the consequences of my decision.

16

Time for Solidarity

After all the anguish and heartbreak of the last days, a feeling of freedom came over me. I recovered the capacity to act and speak as I wished. I could once again set personal goals. My first was to draw closer to my family and to witness the marvellous awakening of love and intelligence in a six-month-old baby. My political program had met an obstacle. I had been used and manipulated. But no one could take away my honour and the respect of my own people.

For now, I had to pick up a lot of loose threads. A minister's time is parcelled out and planned weeks if not months in advance. Before vacating my office, the day of my resignation, I asked my staff to clean up my schedule and to cancel, among other things, an appointment for the next day at the Montreal Chamber of Commerce.

Since the invitation, accepted several weeks earlier, had been addressed to the environment minister, I no longer possessed the required status to give the speech I had drafted on sustainable development. But the Chamber of Commerce refused to cancel: the tickets had already been sold and the expenses for arrangements committed. I sent a message saying I would then have to speak on the political situation. At first they refused, but they finally gave in for lack of any alternative.

Panic overwhelmed me on the way to Montreal the next morning.
I had no written speech, no notes, nothing. Walking along the
corridor in the Queen Elizabeth Hotel to the hall where my audience
was waiting, I had the impression these were the last steps of my
ephemeral political career. Businesspeople scorn noisy resignations.
In 1980, they were almost unanimously in favour of the no side. They
distrust nationalists, and many of them do business with English
Canada. I had a few strikes against me and expected a hostile reaction.

With my courage failing, I entered the room. To my surprise, they
gave me a standing ovation before I had even said a word. From the
podium, I could feel them urging me on. I felt I was in a state of
osmosis with my audience. I described English Canada's inability to
understand the long struggle of Québec society, its imprisonment in
one of the compartments of Canadian federalism, and the inevitability of our collective deployment. The nature of the required changes
went directly against English Canada's conception of the country and
were of such magnitude that they lay beyond the scope of traditional
negotiations. Hence the need to gather together in order to improve
the relative political strength of Québec. To that end, I invited
Québécois to define their political goal, to be sanctioned later by a
referendum. I mentioned sovereignty association as a valid goal.
Otherwise, all we could expect would be more power plays like the
one of 1981–82 and repudiations such as the one that occurred with
Meech. On that point, I even mentioned my grandfather, the settler
from Lac-Saint-Jean, who would have had a great deal of trouble
accepting that one could no longer rely on the signatures of eleven
first ministers. The audience repeatedly interrupted me to show its
approval. I could not recognize in these emotional listeners the
cool-headed administrators who had come to hear a speech on
ecological risks and the appearance of environmental ethics in economic development.

During the long-standing ovation at the end of my speech, I could
not help thinking that important changes were in the making for
Québec. The broken promises of 1980, the isolation of 1981, the
signing in 1982 of the others' Constitution on the lawn of Parliament
Hill, and the reopening of Meech — weren't these more than

Québec's pride could bear? Couldn't we start dreaming again of our own solidarity, ready to be converted into political action? Wasn't Lévesque right to count on such an awakening?

The reaction of these representatives of the Montreal business community was, at least, the beginning of a positive answer.

I got the same reaction, a few days later, at the annual Québec bar association meeting at the Manoir Richelieu in Pointe-au-Pic.

Even though there are many sovereigntists among them, the members of the bar were for me, *a priori,* a hostile audience. The representatives of the federal establishment had a great deal of influence in these kinds of sessions. Moreover, as a professional group, lawyers are close to political and financial power. I remember having worked, in 1977, on a speech that Marc-André Bédard, newly appointed minister of justice, was to give before a meeting of the bar in Montreal. We had discussed at length the opportunity of inserting a presentation of the Lévesque government's sovereigntist commitment. We finally decided to limit ourselves to a brief reference. I was present for Bédard's speech, and I felt the audience tense for the thirty seconds the passage lasted — and the passage was mild compared to what I was planning now.

The agreement with the bar, also made several months earlier, was for a nonpolitical speech. Guy Wells, one of my former Chicoutimi partners, had looked after the arrangements; in spite of the turn of events, he insisted I speak. My reception at the Chambre de Commerce persuaded me to ignore my misgivings. Using basically the same themes as in Montreal, I received the same show of support. Seeing and hearing federalist lawyers I knew noisily applauding and standing, a certain fervour in their eyes, told me that my professional family still considered me one of their own and was telling me to keep going. I never imagined that my colleagues, all rather blasé as speakers and listeners, would react in this way. It was very timely comfort and encouragement, for the spectacle unfolding in Ottawa would plunge anyone into total despair.

It was the week when Meech was dying behind closed doors. Bourassa had made the mistake of joining the others in this snake pit where they merrily nibbled away at Meech day after day. Without any illusions about the effect of my modest contribution, I had advised the premier to avoid this ambush set by Mulroney. The trap was pitifully banal and would never have deceived an experienced negotiator. It consisted of throwing all the cards haphazardly on the table (it was easy to recognize the Charest report), seating the players around the table, closing the doors, raising the temperature and the air pressure, and keeping these beautiful people on the spot until an agreement was reached.

The operation, apart from failing, also resulted in some damage, for Québec traded away the moral legitimacy and historical authority of the accord of June 3, 1987. Bourassa travelled to Ottawa with an agreement to which eleven first ministers had subscribed — something that had never happened in our history — and came back with an indecipherable hodgepodge, full of deletions, additions, and asterisks, stapled to an appendix scrawled by legal experts eager to sanitize Québec's distinct character. Our premier had bartered the signatures of eleven first ministers for the initials of jurists, some of whom were being paid by the federal government. More seriously, he had conceded without any compensation whatsoever the principle of an elected Senate, that is, the recognition of a third legitimacy that would allow a second category of elected Québec representatives in Ottawa to counteract the actions of the National Assembly.

There is also an enigma that defies solution: How could so circumspect an individual as Bourassa, for whom every road is a mine field, lend himself to this outrageous session in which everybody was hugging one another in front of the cameras, pretending to celebrate the conclusion of an unintelligible piece of work that still needed ratification? How could this politician, who fears the power of words as much as the truth of emotion, lapse in such verbal delirium and claim, "Henceforth . . . for all Québécois, Canada is a real country"?

Out of the inexhaustible flux of words and images that television spews out every day, collective memory, unconsciously assuming the role of historian, retains only a few choice ones. The ones surviving the last hours of Meech compose a sequence that says it all, albeit almost subliminally. We see Wells signing during the nocturnal scene at Ottawa's Conference Centre; Bourassa and Mulroney, with fake solemnity, singing "O Canada" together; Native representative Elijah Harper blocking, with a few disdainful strokes of the pen, any desire Manitoba might have for ratifying the accord; and again, Wells, with his intense blue eyes against the red background of the Canadian flag, announcing he would not submit Meech to a vote; Lowell Murray certifying the death of Meech.

The epilogue was Chrétien, falling into the arms of the premier of Newfoundland and acknowledging his debt: "Thanks for all you've done, Clyde."

The signs of political agitation multiplied around me. With no previous consultation, two other members of Parliament, François Gérin and Gilbert Chartrand, resigned from the Conservative caucus in protest against the Charest report. Three others followed in our footsteps after the Meech shipwreck: Nic Leblanc, Louis Plamondon, and Benoît Tremblay. On the Liberal side, Jean Lapierre and Gilles Rocheleau slammed the door, refusing to rally behind Chrétien, their new leader.

The attitude of voters in my riding could not have been more positive. At a brunch that was held on May 27, but organized long before under the banner of my former Conservative association, several hundreds of them supported my resignation. In Montreal, June 25, I walked along rue Sherbrooke to Olympic Stadium, submerged in the immense river of white and blue that seemed unstoppable on its march to sovereignty. Three days earlier, Bourassa, former minstrel of federalism, had hurriedly changed his tune: "English Canada must understand that . . . Québec is, today and forever, a distinct society, free and able to assume its destiny and its development."

Obviously, the wind was rising and pushing Québécois forward. Their political instincts told them the rout of Meech was more than a failure of negotiations. This was not the kind of situation where, after things go wrong, people spit into their hands and start all over again. In this sense, Québécois reaction was not solely one of indignation. Undeniably, there was some. But coming after the encirclement of 1981–82, itself the negation of the commitments of 1980, the repudiation in 1990 of the signatures of 1987 could only bring about a loss of confidence, probably a permanent one, and a deep resentment among a naturally well-disposed population. Banished eight years earlier from the constitutional family, Québec was now being told, when it was making every effort to be readmitted, that it must continue stagnating in constitutional limbo. Many communities would be angry for much less.

The real meaning of the failure, the one that definitively blew up all bridges, lay in its most profound cause. English-speaking Canadians condemned Meech because it threatened the idea they had of their country. The country they carry in their minds and hearts is the present Canada, in which English is clearly predominant and which admires and is nostalgic for the British Crown, institutionalized and personified in a central state, in fact, a state as centralized as possible. Around the centre, there are ten subsidiaries, one of them being Québec. It is one module among ten, quietly keeping its place in a provincial niche, interchangeable with each of the other nine, to whose number Ottawa may add more at will. Such a system is horror-stricken at the thought of "distinctiveness." The word is anti-Canadian.

Our Canadian friends understand that the words in a constitution have a reality of their own and that this reality, whenever it is described as "distinct," will sooner or later take on the meaning of distinct powers. However, power is expected to be concentrated in Ottawa, and what remains for the provinces must be allocated on the basis of strict uniformity.

Québécois see the same country, but reflected in a mirror. Their real state is Québec. For the last thirty years, they have tried to seize as much power as possible from Ottawa. They feel they form a nation, one that is predominantly francophone, to which they pledge their primary loyalty. They have long recognized in the various elements that make up a state the attributes of a country: state, territory, loyalty, people, and culture. It is, in fact, a country that is being artificially kept within the Canadian country. By rejecting Meech, English-speaking Canadians had sent the message that they do not want two countries in one and that, if they had to choose, they would choose their own. This gave Québécois the idea of doing the same thing. English Canada had seen about as much political change in the federal system as it was willing to accept. If Québec wanted to go further, it would have to go elsewhere, meaning home to Québec.

This decision is beyond negotiation and removes us forever from questions of good or ill will, of esteem or contempt, of respect or rejection. The decision is one of logic and political necessity. Instead of constantly worrying about our own feelings and those of others, or going around in circles and tearing ourselves apart, we must take notice of reality and its demands: there is a country missing in this country, and it is ours. The Quiet Revolution stopped precisely at that point. Québec is an unfinished country, one that needs to be completed.

I regularly hear from English Canada that only two provinces scuttled Meech. The brief from the Québec Chamber of Commerce to the Bélanger-Campeau Commission renders justice to this specious argument, which Trudeau will likely use for our benefit whenever he recovers his speech. Technically true, the argument does not hold according to public opinion polls conducted during the debate on Meech. They show that, from one end of English Canada to the other, more than two-thirds of the population rejected the accord (the Gallup poll of May 1990 confirmed that even in the Atlantic provinces the level of rejection was as high as seventy-five percent). If they had not been able to rely on such broad support, McKenna, Wells, Chrétien, Carstairs, Filmon, and Harper would never have been able to mount such a resistance. They rode the crest of a wave.

I came to my decision at the end of June when I crisscrossed Québec with Audrey and Alexandre. I decided to stay in politics to work for the sovereignty of Québec. As I explained in my resignation speech in the House of Commons, I had drained the chalice of the *beau risque* to the last drop and used all my energy to bring about a national reconciliation through a Canadian renewal. I did not disavow the objective I had pursued until then. But I concluded, like many others who had wanted to put their hand on the wound like Saint Thomas, that the whole undertaking was doomed from the start. This time, the verdict rendered by English-speaking Canadians themselves made our sovereignty into an obstacle that could not be avoided. Québec could only move in that direction. By refusing to accept any alternatives, English Canada had shown us which road we should take.

I was not alone in drawing these conclusions. At the end of June, at the instigation of François Gérin, several MPs who had resigned thought of forming a parliamentary group to promote Québec sovereignty. Gérin's rapprochement with the Parti Québécois had taken place a few months earlier. Several MPs and ministers who had stayed in the Conservative caucus had been flirting with Jacques Parizeau's party. The news burst like a thunderclap on Saturday, May 5, 1990, right in the middle of the national Conservative caucus meeting at Mont-Tremblant. We learned that morning, on reading *Le Devoir,* that Bernard Landry was conducting secret talks with the nationalist wing of the caucus.

Such a thorough operation was a surprise for most people, including me. Apart from Gérin, the names of the others who had met with the vice-president of the Parti Québécois began circulating. Though I was on good terms with friends and acquaintances in nationalist circles, I had had no contact with Landry. The idea of sovereigntist representatives in Ottawa had already occurred to Marcel Léger, who had failed to convince Lévesque. All the same, Léger organized the Parti Nationaliste, which ran seventy-five candidates in the 1984 general elections but elected none. Gérin's thinking on this question was more advanced than that of others who had resigned. As for me, as I said, I had originally thought of giving up politics.

At first limited to former Conservatives, discussions broadened to take in two former Liberals, Jean Lapierre and then Gilles Rocheleau. Both had stormed out of the Liberal party within a minute of Chrétien's election as leader of the federal party. Lapierre, thirty-four years old, brought youth and experience. Rocheleau, a great anti-sovereigntist crusader, had turned his animosity against Chrétien and federalists of all kinds. We examined the whole question together.

By having two levels of representation, the federal system created two groups of elected Québécois, one in Ottawa and the other in Québec. Since the two levels of government are invariably in conflict over problems of jurisdiction as well as over policy issues, our elected representatives are systematically in an ambiguous or unstable situation. The fact that Québécois MPs are usually members of pan-Canadian parties within which they are but a minority only makes the problem worse. The law of the majority and the centralizing mentality of federal circles often force them to oppose the demands of their counterparts in the National Assembly. Furthermore, the two groups of elected representatives compete for visibility among the same voters. The winner is the one who turns the most sod, cuts the most inaugural ribbons, and distributes the most cheques. Behind the competition for media attention, there is a bitter struggle to defend and conquer jurisdictional authority. Since the central government's spending power can force the issue, the federal MP wins at the expense of his Québec counterpart, whose credibility suffers.

The system's unforeseen side effect is the fragmentation of Québec's political force. Ottawa knows how to bring it about: divide and conquer. The legitimacy of our federal representatives best serves the federal machine when it needs moral support for its less commendable enterprises. Never would English Canada have dared perpetrate the coup of 1982 without being able to use Québec Liberal MPs as a screen. Louis Duclos, representing Montmorency, was the only one to dissociate himself. Warren Allmand also voted against the resolution of December 2, 1981, but only because he thought the interests of the Anglo-Québec minority were insufficiently protected.

Québec voters must stop voting "for one thing and its opposite," to quote Bernard Landry. "Red in Ottawa, blue in Québec, maybe yes, maybe no," our ambiguity has been harmful to our cause.

We decided to attack this evil and to do so as a block. Our group even took that name, since its purpose was to bring together in Ottawa sovereigntists of all tendencies. Thus was born the Bloc Québécois.

Deliberately renouncing the idea of forming a government in Ottawa, the new party wants to make a supplementary contribution to the sovereigntist cause. For the first time, sovereigntists of all stripes will be voting federally in harmony with their vision of Québec's future. In this perspective, sovereignty brings Québécois together and reinforces their solidarity. As an instrument and product of this unity, the Bloc Québécois will play its most critical role in the wake of a provincial referendum favouring sovereignty. In the federal elections that are bound to follow, a strong contingent of Bloc candidates will be sitting in the House of Commons. This will be the time when the Québec government, vested with a mandate for sovereignty, will repatriate fiscal and legislative powers, recover its part of Canadian assets and assume its fair share of the public debt, and resolve with English Canada the issues of currency and the free movement of goods. Being in the heart of the federal parliamentary institution, the Bloc will be a conveyor belt between the National Assembly and its federal counterpart.

During this transition period, the Bloc will make its presence known. The next federal Parliament will be fragmented between Liberals, New Democrats, and Conservatives. None will be able to form the government alone. With a compact group of fifty to sixty members, the Bloc will make full use of the dynamics of parliamentary procedure to force the federal associate to respect the sovereigntist decision of the people of Québec. Having lost its cohort of elected Québec representatives, the federal government will be unable to prevent its sovereigntist adversaries, democratically elected to the House of Commons, from overwhelming its defences. The sovereigntist avant-garde will displace yesterday's federalist allies. The Bloc will be the enveloping wing of the sovereigntist advance. For a change, we will be united rather than divided: sovereigntist in Québec, sovereigntist in Ottawa. The federalists will be encircled by sovereigntists just as the sovereigntists used to be by federalists.

A referendum on sovereignty is a prerequisite to the success of this strategy. Nothing can exempt Québécois from making their decision. Another Bloc objective is to put an end to delays and equivocation. The Bloc will participate in the referendum debate along with its sovereigntist allies.

In the meantime, the Bloc will promote our interests in the House of Commons and wage timely battles against plans and decisions detrimental to Québec. However, it is not up to the Bloc to formulate government policy for the post-sovereignty period, since it is not involved in electoral activities on the Québec scene proper. This task belongs, for the moment, to the Parti Québécois and, later, to other parties soliciting a mandate to govern Québec. For this reason, and in accordance with the primary objective of gathering all sovereigntists beyond party lines, Bloc members have accepted the principles of free voting in the House of Commons. The only exceptions will be issues relating to the sovereignty of Québec.

The Bloc's avoidance of formulating policy for the post-sovereignty period does not mean that members of the Bloc are disinterested in the widely felt need to define the future of Québec. Here we touch upon one of the poisoned fruits of the interminable constitutional conflict, which has paralysed political thinking for more than ten years. The last years of the Parti Québécois government had all the signs of a rearguard action. Bourassa's Liberals govern for the short term, using the antagonisms and ambiguities of the "national question" to keep themselves in power. Constitutional proselytizing has widened the gulf between the politicians and the people. Voters understand less and less why politicians are locked in hermetic combat over the Constitution while the world around them is changing right before their eyes, with new concerns and hopes coming to the fore.

Although the limits imposed by the nature of the Bloc's mission and rainbow composition do not allow it to make projections into the future, the Bloc believes it can still define the prerequisites of sovereignty. Since a sovereign Québec must be built on democratic foundations and ruled by law, Bloc members acknowledge that the sovereigntist approach carries the obligation to define, right from the start, the democratic guarantees to be enjoyed by anglophone and ethnic minorities, as well as by Native peoples. Similarly, the Bloc's political committee has been asked to spell out Québec's interests and general objectives internationally. Finally, the Bloc also believes it has a contribution to make on future arrangements with English Canada.

Ottawa provides a unique forum from which to address English Canada, not to convince it of the benefits of Québec sovereignty but to make sure it is prepared for it. Québec's voice in English Canada is heard through the appointed loudspeakers of federalism in Ottawa. The people who issue bulletins on Québec's health are Jean Chrétien, Brian Mulroney, and André Ouellet. No wonder our reality and the pan-Canadian perception of it are so dangerously out of sync. It is up to the Bloc Québécois to ensure that messages from Parliament Hill are not distorted. English-speaking Canadians need to know the intensity, determination, and objectives of the sovereigntist vision. Someone has to tell them that, contrary to the reassuring speeches from official sources, Québec has not been anaesthetized. There is broad consensus for a referendum on sovereignty.

If we were to keep our Canadian friends in ignorance or under a false sense of security, we would be setting them up for some nasty surprises. They must be prepared for a referendum whose outcome will be favourable to sovereignty. It is the best way to avoid emotional shock and promote the climate of realism needed for a responsible transition. To speak to English Canada is one of the numerous tasks falling to the Bloc Québécois.

The same thing applies to opinion abroad. The federal capital is host to a hundred embassies and countless visitors from the four corners of the globe. Since we expect the international community to recognize the sovereign state of Québec, it is essential for the Bloc to take advantage of the place and the circumstances to inform and sensitize foreign officials.

Judging from the scope of the job and the number of niches open to persuasion, the MPs who have recently resigned from the federal parties could not have any doubts about the justification and legitimacy of their new political association.

The Bloc's political objectives are reflected in the description of its mission as set out on July 25, 1990:

1. We define ourselves first of all as a group of MPs anxious to represent faithfully the citizens who have elected us.

    We intend therefore to set up in our respective constituencies institutions that will stimulate democratic debate and broad public involvement. We believe that our society must develop within the framework of a true participatory democracy. We are working to this end with all the means at our disposal.

2. Our national allegiance is Québécois. The territory to which we belong is that of Québec, home of a people of French culture and language, whose sovereignty we intend to promote.

3. We consider the National Assembly of Québec as being, in fact and in right, the supreme democratic institution of the Québécois people. The Assembly is where the people will exercise their sovereign authority.

4. We have left our respective political parties and kept our seats in the House of Commons in order to:
   (a) associate ourselves without constraint to the efforts to define and build, in a context of participation, a Québec in full possession of its attributes;
   (b) make ourselves spokespersons of this goal in Ottawa and English Canada;
   (c) ensure the Québécois people free exercise of their right to self-determination by making this right clear to the whole of Canada and respected by federal institutions;
   (d) support Québec by promoting its bargaining power in the new political arrangements with the Canadian associate;
   (e) consolidate, around the exclusive interests of Québec, the strength and political authority of our people in Ottawa.

5. The MPs of the Bloc Québécois are not subject to party discipline, and they freely exercise their right to vote in the House of Commons.

6. Acknowledging that the future of Québec is closely tied to its economic prosperity and stability, we will ask from the federal government for Québec's full share as founding partner and major contributor in the Canadian federation.

7. In every case, we will fully respect and apply the principles of democracy, equity, and social responsibility. We will oppose discrimination in any form, while asserting a favourable bias towards the underprivileged in our society.

Events moved faster than we did. At the beginning of July, before we had a chance to consolidate our discussions into a formal founding document, we were up against our first thorny decision. The by-election called in the riding of Laurier–Sainte-Marie to replace Liberal Jean-Claude Malépart, who had died, forced a first test of our nascent organization.

In many respects, there was matter for concern. The by-election had been set for August 13, six weeks away. We had no candidate, no organization, no party, and no money. Mobilizing support in the middle of summer would be a problem. Many people advised me against entering the race. Already, three or four potential candidates had turned me down. Moreover, as some pointed out, Malépart had successfully held off Conservative onslaughts in 1984 and 1988.

Michel Lepage, the Parti Québécois's infallible pollster, still anticipated a sovereigntist victory in the riding. But even our New Democrat and Conservative opponents were coming out in favour of sovereignty. How could we make sure that the voters could tell the difference between four or five sovereigntists who might run? Nevertheless, Michel Lepage's surveys showed that a "sovereigntist candidate supported by Lucien Bouchard" would have the best chance.

The main reason I jumped into the contest was the question of legitimacy. In spite of the support we had all received in our own constituencies, the Conservatives and many political analysts (not necessarily anglophones) accused us of hijacking our electoral mandate. They questioned our right to promote sovereignty in the House of Commons, to which we had been elected under the banners of federalist parties. Personally, I invoked the polls supporting my resignation and offered several times to put my seat up for grabs. But the attacks continued and threatened to erode our credibility. By taking up the challenge in Laurier–Sainte-Marie to replace Malépart, I believed I could settle the question once and for all. The election, for the first time in the history of Québec, of a sovereigntist to the federal Parliament — and, moreover, a sovereigntist brought forward by the Bloc Québécois — would resolve the whole question of our legitimacy.

But we still had to find a candidate. After several fruitless meetings in a suite at the Queen Elizabeth Hotel, I decided to go out into the field. Remembering that Louise Harel had already spoken to me about one of the electoral pillars of the riding, I went to Bob Dufour's tavern on rue Ontario, in Montreal's east end. In the torrid heat of a late-July afternoon, my host, silent and wary, motioned me to a chair before a tableful of cold draft beers. I knew he was an admirer of Claude Charron and Robert Burns, that he had been a stevedore in the port of Montreal, and that he plunged into every election contest no matter what level. As he examined me with a suspicious eye, I ran off a list of possible candidates, including Gilles Duceppe, the actor's son, whose name had been suggested by Benoît Tremblay of the Bloc. After drawing a picture of the constituency and its heavy players, Bob (his real name was Yves, which he used only on formal occasions) praised Duceppe's "political culture." The next day, he called to tell me that he and other network chiefs would be prepared to work for Duceppe. The latter, a negotiator with the Confederation of National Trade Unions, was winding up a contract on behalf of hotel workers and was not sure he could be available. Finally, there was a settlement on July 9, and later that day he agreed to run.

Two days later, in the basement of Saint-Louis-de-Gonzague church, where fifteen hundred people had gathered, I declared Duceppe the Bloc's candidate. The announcement did not make much of a splash in the media, and for good reason: this was the day Corporal Marcel Lemay was killed at Oka during the Sûreté du Québec's assault on the Mohawks.

The campaign was short but intense. Door-to-door canvassing, poster battles, political debates, bingos, handshakes in subway entrances, corn roasts — the works. On the evening of August 13, after a day of torrential rain, Duceppe won with a majority of 16,818 votes. He had 66.9 percent of the votes, compared with 19.1 percent for the Liberals, 7.24 percent for the NDP, and 4.45 percent for the Conservatives.

I didn't hear much questioning of our legitimacy anymore.

In any case, the scope of the debate was now remarkably broader. Losing interest in Ottawa's muddle and determined to go its own way, Québec was paying more and more attention to redefining its goals.

Beginning in early June, I was able to confirm for myself that many Québécois were eager for a consensus on the shape of their future. This was manifestly the case in business circles where I gave several speeches, similar to those at the Montreal Chamber of Commerce and the Québec bar association. I decided to test the ground elsewhere, especially with labour leaders. The bitter confrontations in the public sector in 1982–83 had hardened my relations with labour's leadership. But because everything had taken place in the open, I believed that relations had never actually been broken off. I met Gérald Larose of the Confederation of National Trade Unions, Louis Laberge of the Québec Federation of Labour, and Lorraine Pagé of the Corporation des enseignants du Québec to discuss the political situation. I also had conversations with Claude Béland of the Mouvement Desjardins and Jean Campeau, who still was with the Caisse de dépôt, which confirmed two points for me: the need to conduct a broad dialogue and rally the Québécois outside of party lines to create a forum for studies and exchanges, allowing participants of all interests to define the broad strokes of Québec's future development.

In late June and early July, these contacts led to a series of meetings bringing together, alternately around Gérald Larose and Claude Béland, representatives of all backgrounds: from Jean Campeau to Denise Crête, president of the Fédération des femmes du Québec (Quebec women's federation); from Jacques Proulx of the Union des producteurs agricoles (farmers' union) to Serge Proulx of the Union des artistes (artists' union). Other participants gathered around Louis Laberge: Pierre Dansereau; Rita Dionne-Marsolais, Québec's delegate-general in New York; and Isabelle Courville, former president of the Parti Québécois youth section under Pierre-Marc Johnson. Even Claude Castonguay attended one of our meetings, though he later informed me he would not come back.

The project we discussed was called Forum-Québec. According to one of the last texts we circulated, its goals were to:

1. Set up a centre for exchanging information, doing research, and gathering data on all activities that would lead the various components of

Québec society to define and put into place a national strategy of sovereignty for Québec.

2. Promote opportunities for broad public debate of fundamental questions relating to the future of Québec, which the population of Québec would be called on to decide.

3. Encourage, in the form of personal participation (membership), the greatest possible number of people from all sections of Québec society to join a massive rally, constituting a broad, nonpartisan, social movement in favour of a national strategy for Québec.

4. Bring about a large assembly transcending political parties and the founding groups of Forum-Québec, of people who wish to contribute actively, within an open and democratic process, to the definition and promotion of a national strategy for Québec.

The resolution was accompanied with a thematic schedule of projected research and a calendar of conferences and seminars.

Meanwhile, an unusual climate of solidarity prevailed in the National Assembly. The politicians reacted to the official demise of Meech by rising against partisan conflicts. Parizeau's cry, "The country before the party," set the tone. Québécois would not say where they stood when Meech collapsed. Whatever the future held for them, they hoped to be able to shape it and reach it together.

Political circles in Québec debated the most appropriate framework for the required discussions: public forums or a restricted group. In the second case, should it be a traditional commission of inquiry or a parliamentary committee? Should this parliamentary committee be composed solely of members of the National Assembly, or should it also include people from different walks of life?

We were on the verge of publicly launching Forum-Québec. However, after developments in Québec, we held back to avoid short-circuiting the rapprochement between Bourassa and Parizeau. At that time, members of our group were starting to receive calls from

Bourassa sounding them out on who should preside over and who should sit on the commission he was putting together. So we decided to shelve Forum-Québec. An enlarged parliamentary committee seemed a more appropriate instrument for achieving the Forum's objectives. Nevertheless, it was not time wasted: eight of us were named to the Bélanger-Campeau Commission, one as co-president. Our summer discussions had laid the groundwork for close cooperation, which was later referred to as "the nonaligned commission."

On July 3, at the end of a conversation on the roof of the "bunker," Bourassa honoured me as the first appointment to the still-untitled commission. Two more were appointed once Bourassa and Parizeau had agreed on the choice of its joint presidents, Michel Bélanger and Jean Campeau. It seemed a symbol to me that both were representative products of the Quiet Revolution: both of them came up through the Québec public service and then crowned their careers with remarkable success in the world of finance.

By September, the roster of the commission was complete and included members of the National Assembly and the House of Commons, as well as municipal and school officials, union leaders, representatives from the arts, and businesspeople.

All these people quietly sized each other up at the initial meetings. Everyone was aware of the invisible line separating the federalists from the fewer but more compact sovereigntist contingent. The atmosphere warmed up quickly as personal chemistry came into play. Old networks soon came to the fore in Québec and in every group, whatever their origins: college friendships, university ties, mutual acquaintances, professional contacts, and geographical or political affinities.

In spite of a general desire to sort out points of convergence, no one had any illusions about agreeing on essential issues. Bourassa never thought he could transform Parizeau into a federalist. Neither did Lorraine Pagé expect Charles-Albert Poissant to turn into a crusader for independence.

It was therefore inevitable that subgroups appeared within the two camps. André Ouellet was supported by Ghislain Dufour, president of the Conseil du Patronat (Council of Employers), Marcel

Beaudry, defender of the Outaouais interests, and other representatives of the business community. Jean-Pierre Hogue, a Conservative MP and the federal government's man on the spot, brought to his group the support of experts in the Privy Council. Ouellet led the group with formidable skill. However, I had the impression that his federalism lost some of its abrasiveness as a result of his contacts with a variety of nationalists, Péquistes, and sovereigntists.

Our initial core of seven sovereigntists (I never understood what the media meant by referring to us as "nonaligned") grew to nine with Roger Nicolet, president of the Union des municipalités régionales de comté et des municipalités locales du Québec (Québec Union of Regional County Municipalities and Local Municipalities) and Jean-Claude Beaumier, vice-president of the Union des municipalités du Québec (Québec Union of Municipalities). We appointed Gérald Larose as our whip. A combative but conciliatory man, Larose grew from the experience. I was proud of our team. Béland, Laberge, Pagé, Turgeon, Nicolet, Proulx, and Beaumier worked in a way that enhanced our preparations. Early on, we pooled our resources. We organized our own little privy council with Yves Martin, whose services I retained, Pierre Bonnet of the CSN (CNTU), Yvan Loubier of the UPA (farmers' union), Guy de Grandpré of the Mouvement Desjardins, and Henri Laberge of the CEQ (teachers' federation). We owe a lot to their intelligence and to the quality of their analyses, strategic studies, and documents. Yves Martin's wisdom and attentiveness were a tremendous help. I have always benefitted from my periodic collaboration with this warmhearted friend, whose integrity equals his judgement, and whose dedication to the cause of Québec rests on his demanding convictions.

For members of the National Assembly, both Liberals and Péquistes, the commission's work simply formed an extension of their own. Caucus discipline, which continued to apply, had the effect of keeping the two groups separate. In spite of joint meetings, any convergence, at least as far as sovereigntists were concerned, took place at the personal level. People often called upon my old ties of friendship with Guy Chevrette and Jacques Brassard.

After an initial period of adaptation, it was really the quality of the briefs and their presentation that got the commission going and brought about a feeling of harmony.

It came out very quickly that a strong majority of Québécois reject federalism in its present form. The brief submitted by the Québec Chamber of Commerce was the most devastating demonstration of Canadian federalism's economic failure. The scope of the changes its sixty thousand members called for (such as the abolition of the federal government's power to spend and the extension of Québec's jurisdiction) set the consensus at about the same level as the Québec Liberal party's Allaire report a few months later. The Chamber of Commerce also complained about the economic and social costs of political indecision.

The chamber was particularly insistent about the need to resolve "the question of Québec's constitutional future speedily and decisively." Many other important briefs, from the Mouvement Desjardins, the Association of Manufacturers ("It is crucial to act quickly"), and the teachers' union, along with other labour organizations, came to similar conclusions.

Here were the foundations of a consensus with serious consequences: the status quo was no longer acceptable. By subordinating their federalist allegiance to the need for profound reform, the last supporters of the federal system were caught in a vicious bind. Though they wished for an expeditious solution, they also wanted time enough to improve federal structures. It was fair game for sovereigntists to say that, given the rejection of Meech's minimal conditions, any new attempt at national reconciliation founded on greater demands was bound to fail. Whoever refuses to concede less will certainly not concede more.

Obviously, the intentions behind these requests for more time were not always pure. Weren't they counting on time to cool sovereigntist fervour?

One group of nine decided to reactivate Québec-Forum, but as a pressure group pushing for a referendum on sovereignty in 1991. Under the name of Mouvement Québec 91, the organization began to act in November 1990. Membership included representatives from various sovereigntist organizations, labour federations, the Bloc Québécois, and the Parti Québécois. It began recruiting new members from the public.

The debate was heating up within the commission itself, as more and more delegations pressed for an early referendum. Péquistes and nonaligned commissioners never missed an opportunity to hammer home the idea of a referendum on sovereignty in 1991.

Nothing in the behaviour of the two presidents, who had been content to preside like a couple of sphinxes, foreshadowed the dramatic turn of events they had prepared. On February 19, 1991, they suggested to the commission that a referendum be held before the end of September 1991 proposing the proclamation of sovereignty by December 31, 1993, failing an agreement on the reform of the federal system that would satisfy Québec.

The sovereigntists accepted the recommendation. They had some merit in doing that because it raised the possibility of further negotiations. The federalists, with Bourassa at their head, rebelled and said no. Ouellet and his allies rejoiced at this firmness. But they did not know, any more than we did, that the no was not categorical. Two weeks later, the Allaire report was released in the presence of Premier Bourassa and with his apparent blessing. The cat was among the pigeons. The new Liberal catechism demanded the elimination of the federal government's power to spend, the abolition of the Senate, the insertion of a secession clause into the Constitution, the recovery of Québec's right of veto, the transfer from Ottawa to Québec of eleven areas of jurisdiction, and the end to federal encroachments in eleven more. The best was yet to come. The report asked the Québec government to commit itself to a referendum, to be held before December 21, 1992, proposing ratification of an agreement along the lines of the report or, failing that, the accession to sovereignty with an offer of economic union administered by confederal institutions.

The twenty-fifth convention of the Québec Liberal party voted to accept the report — with the exception of the abolition of the Senate — on March 9, 1991.

This forward leap gave initiative to the Liberals on the commission for the first time. They took the ball away from André Ouellet, who, until then, had been more or less the federal side's leader. Afterwards, the Bourassa Liberals never relinquished their advantage. Ouellet, who understood better than anyone else the explosive effect of the Allaire reform proposals on English Canada, was abandoned by his circumstantial allies Ghislain Dufour, Marcel Beaudry, and Charles-Albert Poissant and found himself isolated with Robert Libman. But it was mostly in relation to their sovereigntist counterparts that the Liberals had altered the dynamics of the discussions. They now had something to offer, saying to the sovereigntists: "Accept the postponement of the referendum for one year and we will be able to sign the commission's report with you." The offer was an interesting one, since the public expected the commission's work would lead to a consensus.

We were all hoping for that consensus during the last weeks of March, as the report was being drafted. Public hearings throughout Québec, televised live and rebroadcast in the evening, proved a tremendous success. Having been deprived of any opportunity to express themselves about their future for ten years, Québécois took advantage of these "electronic public forums" to resume discussion on their destiny as a nation.

The profound hope, clearly in the majority, was for sovereignty. But there was often more hope than conviction. And further, many people had asked the commission questions that it felt it must answer. But to do so, it should have been more homogeneous whereas, from the outset, its composition made it more closely resemble Jacques Godbout's *Les Têtes à Papineau*.

Divided on essential issues, how could the commission formulate coherent proposals allowing Québécois to make the right decision with any solidarity? At the same time, I could see among most of the commissioners a sincere desire for consensus on all questions, including that of sovereignty. This goodwill enabled us to make considerable headway. For example, it allowed us to recognize the short- and long-term viability of a sovereign Québec. Very few people questioned this assumption, even economists addressing the hearings. Concerns over the economic aspects of gaining sovereignty were mainly limited to economic stability during the transition from one system to another.

Taking this as its cue, the commission was able to limit the range of choices to two basic options: one last attempt at constitutional reform, or the accession to sovereignty. It summed up the general view in the following manner:

> Some believe the first way must be tried first and that, in case of failure, Québec should take the second to accede to sovereignty. Others prefer taking the second way right now. Thus, in case the last attempt at constitutional reform fails, there is only one option left, which is sovereignty [pages 82–83 of the report].

Even for people wanting to give it a last chance, federalism was preferable to sovereignty only if there were "major changes" or "profound transformation." The commissioners agreed to provide a broad description of the changes requested by various people appearing before it: abolition of the federal power to spend, elimination of overlaps, and recovery of Québec's veto right. In a general way, regarding power sharing, the commission supported "the attribution to Québec, by exclusive right, of all jurisdictions and responsibilities related to its social, economic and cultural development as well as to the realm of language" (page 55 of the report).

True, the commission did not give more precise indications about the changes it deemed necessary. But there the Allaire report came to the rescue. It dovetails perfectly with the Bélanger-Campeau report, which, like a Mendeleyev table, leaves open a box for powers after giving them a nomenclature. The Liberal report completes the commission's own by detailing the powers to be repatriated from Ottawa to meet the criteria of profound transformation set out by Bélanger-Campeau.

Only the keystone was missing from this beautiful construction: When would the population be called upon to choose between the two ways? With federalist governments in power both in Ottawa and Québec, for two and three years respectively, it looked as if hedging and evasive attitudes would persist. It was important to insert some rigidity and certainty into this hopelessly fluid process. Otherwise the commission would be nothing more than fireworks in Québec's political sky.

This is why the Allaire report's proposal to put the question to a referendum was seen by many sovereigntists, on reflection, as a significant step. But two problems remained. The first was that no sovereigntist could support a referendum bearing on a federalist agreement. The second was that the Liberals wanted to delay the referendum until 1992, while we wanted it in 1991.

Obviously, consensus on a timetable could only result from compromise. The most realistic solution was to extract from the Liberals a commitment for a referendum on sovereignty, with a concession on our part that it could be postponed for one year, from 1991 to 1992. Delicate and difficult negotiations got under way around these parameters during the last days of the commission, not only between federalists and sovereigntists but also between groups and individuals in both camps.

After many setbacks, thirty-two of thirty-five commissioners (the thirty-sixth, Claude Ryan, never found time to participate with us) finally rallied around the realistic solution. The agreement was due to the open-minded determination of one man: Henri-Paul Rousseau, the commission's secretary. This economist, on loan from the National Bank, was a revelation. Working night and day during the final sprint, he shuttled back and forth between parties, groups, camps, and subgroups. With the help of Chevrette, Beaudry, and Larose, he got the majority of the commissioners to agree.

The federalists, though they were in the majority, could not cross the finish line together. Ouellet, Hogue, and Holden were not among the signatories. In fact, only the sovereigntists were unanimous, but not without first overcoming some thorny problems. The substitution of 1992 for 1991 as referendum year shocked many of the militants recently enrolled in Mouvement Québec 91. Once again, the organization had to change its name and its purpose. It became simply Mouvement Québec, an umbrella organization for parties, associations, and individuals of sovereigntist allegiance.

The Liberals also demanded a parliamentary committee to assess constitutional offers coming from Ottawa and English Canada. Péquistes thought the idea rather unattractive. But they agreed, on being promised that the committee would be activated only after receiving "an offer formally binding the government of Canada and the provinces." They rejoiced over the establishment of still another parliamentary committee, this one with a mandate to look into "all questions relating to Québec's accession to full sovereignty."

The principal gain sovereigntists made was the commission's recommendation to inscribe the Liberal commitment for a referendum on sovereignty in a provincial law. Many of us thought legislation would not be too excessive to reinforce Bourassa's signature.

A few months later, the National Assembly passed Bill 150. All that remains now is to put it into action, which many people think is not as simple as it sounds.

It is still too early to assess the fallout from the Bélanger-Campeau Commission. However, for the moment, one can rejoice at the rapprochement, which rose above parties and interest, it made possible among people and circles who, whatever happens, must resolve their differences through dialogue. The commission also gives Québécois a grid, clarified by the Allaire report, that will enable them to evaluate what Ottawa is preparing for them, whether it consists of offers or a referendum question.

But the commission's greatest service was to lock everyone in Québec and Canada in a decisional framework specifying a timetable and the terms of the choice. In the perspective of Bélanger-Campeau, sovereignty was no longer a bogey or a harebrained scheme.

Among the three federal MPs on the Bélanger-Campeau commission, I was the only one to sign the report. There could be no better way to assert the unique role, attributed de facto to the Bloc, of relaying the will of the National Assembly. The Bloc got its mission directly from the recommendations of the Bélanger-Campeau Commission and from the democratic and legislative consecration the recommendations received from Bill 150.

Its legitimacy and the indispensable nature of its work have allowed the Bloc to take root. In June 1991, the founding convention in Sorel-Tracy formed the Bloc into a true electoral vehicle, with a party organization and a program setting out its goals. In August, Pierrette Venne, MP for Saint-Hubert, left the Conservative caucus to join us. Since then, the Bloc has spread to every region in Québec, with its own membership, party activities, constituency organizations, committees, a national office, financing, and a permanent staff. It will participate in all coming struggles, referendums, and elections. Meanwhile, because of its presence in the House of Commons, it can make ready on the opponent's own grounds.

When the federal government published its constitutional proposal of September 24, 1991, the Bloc was ready to expose the gulf separating the federal government from Québec's requirements. All the easier to do because Ottawa chose that very moment to launch an all-out offensive against Québec's meagre economic powers. The feds' projected changes even threatened certain financial institutions, such as the Caisse de dépôt and the Mouvement Desjardins, as well the budgetary latitude of the provinces.

The rest of the federal proposal could not have been more out of tune: the recognition of the distinct society was only a pale imitation of Meech; there was no guaranteed veto for Québec; Senate reform could go in any direction, none of them good for Québec; there was nothing about power sharing, except for a slim jurisdictional gain in manpower, and even that was exposed to federal intrusion.

No one in Ottawa seems to have thought, after the Bélanger-Campeau and Allaire reports, that Québécois expected more than the microscopic movements at bargaining tables or legal arabesques with which Privy Council scribes disguise English Canada's no to Québec's claims.

The reception given the Beaudoin-Dobbie report was just a repeat of the same phenomenon. Everything is a matter of reference. The prime minister introduced this last effort as "the most generous in 125 years." If the comparison is founded on the constitutional changes of 1982, the competition does not look very strong. Understandably enough, Québécois align themselves on the markers they recently set for themselves.

Bourassa himself was not taken in, though he desperately sought a federal offer exempting him from holding a referendum. The report, the best the federal government and English Canada can do for us, proposes "a domineering federalism," to use the former premier's own words at the time.

Everything is in place for the final curtain: the actors, the spectators, and the scenery. The federal government wants to write the ending and act out the final scene on its own stage. But we can't let it happen. Our stage is ready, and for Québécois, it is the only legitimate one. The moment of truth is approaching.

17

A Country for Our Children

I am not so pretentious as to describe the personal road I have travelled as following an itinerary. At fifteen, I had no precise political intentions. Not only did I have no goals then, but I have not reached any today.

The purpose of this book, while remaining respectful of my personal privacy and that of others, has been to retrace my steps to discover the landmarks and motivation behind my political course. I have written with as much sincerity as possible.

Personal trajectories, and collective ones even more so, seldom proceed in straight lines. I would have liked this return to the past to show that, from the moment of my political awakening, sovereignty appeared as Québec's inescapable destiny and the force governing my activities. In reality, I reacted to collective aspirations rather late in the day, when I was in university and saw the new Québec being built all around me. Then again, I developed at the same speed as the people around me.

I went through the same stages: the Quiet Revolution, once it was under way; the nationalization of electricity; French Power in Ottawa with Marchand and Trudeau; Bourassa's election in 1970; support for sovereignty association in 1972; Lévesque's election in 1976; the yes side in the referendum of 1980; disinterest during 1982 and 1983; *le beau risque* of 1984; reconciliation with Meech in 1987; and the resurrection of the sovereigntist project after the break of 1990.

Today, I realize, after rereading the preceding pages in one stretch, that throughout these years I have been carried forward by a nation on the march.

Whether I like it or not, history made me Québécois of old stock. Nowadays, one almost has to apologize for this. My roots have struck deep into a small part of this earth. I don't think it is better or richer than others, but it is mine. Some may think that it nourishes outmoded values and isolates me from other Québécois who joined us more recently to build here, with us, a new future for themselves. I do not think so. The particular is reductionist only if it prevents access to the universal. But I want my village to be part of a real country that broadens the range of my thoughts and opens to the outside world, starting with the one that has already settled among us, the ethnic communities.

Some believed, in 1867, that this real country might be Canada. There was nobility in the arrangement: two nations developing on the same territory, with equality and mutual respect. But the dream was too good to be true. The dream existed only in the minds of the minority associate. Reality quickly put an end to it. The majority associate soon told the other that there was only one nation divided into ten provincial boxes. Squeezed in its own box, Québec suffered from ceaseless erosion of the powers that it had been granted at the outset. Since political and economic interests were at stake, the greater number could not fail to impose its own law on the smaller one. From one defeat to the next, the front line of language and culture gradually moved back towards Québec, the last francophone haven in North America. Not only were the people of Québec not treated as equals, they were not recognized at all. Governed from the inside by a majority wielding limited authority, fragmented by a divisive system of representation, and considered abroad as a ward of Ottawa, Québec has had its development thwarted. Since awakening thirty years ago, the people of Québec have tried to acquire more space within federation. But their efforts always led to failure, frustration, setbacks, and rejection. The principal associate wants to maintain the supremacy of the federal government — in other words, its own.

From three decades of personal travel through various periods, circles, and roles, I have come to the following conclusions: federal structures hinder Québec's development and deprive it of an opening on the world. The converse is also true: the presence of Québec — always in conflict, demanding, and unhappy — compromises English Canada's own development. Our departure will give it access to everything our presence makes impossible: an all-powerful federal government, a central state embodying national aspirations and will.

If they fail to cut the Gordian knot, Canada and Québec will stagnate and exhaust themselves in navel-gazing discussions. Their natural incompatibility prevents common economic policies and an authentic national enterprise. This same helplessness provides us with a poorly trained labour force, ill-prepared for the requirements of international competition.

We buried our heads in the sand so long as we could live off the abundance of our natural resources. We did not even react when the quality of our human resources, particularly technological expertise and productivity, outstripped natural resources as the leading competitive asset. In a painless and effortless attempt to preserve the living standards of Canadians and Québécois, our governments resorted to a quick-fix solution: tax and borrow.

The alarm bells are ringing and the moment of truth is approaching as the federal debt reaches five hundred billion dollars, public finances are out of control, and fiscal tolerance is close to the breaking point. In Québec, our capacity to finance the social safety net is shrinking when 825,000 adults are out of the labour market and 1.2 million people live in poverty. One figure sums up the crisis: twenty-two percent of our working-age population is inactive. Let us not forget that the federal government has greatly contributed to this mess, exacerbating one of the worst recessions in Canadian history. Even Ontario has suffered, with an unemployment level that has doubled in three years.

This is precisely the moment federalists have chosen to warn Québec about the costs of sovereignty.

My purpose here is not to demonstrate the economic viability of sovereignty, or to propose a national development plan. There will be other circumstances and other platforms for this. In any event, I would never attempt to prove that sovereignty will bring about a heaven on earth. Québec will be what we make it. We have the tools to form a dynamic country with a window on the world: an efficient economic structure, a modern government, a responsible and hardworking population, natural resources, the capacity to adapt with flexibility and cohesion to the globalization of the economy. Everything depends on our solidarity, energy, and collective discipline. In other words, everything depends on us.

For the moment, it is important to climb out of the stagnation that feeds on our indecision and uncertainty. Federalists are under a serious illusion if they believe a constitutional agreement will resolve the current crisis. Only when Québécois take up the challenge of sovereignty will the abscess be lanced. To opt for the ambiguous arrangement Ottawa has in mind would constitute only another refusal to decide. Québécois, including those who might have said yes to such an escape, would never forgive themselves for having given in once more to the merchants of fear and to their own ambivalent demons. They would continue cursing the federal government, fighting its intrusion — and as a compensatory gesture, would rush to elect a sovereigntist government in Québec. Canada, increasingly divided, would pursue its morose downward slide.

The sovereigntist embers will never go out. We know now that the drive to sovereignty will always be reborn from its ashes, even if it takes a decade. The flame will flicker as a result of the inevitable clashes between Canadian and Québécois interests.

Conversely, a majority vote for sovereignty will unleash a new energy, attract to politics people who have shunned it, and release a wave of creativity similar to the one that inspired the generation of the Quiet Revolution.

To provide direction and sustain synergy, a deep reflection must precede this surge. We must rethink Québec, with or without sovereignty. While we are immersed in the constitutional whirlpool, going round and round with a partner determined to keep us inside this infernal circle, the world changes and rebuilds all around us. Even here it has already changed.

The concession road on which my grandfather lived still winds its bumpy way along the Grande-Décharge, but my cousin André has installed a computer in the stable. The GATT negotiations five thousand miles away are dramatically altering his peaceful milk producer's life. He will no longer be content to be one of the best in the parish. His competitors tomorrow will be American, French, and German.

All Québec will experience — is already experiencing — this type of upheaval. Our victories and our defeats will be abroad. We are condemned to exporting fewer raw materials taken from the soil or the forest, and more of our quality products, imagination, knowledge, and ambition. And we must do so at a time of increasing environmental constraint.

Accordingly, school reform and a solid research policy are the first problems that must be tackled by a government fully aware of the stakes. But we must be careful, for there is as much grain as chaff in the educational system; it is the chaff we must shake out. Let us spare what works from the fate that the Parent Commission meted out to the humanities, victims of the clear-cutting syndrome. In this time of global trade, shouldn't we put more emphasis on general education and on a return to the deeper roots of human culture? Wouldn't this be a way of catching up with others abroad? Some will say that the most pressing needs are in the fields of science and technology. But why exclude the humanities for the sciences, whether pure or practical? The higher we rise on the ladder of management, investment, and finance, the more we will need to rid ourselves of the shackles of overspecialization. In any case, we can be sure our competitors will be able to do it. I wonder why we would exclude ourselves from their league.

We must break through the bureaucratic and corporative crust on our educational system. I am sure we can do it with dialogue. Union people see the same reality as their fellow citizens. Elementary social justice compels us to reform in order to provide jobs for young people who want to go to the end of their schooling. Dropouts are caught in a vicious circle. Young people would stay in school if it were what it should be — a passage to the labour market. Nothing hurts a student's motivation more than seeing an unemployed university graduate.

I often visit CÉGEPs and speak with the students. Do not tell me that they refuse to work harder. Many of them know they are wasting their time and it pains them. When they no longer believe they live in a paralysed society, they will be willing to put more effort into their futures.

Similarly, we can't afford to close our eyes to the need to review our economic policies. Why is Québec waiting to launch a national effort for full employment and against poverty? Can we not see that a durable development plan is an urgent task? The social and economic decision-makers and players are only waiting for a signal from public authorities to contribute their desire for dialogue. It is not only a matter of internal urgency, as in 1960. Today, the forces of change are coming abroad and are appearing everywhere with the same effects. These forces require our competitors in Europe, Asia, and the United States to react in unison. We must not miss the boat; there may be no catching up.

The language question, for me, can be examined in the same light. Certain factors are clear and not debatable. Québec is predominantly French. Integrating into Québec society, for an immigrant, means essentially acquiring the capacity to communicate "in French and to subscribe to the most fundamental values of Québec society: values such as democracy, religious tolerance, equality of the sexes." I quote here from *Le Devoir* and support the views of the study entitled "Les Francophones québécois," prepared for the Montreal Island School Council by François Rocher, Guy Rocher, and Gérard Bouchard.

Accordingly, we francophones have an obligation to respect our language and our culture. To show respect for our language we must teach, speak, and write better than we are doing now. As for our culture, we must reinstate the compulsory teaching of history, both our own and others'. At the same time, we must recognize that minority ethnic cultures have "a right to live and express themselves in another language, but as marginal cultures and parallel with the national culture, with the exception of the culture expressed in English, which will always have a special status in Québec" (Rocher et al).

The predominance of French does not imply exclusion or ignorance of English. The almost one million anglophones concentrated in the Montreal area are a historical given. This community will always live in English. But we ask it to recognize and accept, in everyday life, the essentially French character of Québec. I cannot contemplate our future without the vigorous participation of the Anglo-Québécois minority. Our English-speaking fellow citizens will be key players in our attempt to penetrate the great economic and scientific networks of the world.

Which brings us to the delicate problem of our relationship to the English language. When we step up our penetration of foreign markets and our international presence, we cannot simply depend on translating from English. It is true that French, as another international language, opens many doors on the world scene. But wherever we need to speak English, we must be able to do so.

However, I feel somewhat ill at ease in this respect. We may rightly conclude that we also need English to carve out a place for Québec abroad, but we must still learn the language somewhere. Apart from making mastery of English a privilege reserved for the sons and daughters of the upper classes, wouldn't it be possible to improve the teaching of English in francophone public schools? Parizeau, Johnson, Jacques-Yvan Morin, for whom I have a great deal of admiration, speak better English than most English-speaking Canadians. For all that, they have not been assimilated into English culture, and it doesn't prevent them from speaking and writing French perfectly. I know this is slippery ground and that we must continue the struggle for French survival. Still, I do not think we can avoid raising the issue.

Willingly or not, these questions broaden a perspective already modified considerably by pluralism. Many grafts have enriched our Franco- and Anglo-Québécois roots, contributing to the diversification of mainstream Québec culture. By joining in and merging with it, the new tributaries will transform it. Our culture will benefit in scope, in knowledge of the world, in freedom, and in greater sensitivity to others.

Our fundamental values — democratic commitments, tolerance, rejection of violence — will survive. We must consolidate these democratic foundations, always endangered here as elsewhere, within a rigorous constitutional framework. A sovereign Québec cannot fail to provide generous guarantees for individual rights and liberties, and clearly define legislative, executive, and judicial attributes. Anglophone and ethnocultural minorities, as well as Native peoples, will receive from such a constitution convincing assurances that it is possible to build, along with other Québécois, a country that will also be theirs.

It will be impossible to resolve the question of the Native peoples before the dust settles. The events of Oka and the way English Canada used them to undermine the goal of sovereignty have had aftereffects. Ovide Mercredi's refusal, a short while later, to recognize Québécois as a people was considered an insult. No discussion is possible when our counterpart denies our existence. It is a pity, because we have many wrongs to redress with Native peoples and we have already started doing so: the James Bay convention and the recognition, in 1985, of the First Nations' right to self-government were important steps towards more harmonious relations. We must continue from there to resolve our differences when the conditions are right. Until then, we must practise openness and moderation. Accordingly, we must never allow doubts about the indivisibility of Québec's territory. Within a single sovereignty, practically all arrangements are possible, including exclusive rights to ancestral lands. Once these limits have been set, there is nothing to do for the time being other than to reach out and wait, and to stand firm against all provocations. Someday, after signing the appropriate agreements, Québec's commitments to the First Nations can also be sanctioned by the constitution.

It will not be the easiest issue to resolve. The way we do it will say a great deal about our political maturity.

Until then, I fervently hope the referendum will give us the opportunity of speaking and acting as a nation.

This book, which is ending at perhaps the point where everything may begin, can only end with hope.

I watch Alexandre and Simon growing, and I see that history and Québec pride are working for them. And I dream that just as one door closed on part of my past one evening in May 1990, so another and better door will soon be opening for the future of my nation.

Index